Religions of the World

Expressions of Faith and Pathways to the Divine

Edited by F.C. La Spina
James Madison University

Bassim Hamadeh, CEO and Publisher
Michael Simpson, Vice President of Acquisitions
Jamie Giganti, Managing Editor
Jess Busch, Graphic Design Supervisor
David Miano, Acquisitions Editor
Monika Dziamka, Project Editor
Luiz Ferreira, Licensing Associate
Sean Adams, Interior Designer

Copyright © 2014 by Cognella, Inc. All rights reserved. No part of this publication may be reprinted, reproduced, transmitted, or utilized in any form or by any electronic, mechanical, or other means, now known or hereafter invented, including photocopying, microfilming, and recording, or in any information retrieval system without the written permission of Cognella, Inc.

First published in the United States of America in 2013 by Cognella, Inc.

Trademark Notice: Product or corporate names may be trademarks or registered trademarks, and are used only for identification and explanation without intent to infringe.

Cover image copyright © 2012 Depositphotos/StephanieFrey
Interior image copyright © 2012 Depositphotos/StephanieFrey

Printed in the United States of America

ISBN: 978-1-62131-753-1 (pbk)/978-1-62131-754-8 (br)

Contents

Introduction   1

Upholding Indigenous Freedoms of Religion and Medicine   13
    Dennis Wiedman

African Traditional Religions   41
    Mutombo Nkulu-N'Sengha

Hinduism   59
    James Chiriyankandath

Buddhism and Jainism   75
    Eugene F. Gorski

Sikh Dharam   95
    Sushil Mittal and Gene Thursby

Understanding Taoism   117
Russell Kirkland

Confucianism   133
Ray Billington

What is Shinto?   151
Inoue Nobutaka

Zoroastrianism   161
Eugene F. Gorski

Judaism   175
Marc H. Ellis

The Uniqueness of Christianity   195
Eugene F. Gorski

Islam   213
Ifran A. Omar

Dedication

Chris and Mike were brothers, with Mike being two years older than Chris. The two brothers were very close, grew up in western Virginia, graduated from Virginia Tech, married childhood sweethearts and together ran a 500 acre farm. They built their houses 75 yards from each other and were solid partners as well as brothers.

In between their two houses was a ravine that separated their land. One day, Chris was cultivating some land with his tractor and got a little careless. He accidentally plowed into the levy of a dam that bordered the property, and a day's worth of water came gushing out, in effect forming a river between his property and his brother's. Chris really didn't know what to do. He was pondering the situation when his brother came out to survey what had happened and was overcome with anger. When he saw his brother, he said, "How could you have been so careless? Don't you know this water will draw every mosquito between here and West Virginia?"

"Mike, it was an accident!" Chris replied, to which Mike said, "Accidents are caused by stupid people," and he stormed off into his house.

In most cases, anger will dissipate over time, but not with Mike. As the days went on, his anger intensified. In fact, he refused to acknowledge his brother. He was trying to think of a way to blot the river, as well as his brother, out of his life. All of a sudden it came to him: he would build a fence! A fence which would allow no light in and act as a barrier between himself and his brother.

At that very moment, the doorbell rang. It was a carpenter, with a toolbelt slung over his shoulder. He said, "I'm looking for work—do you think you might have some?"

Mike, with eyes wide open, said, "This is your lucky day!" and he brought the carpenter in the back to explain the project. "Remember," he said, "I want the boards to butt up next to each other so no light will come through."

The carpenter went to take some measurements and then came back. Upon reaching Mike, he said, "How much are you willing to pay?"

Mike said, "A thousand dollars."

The carpenter replied, "I'll tell you what. I'll do it for $500, but you have to agree to leave for three days. And when you come back, I will have built exactly what you need." So Mike paid him half the money up front.

Figuring he was now $500 to the good, Mike took his family to the city for the weekend, staying at a hotel, going to a show, and taking them out to dinner. On Sunday evening they headed back, Mike all excited about seeing his new fence.

Mike drove into his driveway, went around back, and that's when it hit him. Instead of a fence, there was a bridge spanning the stream, linking his property to his brother's. And I don't mean any bridge—this bridge could have been on the cover of *Virginia Living* magazine, as it featured benches and shrubs. It was truly a crafted work of art.

Now remember that, even though the bridge was beautiful, Mike wanted a fence. He was livid. He clasped his hands into a fist and was ready to hit something, but then he saw his brother coming across the bridge. Chris exclaimed, "Mike, here I thought you were mad! All the time you were planning to build a bridge to join our houses together!" And he hugged his brother. Mike, overcome and feeling reflective, hugged his brother back. Mike said, "This bridge is truly what we needed." Chris, by the way, paid the other half of the fee.

Now the carpenter was packing up his tools when Chris and Mike said, "Hey, don't leave! We're having a party tonight on the bridge in your honor! We're inviting the whole neighborhood, get you a lot of business!" The carpenter shook his head and said, "No, gotta move on—too many other bridges yet to build."

The above story is adapted from "The Sower's Seeds" by Fr. Brian Cavanaugh, T.O.R. It is told in the Franciscan tradition, and legend has it that if a Franciscan story isn't true, it should be! I've told it many times and am dedicating this book to the premise of the story: It is only through building bridges between those of other faiths that we can truly achieve understanding and harmony.

F.C. La Spina, MTS
Editor

Introduction

THE INFLUENCE OF RELIGION ON THE WORLD

It seems that ever since man has walked the earth—which is in itself sometimes a religious question—people have been influenced by what may be referred to as the divine. We have imagined something greater than ourselves, and almost everyone has speculated on what happens to us upon our death. The funny thing is that no one has any real clue about that speculation.

The word religion comes from the Latin word *religio*, which refers to the fear or awe one feels in the presence of the divine—a spirit or god. It is interesting to note that in Roman Catholicism, one of the gifts of the Holy Spirit (based on Paul's writings) is fear or awe of the Lord.

That definition of religion being as it may, religion has come to mean—most likely due to practicality—a standard of organized beliefs that stem from a certain faith tradition. For the most part, and this is very much in general, for a religion to call itself a religion, it has to have three things: A Creed, A Code, and A Cult. Let me elaborate on this point.

First of all, a **creed**: A religion has to have a set of beliefs or it simply cannot be considered a religion. The one which comes to mind most easily is the Nicene Creed, which originated roughly 1800 years ago and is used by the majority of mainline Christian Churches. It is repeated by many denominations each week and serves to reaffirm what Christians believe as a people. Similarly, Islam has the Shahada, which affirms their belief in Allah as well as the prophet Muhammed. Without a creed, a religion could not stand for or represent anything. Therefore, it is an essential element in a tradition being referred to as a religion. Think of it this way: How could someone be persuaded to become part of a religion if there were no answer to the question of what was believed? The Creed serves as sort of a launching pad for a religion.

Second, a **code**: Religion is generally associated with how one lives his or her life. It has been said that all of the major religions have some version of the Golden Rule—which originates in Matthew's gospel—as part of their moral code. People are considered religious not just because of how devout they are in services or rituals, but how they live out their lives as well. With a belief system comes a way of living out that belief system.

Third, a **cult**: A religion, for the most part, has to have some kind of ritual associated with it, whether it be celebration of sacraments in Christianity, the Amrit ceremony in Sikhism, or the Bar Mitzvah in Judaism. Some sort of ceremony must be part of religiosity. This can be elaborate—such as the Greek Orthodox mass—or very simple, like a Friends meeting in which people sit in silence for sometimes an hour. Ritual has to have some part in religion because it is all part of divination, which will be discussed later.

All of the above raises the question of what religion has done for the world and why mankind has sought it so vehemently, sometimes to a violent end.

There are some other characteristics religions hold in common which have given them impact and influence on the world. First of all, they usually, but not always, deal with an unseen world—i.e. demons, spirits, or ancestors. One need only look at the Judeo-Christian belief in the afterlife to see this. Second, religions usually have a way of communing with the unseen world through ritual—this is sometimes called divination. Third, generally there is a system of scripture and hierarchy of priests and temples in which to worship. Fourth, most religions have some statement about the hereafter: either reincarnation or, as in Christianity, resurrection. Fifth, they have a moral code (see above), and sixth, they have attracted a following.

Let me mention something about the above: it seems that for a religion to take hold, it has to have staying power or longevity. This characteristic of surviving through adversity and still being around for centuries seems to give religions their credibility. This is also probably why religions that are new undergo great persecution. All one need do is look at the book of Acts in the Christian scriptures. Judaism had been around for 2000 years and was therefore accepted. Christianity, called "The Way," became the new scapegoat.

When we look at a religion, we have to look at various issues and answer some basic questions. What culture did the religion emerge from? As we know, traditions are influenced by the environment in which they grow. Judaism came out of a culture in which mercy and forgiveness were considered to be for the weak. Therefore, the Hebrew scriptures contain much about punitive, violent action against the violator. Also, was there a founder? What contributed to the discovery? For instance, Muhammed received the revelation of the Quoran during a time in which Saudi Arabia was in the midst of polytheism.

We also have to ask ourselves, are there texts from which to base our belief in this religion? How has the religion progressed, and in some instances changed, over time?

In just the same way that religion has caused as much good as destruction in our world, it still remains the most pervasive phenomenon of culture. It seems to be the basis for what people will live for, stand for, and even die for—and they will defend their beliefs and challenge anyone who won't allow their traditions or, in some cases, who think differently. In this regard, it is truly, as Paul Tillich said, the ultimate concern. Unfortunately, some religious differences are so great that people resort to violence and even go to war.

This collection, however, while being realistic, will take the high road when talking about religion and religious differences. We will try and examine the benefits and good that various religious traditions have given to the world.

Earliest Theories on the Origin of Religion

Someone once said that there are two types of people—those who have an abundant faith and those who have none. This theory can apply to how one considers the beginning of religion. Some believe that religion is nothing more than a crutch that man made up to help him through the pitfalls of life, providing hope. Others, namely Karl Marx, felt that religion was an opiate by which to control the masses. Still others feel that religion was created to justify behavior—i.e., killing a people in the name of faith. Those who have a grounded belief generally feel that their religion has been revealed by the actions or words of a chosen person. For people of the Book—Jews, Christians, and Muslims—this is in the persons of Abraham, Jesus, and Muhammed. For Buddhists (literally "the awakened ones") it is in the teachings of Siddhartha Gautama. For Hindus, it is not so much a revelation as it is an understanding of how the universe works. It is safe to say that those who have an impact on religion embrace it with passion, not from a lukewarm posture.

Different Forms of Religion

Base Religions

For the most part, the terms *base* or *basic religions* refer to those religions that are indigenous to a region or area and cannot be traced back to a founder or revealer. Simply put, the belief is that the people have just always done these things for as long as people can remember. One could put "The Lottery" by Shirley Jackson in this category.

This category embraces beliefs such as animism (everything has a spirit), totemism (a symbolic allegiance to an animal by a tribe), polytheism (belief in many gods), and henotheism (belief in the possibility of many gods). Because of the loose structure and lack of defined revelation in these basic religions, one can see how religions such as Christianity and Islam made inroads and took hold. Saudi Arabia at the time of Muhammed was strewn with polytheistic beliefs, and Christianity was born out of pagan emperor worship.

Religions from India

Hinduism, Jainism, Buddhism, and Sikhism all hail from India and are similar in that they seek escape from this world either in one life or in several—or hundreds of—lives. Each believes in many gods (except for Sikhism, which takes its God from Islam), but the primary goal is release, either by actions, meditation, or a prayerful life. This is one fundamental difference between eastern religious thought and its western counterpart—reincarnation verses resurrection.

Religions from the Far East

With regard to China and Japan, the three pervasive faith traditions are Taoism, Confucianism, and Shinto. Each has a belief in many gods, as well as ancestor veneration, honor of nature, and honor of country (Shinto).

Religions of the Middle East

Sometimes referred to as the cradle of civilization, the Middle East has produced the religious traditions that have affected the world the most taken as a whole. Zoroastrianism, Judaism, Christianity, Islam, and Baha'i all stem from this region. All believe that people have only one life and are judged in accordance with it. And all believe in one Supreme Creator God—in essence, the God of Abraham. Christianity and Islam alone make up roughly 60% of the world's population.

Religion: A Force for Good and Peace or Evil and Violence?

Religion and violence at first glance seem oxymoronic. But the fact is that more people have been killed in the name of religion than for anything else. However, we have to distinguish between religious acts which serve as punishment for those people believed to be evil; violent acts which are, in and of themselves, religious; and clashes between religious communities/traditions. We need only to look to New England and the witch trials, which somehow justified violence. Nazi Germany, at least partly, justified the Holocaust by calling Jews "Christ killers." In this respect, the violence seems to be the result of finding a scapegoat.

When religious communities exhibit violent behavior toward one another, it usually is the result of one of two things: either a group has threatened another group by believing differently or political agendas are masked by religion. Examples of this would be the violence in Northern Ireland in the 1980s, which resulted in people going on hunger strikes. The surface reason in Belfast might have been Catholicism against Protestantism, but the underlying root cause was clearly Irish freedom from British rule. The Crusades of the Middle Ages were ostensibly to retrieve the Holy Land from Islam, but the cause was as political as it was religious.

At times there is backlash—If Hindus defile a mosque by killing a pig in it, Muslims may come back and sacrifice a cow in a Hindu Temple. At this point it becomes difficult to find religion in any of these actions as foolish pride and personal agendas take over. As someone wise once said, religion can bring out the noblest traits of humanity but can also motivate and justify the most twisted and depraved among us. For this reason we must look at becoming a pluralistic society when it comes to belief—it is the only way as a people we will survive. This text contains material that lends itself to this belief.

The Need for Religion Today—Yes or No?

Society is beginning to ask itself: do we really need religion today? Another less severe way to put it is to ask whether or not religion has a place in modern life.

Paul Tillich (1886–1965), a German theologian, gave the world many definitions for which he became well known—defining religion as the "Ultimate Concern," the "ground of being" when discussing God, and "the new being" when discussing Christ. But while definitions help, they fall short when it comes to religion becoming part of who a person has become. For instance, do we attend a house of worship because we are told to through a set of rules set up to be a hierarchy, or have we truly made it our ultimate reason for living? Do we attend halfheartedly—on Christian and Jewish high holy days—or has worship taken a front seat in our everyday existence? Is God truly a ground of being for us or something that we reach out to when we have a need? Do we practice a religion in order to "get to heaven," which is in and of itself self-serving? The final question is, can religion get us out of our egocentricity into a state of other-centeredness—which was a characteristic of those through which the major religions were revealed?

We have seen the decline of some organized religions ("I don't get anything out of it") and the emergence of some others. The so-called "megachurches" have begun to make themselves known, drawing upwards of 30,000 people. These churches are for the most part non-denominational Christian, but they offer an intangible to the masses—they all feel good when they leave. People literally fight to get into these places, partly because of the message and partly for their entertainment factor. This should not come as a surprise: our movie industry has never been bigger and the Super Bowl is watched by half of humanity.

One factor that seems to have had an effect on the faith of people, and ultimately their involvement in religion, is the retreat experience. Regardless of the faith or denomination within that faith, whether it be the Vision Quest of Native Americans or the Cursillo experience of Christians, a voluntary time away with one's faith tradition can serve as a spark to get people thinking seriously and more deeply about what they believe. Theologians have begun to call this the "leap of faith," which causes people to fully embrace what they have been a part of—totally on their own volition.

Still others have said religion is needed for the morality it teaches. Every major faith discussed in this text has some version of the Golden Rule (Matthew 6), and, in some more than others, the body is seen as the temple of the Holy, which leads to living a moral, chaste, and monogamous life. Could these values exist without religion in their corner? Maybe, but religion gives mankind a basis from which to start and from which to refer back.

Why Study Religion?

This fundamental question leads to another question: Why don't we leave the study of religion to religious communities? After all, that's where it belongs! While that argument may hold some weight with some, it doesn't provide for objectivity. A person teaching a faith that he or she is part of in a religious setting by definition cannot be objective. He or she is simply expounding and proselytizing. On the other hand, when religion is approached as an academic study or discipline, it makes no difference what faith tradition the researcher is—it is merely an objective study.

To fully understand, appreciate, and gain insight, a person studying religion has to be without bias. In our American society—which is roughly 50% Christian—it is almost impossible to be objective when learning about a faith that is foreign to us. However, as searchers for the facts, we must strive to be empirical and remain completely objective. There is a huge difference between a study of religion and a religious study.

Religion has been seen by some to be a projection of human needs—i.e., a primitive community needs rain to grow crops, so they submit to the god of rain, which they either created or has been handed down to them; human sacrifice is committed to appease a god that a community fears; a person is designated a "sin eater" to symbolically take away the sins of a person who has died. Each of these situations speaks to a need met through a religious statement or practice. Greek and Roman mythology exhibit this perfectly as well—Atlas holds up the world and Neptune commands the sea.

Ludwig Feuerbach (1804–1872) said that religions were essentially projections of the wishes and needs of humanity. According to Feuerbach, people tend to see themselves as helpless and dependent when faced with the challenges of life. They therefore seek to overcome their problems through imagining a power of goodness who can help them. Put another way, humanity is not created in the image of God, but God is created in the image of idealized humanity. He believed that people seek in heaven what they cannot find on earth. Thus, religion is reduced to a form of wishing. Feuerbach further believed that when people become knowledgeable or powerful, religion is replaced by technology and politics.

Obviously, the above author is coming from an atheistic standpoint, but he does make some interesting points. For instance, is religion still viable when it is reduced to merely asking for what we want? Isn't that the same as believing in one giant benefactor who gives us everything? For the Christian, Jesus accepted the cross even though he could have run away, which proves that this faith—which is based on his teaching—has nothing to do with selfishness and everything to do with selflessness. In the case of many, even when it comes to religion, the question that remains is, "How can I get what I want?"

The famous author Karl Marx stated, "Man makes religion, religion does not make man ... it is the sigh of the oppressed creature, the heart of a heartless world ... it is the opium of the people." Marx was trying to say that religion offers hope and can be used as manipulation, or opium, if you will. This is seen most vividly in some cult situations in which people are asked to give everything they own for a great reward—either monetary or a place in heaven. To be sure, religion has been used for unscrupulous reasons and will continue to be as long as people seek escape.

Theories abound calling religion a crutch for people who can't stand on their own two feet and saying that when one matures he or she can face the world without God or religion (Sigmund Freud). However, people of religious faith are not all in it for self-serving reasons. Countless millions sacrifice much of their lives for the benefit of mankind and not for any personal after-death benefit. They are simply living a religious life and following a moral code. Their philosophy is that whatever happens after this life is up to God. I call that more of a realistic faith than a self-serving one.

There needs to be something said at this point regarding two concepts: religion and martyrdom and religion and being self-serving. First, martyrdom seems to be an integral part of many religions—to be a martyr is to be, in effect, a witness to the faith by what a person says and does. In the Roman Catholic baptismal rite, parents and godparents are asked to be an example to the child being baptized through the witness of their faith "by what they say and do" (Roman Canon Baptismal Rite). However, the term "martyr" has come to mean someone who actually dies for his or her faith and, by so doing, becomes an eternal witness inspiring others.

Some witnesses die for questionable causes and even seek suicide as a way of becoming a martyr. Others decide to take unwilling others with them; a case in point would be the suicide bombings of 9-11. The true sincere martyr, however, faces the adversary without fear and accepts death if that's what it takes to advance the cause. The martyr does not include other unwilling people in the action. From the Christian perspective, Jesus was a true martyr—going to Jerusalem in the midst of Passover and turning over the Temple tables—and faced both the Roman government and the Jewish religious hierarchy. Mahatma Gandhi exhibited martyrdom behavior when he stood up to Great Britain in a non-violent protest and was killed by an assassin's bullet. Martin Luther King, who fashioned his actions off of Gandhi, was martyred during the Civil Rights Movement. What was unique about these three individuals was that they didn't back down, but in fact embraced their roles as martyrs.

The second, and polar opposite, view of religiosity is being self-serving. We live in a society today that is strewn with two things—comfort and speed. We communicate at the touch of a button, and we seek to avoid struggle. And we like what we like. I would submit that this is why people will "shop" for a good preacher or seek a house of worship that fulfills their needs. To a great extent, religion competes with other facets of our society, and much of it is based on entertainment. The obligation card works for fewer and fewer these days, and people will seek a "product" that serves them the best. As harsh as that sounds, it is a function of today's society. The question all people have to ask themselves is: are you one who seeks to serve for the benefit of mankind (the extreme among us becoming martyrs) or do you wish to be served?

Religious Response

Religious affiliations can be sources of both comfort and conflict. Religion in its purest form can provide people with meaning and consolation in difficult times of life. I can recall being summoned to the hospital at 3:00 a.m. for the wife of a man dying of liver failure. She only wanted to know if, when he died, he would be with God.

However, with the new globalization making our world smaller than ever before, there has arisen an urgency to understand others' beliefs. For many people around the world, religion is the central aspect of meaning in their lives. Religious experience may inspire courage and charity, but may also breed hatred and violence toward others. In general, the latter is caused by people behaving in their own self interest or trying to shape the divine to suit their own purposes.

Although we look at a religion as a way to communicate with a divine being or the supernatural, Buddhism qualifies as a religion and has neither of these characteristics. Perhaps we could substitute the term "sacred" for "divine" when speaking about being in a religious presence. In this one example, we can see how difficult a religious response can truly be.

Basic Religious Thought

Mythology

When we use the terms *myth* or *mythology*, we immediately think of a falsehood. But one should be careful to note that there is a huge difference between fact and truth, and many myths, while lacking in the facts, possess a great deal of truth. For instance, in the story of Pandora's Box, it makes very little difference whether or not there was a real Pandora or if she even had a box. What is important is the truth the story tells us—that the temptation of being curious can have serious consequences. The same can be said of the Garden of Eden story in Genesis 2. It makes very little difference if one believes in an actual Adam and Eve and an actual Garden; what is important is the question, faced with the same choice and temptation as the two of them, what would we have done? It has been said that a well structured myth contains more truth than factual evidence. Many pieces of religious literature—Judeo-Christian scriptures and Shinto writings, among others—have within them learning points disguised in myth.

Magic

Many non-religious people, and that is not said in a disparaging way, tend to equate magic with religion. After all, you ask for something and—Presto!—you get it. If people reduce religion to merely asking for things and expecting something in return, they truly have crossed over into what might be termed magic. This is not to say that petition prayer has no place in religion; after all, many people practice only this type of prayer. The problem enters when one either gets what they want, or they leave or turn away from the religion. It is clearly a form of manipulation, and that is the root of magic.

Religion, on the other hand, is about asking for guidance and strength to somehow find within ourselves the solution—on our own merit. Clearly, we are a results-oriented people: if something happens that we like, God loves us. However, if the opposite happens, we doubt his love or even at times his existence. One thing that should be remembered is that in the three Abrahamic religions (the People of the Book), at no time does the deity in question say things would be easy or that life would not contain struggles. The rule of thumb is that if one is looking for a quick fix, one is most likely on the magic bandwagon.

So why, one might ask himself, is anyone religious? If we don't necessarily get what we want (Jesus did not run from the cross, but he certainly did not want it), why be religious? There seem to be various reasons why people seek a religion or to lead a religious life. First, religion provides a moral compass for a certain lifestyle. Second, it states a belief, something on which people can rely. And third, there is a certain ritual component that puts people some way in contact with the eternal. Notice that the truly religious person does not expect anything from the deity. Unlike magic, a religious person does his or her best and worships the deity merely because that deity exists in one's mind and heart. A truly religious person is not self-centered but other-centered. Instead of "If I do this and this will I get to heaven," the religious person might ask, "How can I make this world a better place by practicing my religion?"

Divination

The practice of divination is very much a part of many religious traditions, as it deals with predicting the future and therefore carries with it many "shaman"-like qualities. In ancient Rome, a *haruspex* would read the entrails of animals to see what the future held. Even in the Hebrew Scriptures, prophets were called on to choose the king through sacred dice, a form of divination. As the word "priest" has evolved, the word now describes in many faith traditions an intermediary between the human and divine, and not a soothsayer or clairvoyant.

Rites of Passage

Key parts of many religious and even secular societies are rituals or rites of passage. Generally, these rites deal with the main parts of a person's life—birth, puberty, marriage, and death. Societies use these times to mark transition from one stage to the next, and in so doing see the faith tradition permeate through the entire life of the individual.

At birth, Judaism celebrates being one with the covenant by having each male circumcised on his eighth day. Females join the covenant through their fathers. At its very root, this symbolizes complete faith in God, as it is defilement of a body part. Today, this ritual has turned into a secular procedure, which some believe protects the child from disease. In the more ritualistic Christian churches, babies are baptized with water, following the command of Jesus. In some more primitive cultures, a rite of passage might be an ordeal of some kind. For instance, in some Native American tribes, young males who are going through puberty are encouraged to go on a Vision Quest, which might show their ability to withstand physical and emotional hardship for a three- or four-day period.

It is worth pointing out here that rites or rituals of passage usually involve critical points in a person's life and, correspondingly, these crisis points are when religion is sought out. Some rites of passage, for instance getting a driver's license, are a passage but secular in nature. Depending on the severity of the faith, religious passage rites take on different weight for different people or different societies.

Taboos

In some societies, certain actions are to be avoided in order to be faithful to the religious tradition. One of the most familiar taboos is the avoidance of pork by the Muslim or Jewish person. This taboo, although taken seriously, is actually based on dietary law and for health reasons. In some cultures, touching a dead person is considered unclean, as is associating with women who are in their menstrual cycle. Some ultra-Orthodox Hasidic Jews consider it taboo to even touch a woman other than one's wife. While this is not necessarily considered a taboo, the Roman Catholic Church used to forbid its members to eat meat on Friday in observance of Jesus's death. Still other cultures see twins as taboo, while at the same time some see them as a blessing.

Sacrifice

One of the oldest expressions of religious ritual is that of the sacrifice. We see in Leviticus that the Hebrews offered sacrifices of different animals depending on the severity of their offenses. While animals are a common form of sacrifice, grains and milk products have often been used. These sacrifices are for the precise reason to appease the gods. At times, there has been what is called a "shared sacrifice," in which some commodity is left for the gods and the rest is consumed by the person who made the offering.

Ancestor Worship

Most religious services wind up in one way or the other at a grave or final resting place. A Christian may have what is called an internment service; a Jewish person may have Kaddish prayers prayed over his or her grave. We put flowers on a tomb for one reason—to honor those who have gone before us. Probably the most common element among religions is the tradition of reverence for family members who have passed away. Native Americans believe that people really don't die, but that their spirits live on through the people they touched. On Sunday afternoons, people visit the graves of family who have gone before them.

Symbolism

The last introductory item I wish to deal with is the use of symbols in religion. When you think about religion—almost every type of religion—you think of symbolism. Perhaps this is because symbols evoke thoughts of what the religion means. For instance, the cross was an instrument of execution in ancient Rome and other countries. However, many Christians wear crosses around their necks and even have the symbol hanging up in their homes. The symbol has been transformed from just a method of killing to a symbol of hope for those who believe in the resurrected Jesus. In Buddhism, the symbol of the wheel with eight spokes around it becomes a symbol for the eight-fold path to Nirvana. In Sikhism, the Khanda is the symbol of complete Sikh belief and implies that the sword does not have to be an instrument of violence.

Symbols permeate our culture; from stop and yield signs to the American flag, it isn't merely the object itself, but the symbolism behind it. For instance, to a child, the American flag may conjure up the fourth of July, swimming, and a picnic, while to a veteran of war it may evoke an entirely different image and meaning. Religion is the same way, affecting people in different ways—for some a religious symbol is merely a signpost, while to others it touches the very fabric of their being.

As we embark on this collection of religious studies, let us remember that for the most part religion has provided a moral compass for much of the world, given people a ritualistic way of celebrating, and helped to join the human and the divine in cultures. Also, I am deeply indebted to the Hopfe and

Woodward text *Religions of the World* (Pearson), which is the textbook I used for the previous five years to teach World Religions.

Upholding Indigenous Freedoms of Religion and Medicine

Peyotists at the 1906–1908 Oklahoma Constitutional Convention and First Legislature

By Dennis Wiedman

In February 1908 newspapers throughout Oklahoma reported that the hotel lobbies of Guthrie, the capital of the new state of Oklahoma, were crowded with Indian men, women, and children. At the thirty-sixth day of the first Oklahoma legislature, just sixty days after the state was established by merging Indian and Oklahoma Territories, more than a hundred prominent representatives of the Comanche, Kiowa, Cheyenne, Osage, Ponca, Arapaho, Iowa, and Sac and Fox tribes filled the legislative hall. On four occasions, twice during the constitutional convention and twice at the first Oklahoma legislature six months later, Indian leaders assertively voiced their concerns about laws that restricted their rights to practice their medicine and religion.

At the Senate legislative hearings, Chessie McIntosh, a member of the Creek Nation, a lawyer, and a delegate at the earlier constitutional convention for the unsuccessfully proposed state of Sequoyah, expressed the importance of the moment:

Dennis Wiedman, "Upholding Indigenous Freedoms of Religion and Medicine: Peyotists at the 1906–1908 Oklahoma Constitutional Convention and First Legislature," *American Indian Quarterly*, vol. 36, issue 2, pp. 215–246, 255. Copyright © 2012 by University of Nebraska Press. Reprinted with permission. Provided by ProQuest LLC. All rights reserved.

Ladies and Gentlemen, in conclusion, I thank the people of the great State of Oklahoma for the consideration given the Indian in the late Constitutional Convention; I thank you for what I have never seen in any Legislature before, and I have been to the assembling of more than one state legislature—I have never seen where the Indians were invited into the Legislative Chamber and asked to present his wants. I thank you for that, and for the perpetuation of the souls of the different Nations to agree to come as you have done in the Great Seal of the State of Oklahoma, and I hope and trust that the Indian will make one of the best citizens of this State.[1]

These debates and discourses at the juncture of state formation structured the chartering of the Native American Church (NAC) in Oklahoma ten years later in 1918, creating the legal foundation for the practice of Peyotism throughout the United States and Canada, where it is now the largest intertribal Indigenous religion in North America.

In the five hundred years of European and American globalization of the world, seldom have Indigenous peoples been invited to a constitutional convention and first legislature to express their perspectives and concerns. The use of peyote by the Indigenous peoples of the southern plains and northern Mexico is ancient, dating back thousands of years to at least 5200 BP.[2] Indigenous peoples expressing their desires to practice their traditional medicines and religions directly to lawmakers at the formation of a state is a rare occasion in the United States or elsewhere in the world. Rarely in the five-hundred-year history of the European and American colonization of the world were the rights of the Indigenous peoples considered at the juncture when new political entities established their constitutions and first laws. Typically, nation-states attempt to extinguish Indigenous rights to land and resources, refuse to grant their political legitimacy, and severely persecute traditional healing and religious practices. Not until 1978 did the United States grant religious freedom to Native Americans.[3] Peyotists were not protected by federal law until 1994, when President Clinton signed the amendments to the American Indian Religious Freedom Act.[4] Not until September 2007 did the United Nations declare that nations recognize Indigenous rights to their spiritual and religious traditions as well as their traditional medicines and health practices.[5]

This article portrays this critical juncture in 1907 when the American nation-state imposed its full legal, economic, political, and value system upon more than forty Indigenous nations by merging Indian Territory and Oklahoma Territory into the state of Oklahoma. This critical political and cultural event, where Indigenous peoples expressed their rights for religion and medicine, is not documented nor analyzed in the literature. Even though Sidney Slotkin in his 1956 book, *The Peyote Religion*, details many of the legal and political events in defense of Peyotism, there is no mention of these hearings at the formation of the state of Oklahoma.[6] A photograph and six paragraphs in the 1987 book *Peyote Religion* by Omer Stewart briefly mention this historic event in the chapter on how Peyotism was suppressed.[7] Only a few sentences are in the latest book on Peyotism by Thomas Maroukis.[8]

Indigenous scholars such as Seminole/Shawnee historian Donald Fixico criticize the long history of academic literature that portrays Indigenous peoples as responding, accommodating, and assimilating to non-Indians and the US government.[9] These events at the founding of a new state demonstrate the proactive and strategic actions exhibited by Native Americans in defense of their rights within the political system that was being imposed upon them. This analysis of Peyotists meeting with the constitutional convention and first legislature is evidence that, ten years before the chartering of the NAC, Natives were fully engaged in the political process and that the discourses from these meetings then set the political, legal, and cultural structures that exist today in upholding these Indigenous freedoms of religion and medicine.

Considering the lack of information surrounding this important historical juncture, this article documents these untold events in Native American and Oklahoma history and highlights the proactive, strategic, and coordinated actions of Peyotists at the inception of a nation-state to influence laws for the acceptance of Indigenous forms of religion, healing practices, and medicines.

Methods

Using ethnohistorical research methods, I analyze an array of sources primarily located in the Omer Stewart Native American Church Archives at the University of Colorado Library, at the Fort Sill Museum Archives, and in the Oklahoma Historical Society (OHS).[10] The OHS Indian Archives contain tens of thousands of documents composed by Indian agents, Christian ministers, and Oklahoma legislators. Because of their power and the enormity of their written records, their stories and perspectives dominate the historical record, while the Peyotists' perspectives are obscured and nearly silent. Discourse and content analysis of these documents reveals the cultural themes expressed by Peyotists in their interviews, speeches, and dialogues with federal Indian agents, missionaries, courts, newspaper reporters, and elected Oklahoma legislators. This article builds the sequence and context of how these events were portrayed to the public and the specific purposes and positions of Peyotists before, during, and after the events. Transcriptions of the 1907 Constitutional Convention and the 1908 Oklahoma legislative hearings are the earliest recorded documents where Peyotists openly express their beliefs and views about their use of peyote. These have not been evaluated, analyzed, or discussed at any length in the existing literature on Peyotism or the Native American Church.

NATION-STATE BUILDING IN INDIAN AND OKLAHOMA TERRITORIES

Imposition of the nation-state both unifies and separates people, creating similarities and differences.[11] Nation-states attempt to establish social, economic, and political structures that standardize and homogenize diverse cultural groups. In order to maintain a distinct identity and legal status, each cultural group negotiates its particular place and interpretation of the universalizing precepts. Resistance of groups at the time of nation-state imposition produces important similarities and differences that persist for generations. This analysis of Peyotists at the formation of the state of Oklahoma is about Indigenous people strategically and collectively taking actions to create and shape their place in the nation-state.[12]

With the western expansion of the American frontier, enormous numbers of people arriving from Europe sought land and a new life in America. The story of dispossession of the Indigenous peoples from their land, resources, religions, and way of life has been retold in many books.[13] Proposals for an Indian state were recurrent from the first US treaty with the Delaware in 1788 to the state of Sequoyah in 1905.[14] In the very first treaty between the United States and an Indian nation, the Delaware in 1788 established trade and peaceful relations. The treaty specifies that other friendly tribes could join their confederation "to form a state whereof the Delaware nation shall be the head, and have a representation in Congress."[15] With the expanding European American populations, the Delaware and most eastern tribes were forced to move farther west. By the time of the Louisiana Purchase from the French in 1804, the United States had gained political power over the lands west of the Mississippi. A section of the US congressional act of March 26, 1804, forming the legal foundation for governing the vast lands obtained from the Louisiana Purchase sets in place the removal of eastern Indians west of the Mississippi river by authorizing the president to propose this to the tribal authorities.[16]

Initiating this forced removal language in the first paragraph of the treaty of 1828 with the Western Cherokee assured national sovereignty over their own lands in Indian Territory. Similar language soon appeared in treaties with other tribes.[17]

> under the most solemn guarantee of the United States, be, and remain, theirs forever—a home that shall never, in all future time, be embarrassed by having extended around it the lines, or placed over it the jurisdiction of a Territory or State, nor be pressed upon by the extension, in any way, of any of the limits of any existing Territory or State.[18]

With the 1830 American Indian Removal Act, President Andrew Jackson transformed the US policy of warfare and extermination of Native peoples to relocation and segregation. Indigenous peoples on the western borders of the United States were then forcibly moved by the US military farther west primarily to lands designated as Indian Territory. Through treaties with the US government and reinforced with the Supreme Court decision of 1835, Indian tribes were recognized as separate but dependent nations.

Those moved west to Indian Territory were given the hope of governing their own peoples. Numerous tribes were moved to lands now known as Nebraska, Kansas, and Oklahoma. Known as the Five Civilized Tribes, the Cherokee, Seminole, Choctaw, Creek, and Chickasaw moved to Indian Territory, establishing distinct democratic republics and governing their own schools, legal systems, newspapers, and so on.[19]

FOUNDING OF INDIAN TERRITORY AND THE OKMULGEE CONVENTION

Members of the five tribes participated with both the North and the South during the Civil War. Since some participated with the Confederate States of America, after the Civil War the US government declared all former treaties with these Indian governments abrogated. In 1866 the United States procured new treaties with each of these tribal governments, resulting in concessions that further restricted their authority as separate nations. Common to each of these treaties was that a council consisting of delegates elected by each tribe would be annually convened and presided over by the superintendent of Indian affairs. This council, known as the Okmulgee Convention, was given the power to enact laws for the government of all the Indian tribes in Indian Territory; it allowed railroads to be built through their lands, thus bringing in more settlers from the East; and it ceded approximately half of their western lands to the United States. The first general national council of Indian Territory convened at Okmulgee, then the capital of the Muskogee Nation, on September 27, 1870.[20] The first paragraph of the 1870 Constitution of Indian Territory defines its purpose to form a union of tribes to implement the treaties of 1866. Section 2 of the "Declaration of Rights" specified religious freedoms:

> 2. The free exercise of religious worship and serving God without distinction of creed shall forever be enjoyed within the limits of this Territory. Provided that the liberty of conscious shall not be construed as to excuse acts of licentiousness or justify practices inconsistent with the peace, safety and good morals of this Territory.[21]

THE FOUNDING OF OKLAHOMA TERRITORY

The annexed lands that were previously the western portion of the Five Civilized Tribes of Indian Territory were then used by the federal government to forcibly resettle tribes to defined reservations. Many of these tribes had already been forcibly removed to lands in Kansas and Nebraska a generation before. Tribes settling on these lands included upper midwestern tribes (Otoe-Missouri, Sac and Fox, Iowa, Kickapoo, Pottawatomie-Shawnee); prairie tribes (Osage, Pawnee, Kaw, and Wichita-Caddo); the Delaware from the Northeast; and the southern plains tribes (Comanche, Kiowa, Plains Apache, Cheyenne-Arapaho, and Tonkawa). These tribes were then supervised and managed by Indian agents appointed by the Office of Indian Affairs in Washington, DC. Tribal political and legal structures were suppressed, as the Indian agents monitored individual behaviors, provided food rations and supplies, and with missionaries from a variety of Christian denominations enforced assimilation policies to prohibit traditional languages, beliefs, clothing, marriage patterns, medicines, and healing and religious ceremonies.

Furthering the dispossession of Indian rights to lands and resources, the Dawes Act or General Allotment Act in 1887 divided up reservation lands for individual Indian use. Allotments generally of 160 acres were to provide an agricultural economic base for a family, even though in most of the arid plains of western Oklahoma subsistence agriculture was not environmentally feasible. This US assimilation policy forced communal, tribally owned lands into individual ownership. Indians who accepted allotment became US citizens with the right to vote. The allotment of Indian lands took place over many years, beginning in 1898 and ending before statehood in 1907. With much resistance by tribes and individuals, lands were divided among persons whose names appeared on tribal rolls. Once lands were allotted to individuals and set aside for town sites, schools, and other public purposes, the surplus lands were to be opened for others. While there were little surplus lands for non-Indian homesteading in Indian Territory, hundreds of thousands of acres were available after allotment in Oklahoma Territory.[22]

On completing allotments, vast sections of Oklahoma Territory lands were opened to European American homesteaders, with some tracts being claimed in a single day by thousands of non-Indians during the now famous Oklahoma land runs. Almost immediately these new non-Indian citizens began forming a territorial government to administer schools, roads, and bridges and to provide legal and judicial protections. The first Oklahoma territorial convention of ninety-six delegates met in Guthrie on July 17, 1889, after which they prepared a petition to the US Congress for recognition as a territory. The US Congress responded on May 2, 1890, by implementing the Oklahoma Organic Act, which guided the development of a government for Oklahoma Territory with a structure similar to that of prior states, with a governor, a legislature, and a supreme court.[23] Without the time for careful deliberation, there was a wholesale adoption of the laws of Nebraska. These served as the laws until revised by Oklahoma territorial legislative actions. The territorial government met for seventeen and one-half years, from May 22, 1890, until Oklahoma statehood on November 16, 1907.

Indian involvement was minimal, while corporate interests and Republican politics dominated Oklahoma Territory. This is in contrast to Indian Territory, where Indian involvement was great and where farmer/family interests and Democratic politics dominated. Oklahoma territorial officers were appointed by the Republican US president for thirteen of its seventeen years. Appointed governors were Republicans, usually from outside the territory.[24]

With the famous land runs, cities were built in a day, and the population of western Oklahoma increased dramatically. The population of Oklahoma Territory went from 78,475 in 1890 to 733,062 in 1907 at the time of statehood, a tenfold increase.[25] As Indian reservation lands were allotted, not only did

Indians lose their substantial economic resource base to non-Indians, but a major political power shift occurred as both Indians and non-Indians became citizens and voters in the new territorial government. Once accepting an allotment, Indians became US and territorial citizens living on private property rather than living on reservations under Bureau of Indian Affairs jurisdiction. During this transition federal Indian agents lost their power to enforce BIA policies on Indian-owned private property, shifting the legal base of enforcement from federal BIA policies to territorial laws and statutes.

Peyotism in Western Oklahoma

The basic beliefs and social structure of Peyotism were refined and standardized in southwestern Oklahoma among the tribes forced to live on reservations under the governance of federal Indian agents and Christian ministers. Two major forms of Peyotism developed in southwestern Oklahoma from the 1860s to the 1880s, known as Little Moon and Big Moon Peyotism. Little Moon Peyotism developed first among the Comanche, Kiowa, and Kiowa-Apache. Big Moon Peyotism developed among the Caddo and Delaware living on the adjacent reservation to the north. The basic structure of both these forms derived from the Lipan Apache, who traditionally resided where peyote naturally grows along the Rio Grande of western Texas and northern Mexico. The Comanche and Kiowa formulated the Little Moon version based on the teachings of Chevato, a Lipan Apache who moved to the Comanche reservation.[26] Little Moon Peyotism is based on members praying and singing in an all-night ceremony held in a teepee led by four leaders using a staff, fan, rattle, and drum as ritual instruments. A temporary crescent moon altar made of earth surrounded a fire in the center of the teepee. An 1891 drawing book of Kiowa artist Silverhorn provides evidence that the Little Moon ritual form and leadership structure that are current today were standardized by at least the late 1880s.[27] During the 1890s, Comanche and white Texan Quanah Parker became the primary public figure for Little Moon Peyotism, while John Wilson of Caddo, Delaware, and French background was the Big Moon leader.[28] John Wilson traveled from his reservation adjacent to the Comanche to northeastern Oklahoma, where he introduced Big Moon Peyotism to his Delaware relatives and then to the Quapaw and Osage. John Wilson built upon the Little Moon ritual structure, adding Christian biblical beliefs and symbols with a permanent concrete altar often housed in a wooden building.[29] The Osage rationally and purposefully transformed their traditional religious and political system, adopting John Wilson's Big Moon Peyotism as the focal point.[30] Little Moon and Big Moon Peyotism are the foundations for the major forms of Peyotism practiced throughout North America today. In the late 1880s, when Peyotism came to the attention of the Indian agents and missionaries, Peyotism was already being practiced by the tribes throughout Oklahoma Territory.[31] By the 1940s variations of both versions were practiced by reservation Indians throughout the western United States and Canada.[32]

Federal Involvement, Policies, and Actions

On every reservation there were aggressive actions by the US Indian agents of the BIA and Christian missionaries to restrict Native religious practices, dances, medicine men, and political self-governance.

In 1888 the use of peyote was brought to the attention of the BIA commissioner by the agents governing the Comanche, Kiowa, Caddo, Kiowa-Apache, and Delaware.[33] In order to suppress traditional religion and medical practitioners, an 1889 BIA policy specified arrest and jail time for those identified as practitioners. By 1890 Indian agents reported Peyotism among so many western tribes that the BIA commissioner instructed agents that it was the government's duty to stop the use of the "mescal bean." It should be classified as an "intoxicating liquor," and its sale by traders should be prevented: "The court of Indian offences at your agency shall consider the use, sale, exchange, gift, or introduction of the mescal bean as a misdemeanor punishable under section 9 of the rules governing the court of Indian offences."[34]

By 1892 the BIA had formalized a system of Indian courts throughout US reservations with Indian judges appointed by the Indian agents. BIA commissioner Thomas J. Morgan issued standard rules for Indian courts to be enforced on all the reservations. Among these are specific rules outlawing traditional activities related to social gatherings for religious and healing purposes.

> Dances—Any Indian who shall engage in the sun dance, scalp dance, or war dance, or any similar feast, so called, shall be guilty of an offense, and upon conviction thereof shall be punished for the first offence by withholding of his rations for not exceeding ten days or by imprisonment for not exceeding ten days; for any subsequent offense under this clause he shall be punished by withholding his rations for not less than ten days nor more than thirty days, or by imprisonment for not less than ten days nor more than thirty days.
>
> Medicine men—Any Indian who shall engage in the practices of so-called medicine men, or who shall resort to any artifice or device to keep the Indians of the reservation from adopting and following civilized habits and pursuits, or shall use any arts of conjurer to prevent Indians from abandoning their barbarous rites and customs, shall be deemed guilty of an offense, and upon conviction thereof, for the first offense shall be imprisoned for not less than ten days and not more than thirty days: Provided that for subsequent conviction for such offense the maximum term of imprisonment shall not exceed six months.[35]

Following individual land allotments, the federal Indian agents lost significant power to regulate individual Indian citizens, so they initiated efforts to insert their policies into the laws of the new Oklahoma territorial government. The May 21, 1896, edition of the *Hennessey Clipper*, the newspaper that served northwestern Oklahoma, communicated to the general public on its front page that Captain Woodson,

Indian agent of the Cheyenne and Arapaho at Darlington, had received instructions from the BIA commissioner to inform the Indians that unless they abandoned the use of mescal, their rations would be cut off.[36] With the full support of the BIA commissioner, Indian agent Colonel Woodson at the Cheyenne and Arapaho Agency worked with political leaders to introduce a law at the 1899 session of the Oklahoma territorial legislature to prohibit Indian medicine men from practicing their incantations and using "mescal beans."[37] On March 7, 1899, a bill passed the House prohibiting the practices of Indian "medicine" men and the sale of the mescal beans to Indians. With an array of other laws, Governor George Bellamy signed Bill 224 on March 14, transmitting it to the secretary of the territory and making it a new law.[38] The *Session Laws of 1899*, chapter 12, article 2, read:

> Section 1. That it shall be unlawful for any so-called Indian Medicine Man to practice among the allotted Indians of the Territory, who is not legally authorized under existing Statutes to do so, or to hold incantations over the sick, or to maltreat, or in any manner whatsoever abuse the sick, or to commit immoral practices upon sick persons, or to demand payment for such services.
>
> Section 2. It shall be unlawful for any person to introduce on any Indian Reservation or Indian allotment situated within this Territory or to have in possession, barter, sell, give, or otherwise dispose of any "mescal beans," or the product of any such drug, to any allotted Indian in this territory: Provided, That nothing in this Act shall prevent its use by any physician authorized under existing laws to practice his profession in this Territory.
>
> Section 3. Any person who shall violate the provisions of this act in this Territory, shall be deemed guilty of a misdemeanor, and, upon conviction thereof, shall be fined in the sum not less than $25.00, nor more than $200.00, or confined in the County Jail for not more than six months, or be assessed both such fines and imprisonment at the discretion of the Court.[39]

Federal Indian agents actively took actions to restrict peyote use by limiting the travel of Peyotists and by limiting their economic resources. OHS records show that Indian agents penalized Peyotists and their families by denying food rations, requests for tools and labor to work their land, and requests to travel off the reservation.

The most-targeted federal effort to suppress Peyotism was begun on August 17, 1906, with the appointment of William E. Johnson as "special officer" to work with federal Indian agents in the prohibition against intoxicants. He was directed by the BIA commissioner to specifically focus on Oklahoma and Indian Territories "to suppress this illegal traffic and turn the two Territories, as far at least as the Indian parts are concerned, over to the new State in as clean a condition as possible."[40] Johnson included the "mescal bean" as an intoxicant and immediately set to work to restrict its use with surveillance of peyote meetings and by arresting Peyotists.[41]

THE PROPOSED STATE OF SEQUOYAH

Many citizens of the Five Civilized Tribes and other residents of the Indian Territory, fearing that the residents of Oklahoma Territory would dominate if the two territories were combined, moved to establish the state of Sequoyah. Gen. Pleasant Porter, principal chief of the Creek Nation, and Charles N. Haskell, a forty-six-year-old native of Ohio and railroad promoter, prevailed upon the leaders of the other Five Civilized Tribes to call the convention to write a constitution. Meeting during the summer of 1905 in Muskogee, Indian Territory, the Sequoyah convention completed a constitution that when brought to the voters on November 7, 1905, was overwhelmingly ratified by a vote of six to one. A month later, on December 4, 1905, the bill to admit the state of Sequoyah was denied by the US Congress and Republican president Theodore Roosevelt. This ended the possibility of an Indian state as stated in many treaties that removed eastern tribes to the west.

Following this refusal to recognize the predominantly Indigenous state of Sequoyah, the president then signed the Enabling Act, specifying the procedures for the formation of a constitutional convention for the new state of Oklahoma, merging Indian and Oklahoma Territories.

OKLAHOMA CONSTITUTIONAL CONVENTION DELEGATES AND MAJOR ISSUES

Approved by President Theodore Roosevelt, the Enabling Act of June 16, 1906, stipulated that a constitutional convention of 112 delegates should convene at Guthrie: 55 from each of the territories and 2 from the Osage Reserve. By this time the reservations were dissolved and the lands had been allotted individually, making allotted Indians voting citizens. Eligibility to serve as a delegate was limited to male citizens of the United States or of one of the Indian tribes, twenty-one years of age, and a resident of the area at least six months before the election. Women and blacks were restricted from being delegates. The thirty-four delegates who were members of the prior Sequoyah convention enhanced Native perspectives, interests, and power during the constitutional convention. William Murray, president of the convention, and Vice President Charles N. Haskell were active leaders in the Sequoyah convention.[42]

At least five major issues dominated the discussions at the constitutional convention and first years of the new state. Each of these had organized lobbying groups expressing their interests directly to the delegates in Guthrie. These issues dominated the debate and time of the members at the convention, the committee meetings, and the legislative hearings: (1) controlling the power of railroads and corporations;

(2) woman suffrage; (3) segregation of blacks; (4) prohibition of alcohol; and (5) formation of county boundaries. These issues, the personalities involved, and the context within the larger US issues at the time are well documented in the Oklahoma history books, while the Native American pursuit to uphold religious and medical beliefs is an untold story.[43]

Peyotists at the Oklahoma Constitutional Convention

The Oklahoma constitutional convention convened on November 20, 1906, and adjourned a year later on November 16, 1907, when officers of the new state were sworn in. The official proceedings of the convention record only one address to the convention members by a speaker noted as from a tribe. Quanah Parker spoke on the morning of the twentieth day of the session, Monday, December 17, 1906, at 10:00.[44]

Earlier in December, Comanche leaders held their own convention, a peyote meeting, to deliberate the issues and formulate their strategy to address the new Oklahoma government for the common welfare of the Indians. They selected Quanah Parker to present their interests before the convention. A non-Indian observer commented on the equality of the speakers and compared it to mass meetings, caucuses, and political conventions among white people.[45]

From the official typed minutes of the constitutional convention for Monday, December 17, 1906, after a formal vote to allow Parker to speak, President Murray introduced Chief Quanah Parker of the Comanche and several of the subchiefs of the various tribes as attending this convention to express matters of interest to them. Parker begins by expressing concerns against forming two counties from the one in which the Comanche live. He then expounds upon the Indian desire not to enact laws against Indian medicine.

> CHIEF QUANAH PARKER: Gentlemen, I am glad to meet you all this morning. My name is Quanah Parker. My Indians just the same as you people settled in the United States. I look after my Indians. My Indians pay taxes. That is what I come here for, relative to my people's interests, and two or three of my head men are over there, of the Kiowas, the Comanches and the Apaches, and the Cheyennes too are here. I say to, you gentlemen, just as I said while ago, that I pay taxes just the same as you people. There is one matter about Comanche county and Kiowa county. They want to cut those counties up, and make a poor county, maybe. That is the reason me come here for I don't want them to cut that county off of Comanche county, and my people, they pay taxes. The taxes are too high for my people. That is one matter that I came here for. Here is another matter. I am an Indian myself; I am half white. My mother was a white woman; I attend to the government business for a good many years. All kinds of papers and agreements with the government I signed, about my country; the big pasture, four hundred

thousand acres, all of that matter, I attend to that. I help all kinds of business. That is the kind of man I am. Here is another matter. I am pretty near fifty years old; maybe over fifty years old, and my Indian ways are going out; they will not last maybe forty or fifty years yet. Here is another matter I came here about. My Indians use what they call peotus; some call it mescal; all my Indian people use that for medicine. That is a good medicine and when my people are sick they use it. It is no poison and we want to keep that medicine. I use that and I use the white doctor's medicine, and my people use it too. I want to keep this medicine. I said while ago, my ways in time will wear out, and in time this medicine will wear out too. My people are citizens of the United States, and my people keep the right way; they go to school and teach school; I wish you delegates will look after my people—look after my Indians. My delegates look after my people, look after my Indians. My Indians, just the same as you people are citizens of the United States. That is all I will say to you Gentlemen.[46]

After hearing Parker's appeal not to split the county, members of the committee on boundaries requested permission to retire and proceed with their work. President Murray then asked the committee on public health and sanitation "to meet that afternoon to let Chief Parker come before them and present his views on medicine in his own way, because he says he came here on his own expense, and that is the primary object of his visit."

He stated to me yesterday that he had been told by the Indian Agency that this Convention intended to prevent their use of mescal, and he wanted the right to continue that use, the same as white doctors, as he explained here, as a medicine. He has evidence and I should like the Committee to meet at one or one-thirty and let Chief Parker tell them what he and his people want.[47]

A photograph commemorating Quanah Parker, the leading Peyotists, and members of the medical committee of the Oklahoma constitutional convention portrays eleven Kiowa, Comanche, and Cheyenne Peyotists and the sixteen members of the medical committee and legislature. Omer Stewart published this photograph and reported that the medical committee was sympathetic to the Indians and impressed by their demeanor and intelligence. The committee told the chiefs: "This is your religion like my white church. Keep it for your younger children that they too will preserve it for the future generations."[48]

Four months later the constitutional convention ended with the 106-page constitution signed by the delegates. The handwritten Oklahoma Constitution of April 19, 1907, is now on display in the foyer of the Oklahoma state capitol. Visible to the public is section 2 on the first page, which reads: "Perfect toleration of religious sentiment shall be secured, and no inhabitant of the State shall be molested in person or property on account of his or her mode of religious worship, and no religious test shall be required for the exercise of civil or political rights."[49]

A month after Quanah's address to the convention the *Daily Oklahoman* reported that Quanah had met with success.

> Quanah Parker, chief of the Comanche Indians, has returned from Guthrie with the assurance from President Murray and other delegates to the constitutional convention that no provision of the constitution will prevent the sale and eating of mescal beans among the Indians of the new state. Parker states that he was treated very courteously by the constitutional delegates.[50]

Even with these concerted efforts by Indian leaders at the constitutional convention, the anti-medicine men and anti-mescal bean laws that were in the Oklahoma territorial laws were essentially repeated in the first 1907–8 laws of the state of Oklahoma. The federal Indian agents had prevailed, showing the power of the federal government and the BIA in influencing state laws continuing federal assimilation policies.

THE ARREST AND TRIAL OF CHEYENNE AND ARAPAHO

Not even a month after Quanah Parker's appeal to the constitutional convention, on January 11, 1907, federal Indian agents sent letters to Peyotists telling them it was against Oklahoma territorial law.[51] Then on February 9, in northwestern Oklahoma Territory, a peyote meeting was disrupted by Indian police, and the first arrests were made. In *Territory of Oklahoma v. Reuben Taylor, Howling Wolf and Percy Cable*, complainant Charles E. Shell, Cheyenne and Arapaho Indian Agency superintendent, says that these three "willfully and unlawfully have in their possession 'Mescal Beans' and dispose of said 'Mescal Beans' to other allotted Indians all of which is against the peace and dignity of the Territory of Oklahoma."[52] The Cheyenne Peyotists, led by Reuben Taylor, hired attorney D. K. Cunningham, whose letter to Indian Agent Charles Shell defends the use of peyote for its medical and healing properties and also as a way to worship God. Reuben Taylor and the two others faced trial, were found guilty, and were fined $25 each. On appeal, no judgment or sentence was ever filed.[53]

Many other court cases were tried in 1907. Most ended in the acquittal of the Indians, who claimed that they consumed "peyote," not the "mescal bean," which was prohibited by the law. Mescal beans (*Sophora secundiflora*) are small red beans that grow on small trees, while peyote (*Lophophora williamsii*) is a small green cactus that grows on the ground. Both grow in southern Texas and northern Mexico.

New State Citizenship and First Laws

In the new state constitution Native Americans received citizenship equal to whites. "Colored" or "Negroe" applied to all persons of African descent, and the term "white race" included all others.[54] This definition of citizenship entitled Indians to a voice at the constitutional convention and first legislature. A census at the time of state formation indicated a total Oklahoma population of 1,414,000, with the 75,012 Indians composing only 5.3 percent of the total population.

On November 16, 1907, President Roosevelt signed the official proclamation declaring Oklahoma a new state, and Charles Haskell, the new governor, was sworn into office at Guthrie, the new state capital.[55] The first legislative session began in January 1908 with its primary task to implement the recently approved constitutional convention.[56]

Three of the 1907 general statutes of the new state of Oklahoma restricted Native American medicine and religion.[57] They were basically the same wording as in the Oklahoma territorial laws from 1899. To modify or remove these statutes was the focus of the special meetings of the constitutional convention held in 1907 and the first legislative session. Section 1860 of the first set of Oklahoma statutes made it unlawful for medicine men to practice among allotted Indians of the state, to hold incantations over the sick, or to demand payment for services. Section 1861 outlawed the possession, bartering, selling, or giving of any "mescal bean" to any allotted Indian in the state. The third statute, section 1863, legislated that a person guilty of either statute would be committing a misdemeanor, with fines from $25 to $200 or confinement in the county jail for not more than six months.[58]

The First Legislative Session

Wanting to continue the Oklahoma territorial laws, Indian agents, organized and led by federal Indian Agent Charles Shell of the Cheyenne and Arapaho Agency, pushed for a bill outlawing medicine men and mescal use in the new state laws. Opposing these efforts were Quanah Parker, Peyotists who attended the earlier constitutional convention, and those they had organized from tribes throughout Oklahoma.

> Guthrie, Okla. Dec 17. Quanah Parker, chief of the Comanche Indians will be in Guthrie early in January for the purpose of lobbying with legislative committees in behalf of his people. A bill has been introduced in the house providing a prohibition against the sale of mescal beans to Indians. To this bill Parker does not object but he fears that the legislature will go further than this and deprive the Indians of the use of a medicinal herb known as beyoute.

In a letter to a friend here Parker says "The Indians here use beyoute, no use beans at all. I am the man that knows this beyoute business well. These Indians use it when they are sick and they don't use it when they are not sick."[59]

Lieutenant Governor George Bellamy asked for the Indian agents to appear before the Oklahoma legislature to show why the measure should pass, and he wanted the Indians to also be heard.[60]

The mescal bean bill introduced at the first Oklahoma legislature by Charles Shell, Cheyenne and Arapaho Indian agent, attempted to strengthen the Oklahoma territorial laws outlawing medicine men and mescal bean use by amending sections 2651–53 of Wilson's statutes. Analysis of the documents and correspondence of Agent Charles Shell indicate he had a wide array of supporters. Federal government supporters included the BIA commissioner in Washington, BIA Special Officer William Johnson, and numerous Oklahoma Indian agents, but not all of them. National organization supporters included the Lake Mohunk Conference, Friends of the Indians, and the Indian Rights Association. Oklahoma legislative supporters included Lieutenant Governor George Bellamy and A. Frank Ross, member of the House of Representatives from Durant. Religious organization supporters included the Independent Order of Odd Fellows, the Reformed Church in America, and the Baptist Church.

By January 7, 1908, sixteen Indians had registered as lobbyists.[61] On the days before the legislative hearings, hundreds of Indians merged on Guthrie. Newspapers from around the state reported on at least three Indian lobbying groups. Newspapers contained interviews with spokespersons who expressed their positions to the Oklahoma public. Quanah Parker represented the southwestern Oklahoma tribes of the Kiowa, Comanche, and Apache; a second group from the Cheyenne and Arapaho of northwestern Oklahoma was represented by Reuben Taylor; and a third group from the Osage of northeastern Oklahoma was led by Black Dog. Numerous tribal leaders mentioned in the news stories reflected on the importance of why so many important Indian leaders, who had often traveled to Washington to speak for their tribes, were now descending on the capital of Oklahoma.

On January 20, the day before the legislative hearings, Black Dog, with members of the Osage, Iowa, Otoe, Cheyenne, Sac and Fox, and Ponca, met with Speaker Murray and Representative William A. Durant in Speaker Murray's office for an hour discussing how the bill prohibited their religion.[62] William A. Durrant, Choctaw, was the only full-blood Indian in the legislature.

A newspaper interview with Reuben Taylor summarized his position that the Indian people did not care much about the mescal bean, but they did not want their religious rights disturbed.

> The Indians do not seem to care so much for the suppression of the mescal bean, as they do not use it to any extent only as a medicine. But the peyote, they claim is a part of their religious ceremonies, and they want their religious ceremonies, and they want their rights protected. Peyote is to the Indians in their communion services, as bread and wine are to the white man.

The wine is represented by water, being the blood of Christ, while the peyote is the bread, representing the body.[63]

On January 21, 1908, there were two hearings: one before a committee of the House of Representatives in the morning presided over by Representative H. Ashby, and another before the Senate that same afternoon led by Lieutenant Governor Bellamy with forty-one of the forty-four Senate members present. A transcriptionist produced typed minutes of Senate and House discussions (committees of these bodies did not have formal transcriptionists). Therefore, excellent verbatim typed minutes exist for the Senate hearings; fortunately, handwritten notes are extant from the morning hearings before a committee of the House.

Hearings Before the House of Representatives

During the morning meeting with House of Representative members, the Indian agents were kept out at the discretion of Governor William H. Murray, so the Indians were much freer in expressing themselves. In the Indian Archives of the Oklahoma Historical Society, six handwritten pages on stationery of the first legislature are in an envelope upon which is written: "Notes of an Indian Convention before a Committee of the House of Oklahoma, January 21st, 1908 by A. Frank Ross." On the top of the first page is written: "Report of Indian Pow-wow Jan 21, 1908 considering the 'Mescal Bean' Bill." These notes record the key points made by seven speakers: three Peyotists, Quanah Parker (Comanche), Otto Wells (Kiowa), and Black Dog (Osage); an Indian non-Peyotist, Joseph Pointer (Cheyenne-Arapaho); the Indians' lawyer, T. K. Cunningham; and a response from Albert Riddle, a member of the House of Representatives.[64]

Key points made by the Peyotists illustrate the defense of their values by distinguishing peyote from mescal while explaining their use of peyote as both medicine and religion. Quanah Parker began by saying: "The Mescal Bean cannot be eaten, a drink is made of it but it is the piote bean we eat or use as a medicine."

Otto Wells, a Kiowa Peyotist, stated:

> The piote bean is good if used right. My wife was sick and pronounced incurable, so I got the peyote bean and we attended their meetings where we all prayed for her recovery and she was restored to health after having been so low for six years. She is now well and fat and we have [come] here to ask you to allow us to have piote as a medicine and for our religious services.

Black Dog of the Osage spoke last, saying that he had used peyote for years but not the mescal bean:

I have used the peoti bean for ten years but not the mescal bean. I use the peoti bean in my religious ceremonies. We use it in our meetings same as you white people worship God in your churches. It does not make us crazy or cause us to do any harm and I can see nothing wrong in it. When I eat it I feel happy and good and thank God for his many gifts. As we use peyote in our meetings we realize that we have to die and it aids us to do right, it helps us to live and enjoy happy experiences and we trust you will allow us to retain this channel through which so many gifts flow.

Dr. Albert S. Riddle, member of the House of Representatives and member of the public health committee, stated: "I have been almost overcome by the talks of these Indians and I do not believe any legislator wants to rob these Indians of their religious rights. If I have regard for any person on earth it is for the aborigine of our country, it is our duty to protect their rights religiously and otherwise."[65]

HEARINGS BEFORE THE SENATE

During the afternoon open session before the Senate, both Indian agents and Indians were permitted to speak. The official published *Journal of the Proceedings of the Senate* does not provide the content of the discussions but does list the order of the eleven speakers.[66] Four federal Indian agents spoke first: Charles E. Shell of the Cheyenne and Arapaho Agency; Mr. Edsen Watson of the Kaw Agency; Mr. Hugh Noble, agent of the Ponca Agency; and W. C. Colbert, agent of the Sac and Fox. They were followed by Quanah Parker (Comanche), Paul Boynton (Arapaho), Otto Wells (Comanche), Chessie McIntosh (Creek), Joseph Springer (Iowa), James Waldo (Kiowa), and D. K. Cunningham, the Indians' lawyer.[67] Among the six Indians were four Peyotists (Waldo, Parker, Wells, and Springer) and two non-Peyotists (McIntosh and Boynton). Two of the Peyotists, Quanah Parker and Otto Wells, had attended the medical subcommittee of the constitutional convention the prior year.[68]

Those against the use of peyote based their arguments on the supposedly detrimental effects of long-time usage of the mescal bean and the amount of time the Indians spent in peyote meetings. Indian Agent Charles Shell began the discussion, dwelling upon these points, followed by Agents Noble, Watson, and Colbert. Defending the use of peyote was Quanah Parker, who spoke of three kinds of mescal: one like a bean about the size of a peanut; one plant about as high as the top of a desk, which is the one from which they make whiskey; the third peyote, which is the one he uses. He recommended that three men be selected to go to Mexico and see the differences themselves.

Mr. Springer, a Peyotist from the Iowa tribe, stated that his tribe uses the little red mescal bean as an ornament, and they call it "red medicine." He has a vest with the beans on it for buttons, and when he dresses up he puts it on in addition to his leather leggings. He said that his people were "trying to reach

Jesus Christ: we worship him and use this medicine, as the Catholic people use wine as a sacrifice. It is good medicine if taken only a little of it. If Mr. Shell would take a gallon of soup it will hurt him, too. We all know that too much of a thing is no good."

Kiowa Peyotist James Waldo talked about the difference between mescal and peyote. He said that they could make a law against the use of mescal, but the peyote was used in his religion as a medicine, and he did not want it taken away.

Comanche Peyotist Otto Wells commented on the agents' claim that the Indians become lazy and lie around for two or three days at a time during peyote meetings. He asked, "How is it that the missionaries hold their camp meetings a week at a time?"[69]

When called to the stand, the Arapaho, Paul Boynton, claimed that he was not a believer in Indian religion or in the use of peyote. But he told the Senate to see this peyote society as a certain denomination:

> It is known that there is a great many denominations, but let us call this one of them—let us try to recognize it as one of the ways that the great spirit is talking to the Indians.
>
> I thank you all that you do not pass a law in regard to this just because one or a few men do not like this—just because a few men do not like this at all why do you go to work and make a law? No, you have no reason whatever—common sense will always tell us that any religion that might be existing among the Indians would be constitutional.
>
> If you think they have a religion of their own, give them a right—that is what I am after—if my people think they have a religion of their own, give them a right to worship their religion. Give them a right.
>
> I do not think you got any right whatever, or any other denomination to interfere with this right. Let my people have a right—let them have their right because I have seen that it does them good.[70]

Chessie McIntosh, a non-Peyotist of the Creek Nation, then spoke, carrying on Boynton's forceful talk about rights. McIntosh spoke about how the Indian, according to the constitution of the state, was on an equal footing with and given the same opportunities as the white people. He thanked the legislature for what he had never seen in the legislature before, and that was to see that the "Indians were invited into the legislative chamber and asked to present his wants."[71]

Indian Agent Charles Shell returned to the stand to defend what had been said against him. He said that he was in charge of certain affairs of the Indians and that he had found a statute that was being violated. He considered it his duty to prosecute them for violating this law:

> As I said in the beginning, if you see fit to refuse to pass this amendment to bill No. 49, I shall certainly say that is right. I never question the action of the judge and jury. If you shall decide

that it would not hurt these Indians, all right. I believe it does, for I believe that no person can take a strong alcholoidal poison into their systems without harm, but if you say they shall do it, I will not raise my hand against it.[72]

No formal legislative vote or decision is recorded in the minutes, the newspapers, or the Indian agency correspondence. A month later, on February 25, 1908, Lieutenant Governor George Bellamy wrote to Indian Agent Charles Shell, transmitting typed copies of the speeches at the Senate hearings. In his cover letter he writes: "There is nothing done with the matter as yet." Then in an indirect way, noting defeat of the bill, he asks: "In your opinion would present law be effective if it is not amended?"[73]

THE EMERGENCE OF THE NATIVE AMERICAN CHURCH

Peyotists met with success: the three statutes outlawing medicine men and mescal use do not appear again in the 1908 edition of the Oklahoma state statutes. But even after the legislature's action not to continue these laws by the new state of Oklahoma, federal Indian agents continued to persecute Peyotists. Within weeks after the legislative hearings, federal Indian agent William E. Johnson shifted his efforts to prevent the importation of peyote from Mexico, where he purchased the entire peyote crop of southern Texas.

The federal government's continuing antipeyote activities stimulated the emergence of a variety of Peyotist defense organizations from Oklahoma to Nebraska. Anthropologists James Slotkin and Weston La Barre discuss organizations with titles such as Peyote Societies, Union Church, American Indian Church Brother Association, Kiowa United American Church, and the First Born Church of Christ.[74] Several of these consisted of "lodges," with elected officials indicating the adoption of European American forms of democratic governance. Slotkin described this organizational development:

> (a) The use of the white term "Church," with all its connotations, is an attempt to put Peyotism on a par with White religions. (b) The name reveals an attempt to accommodate to White patterns of religious organization. (c) It is a more dignified name according to White standards, reflecting the sensitivity of marginal people to the opinions of the dominant ethnic group.[75]

The first of these organizations to take the step to seek legal security for freedom of religious worship was in 1914, when Peyotists and their Otoe leader, Johnathan Koshiway, incorporated the First Born Church of Christ in Oklahoma.[76]

Failing to have an Oklahoma state law, Bureau of Indian Affairs agents and missionaries then moved their efforts to the national level by attempting to have the US Congress pass an antipeyote law in 1918. A federal law would pertain to Indians in all the states. The House Committee on Indian Affairs held hearings on H.R. 2614 in February and March 1918. This motivated numerous meetings and conferences of Peyotists to discuss defensive actions. James Mooney reported during the summer that these intertribal conferences debated "the matter of organizing their own native religion on a regular business basis, like any other church or society, as American citizens."[77]

Following the failure of H.R. 2614 to pass at the federal level, Oklahoma delegates from a variety of tribes met at Calumet, Oklahoma, on Cheyenne and Arapaho lands, to discuss actions they could take in defense of Peyotism. Here they settled upon the name Native American Church, and they then proceeded to incorporate with the state of Oklahoma as a church under this name on October 10, 1918. The chartering leadership was intertribal, representing tribes throughout Oklahoma, with Maack Haag (Cheyenne/Arapaho) as the first president.

Discussion

The formation of the state of Oklahoma was a culmination point for the dispossession of Indigenous rights to lands, resources, and traditional political, religious, and medical systems. Early treaties with the United States promised that by moving to Indian Territory tribes would never be under a territorial or state organization; later treaties implied that if their nations congregated in Indian Territory, they would one day have their own state. With the US Congress' denial to support the Indian petition for the state of Sequoyah, the merging of Indian and Oklahoma Territories was quickly brought about. Through placement on reservations and then the allotment of lands individually, Indians had been disenfranchised from their traditional lands and natural resources. Federal Indian agents, aggressively pursuing the federal assimilation policy, sought to keep Indians from speaking their traditional languages, performing their dances and ceremonies, and practicing their traditional religions and medicines.[78]

Once the land was allotted individually, Indians in eastern Oklahoma became citizens of Indian Territory, and those on the west and north became citizens of Oklahoma Territory. With territorial citizenship, the federal Indian agents lost their power to assert BIA policies over individual Indians on Indian lands. To retain this power, Indian agents successfully placed anti-medicine men and antipeyote statutes in Oklahoma Territory law. When the two territories merged to become the state of Oklahoma, the Indian agents sought to have the Oklahoma territorial laws continued as state law. At this important juncture during the constitutional convention and the first legislature, Peyotists attempted to retain two of the few things they still had left, their medicine and their religion.

These very public political forums at the constitutional convention and again at the first Oklahoma legislative assembly provide a unique view on the values and perspectives of Peyotists in defense of their religion and medicine. Ethnohistorical evidence from the sequence of events and the purposeful public presentation of positions demonstrates that the Peyotists strategically coordinated and planned their discourses and dialogues. They were proactive rather than reactive in their behaviors; they made strategic decisions on what to say, to whom and when; and they coordinated events rather than letting them happen.

Prior to these major events, reports in the newspapers and Indian agent correspondence reveal that peyote meetings were called, serving as conferences where speakers spoke, justifications were developed, and actions were planned well in advance. In the few days prior to the legislative hearings, newspaper interviews clearly presented the Peyotists' positions. In the fashion of well-organized lobbying groups, Peyotist leaders met with lawmakers the day before legislative hearings, educating them on their concerns. At both the constitutional convention and the first legislative hearings before the House committee and full Senate the selection of speakers carefully presented the range of opinions and perspectives, using personal stories, reference to people's experiences present in the audience, and written evidence from outside experts.

Throughout these events there is no evidence to show that citizens of Oklahoma responded to these issues or expressed opinions one way or the other. There were no opinion sections of newspapers written and no newspaper stories reporting resistance groups opposing the Indians' use of peyote or the federal agents' proposed law. Newspaper stories based on objective firsthand interviews often had a sensationalized headline, probably created by an editor to sell papers. This was not a local issue of the general Oklahoma population; it was mostly external from the federal government through the Indian agents, medical professionals, Christian churches through legislators, and Friends of the Indians national organizations that pursued an assimilationist agenda.[79]

These historical documents demonstrate that when first confronted by the Oklahoma legal, medical, and political system, Peyotists represented peyote as a medicine. Even though Indian leaders specifically voiced peyote's therapeutic use, the 1907 medical subcommittee of the Oklahoma constitutional convention concluded that the Indians should carry this "religion" on to their children. Subsequently, the 1908 speeches before the Oklahoma legislature showed that the political and legal systems would not recognize Peyotism as a medical system, yet it could be tolerated as a religion.

These events transformed Indian-white relationships, identities, and social structures in the political order of the new nation-state. The refinement of their discourses as the events unfolded narrowed and defined their positions even further within the political and legal structures being imposed on them. Most importantly, this juncture had long-lasting effects leading up to today. It upheld Indigenous religious rights, built broad intertribal solidarity for a common purpose, empowered an Indian voice to counter the power and hegemony of federal Indian agents and the BIA, promoted engagement of Indians as citizens of the new state using their own lawyers, established long-term political influence through direct communication with Oklahoma and national legislators, and structured the emergence of Peyotism as a religious organization ten years later in 1918 as the Native American Church.

Ethnohistorical methods reveal this important juncture in Oklahoma and Indian history that is missing from the history books. In a postmodern pursuit of the subjective views, perspectives, and positions of Peyotists, these methods reconstruct one-hundred-year-old personalities, positionalities, and political realities. Having been forcibly removed from their distant tribal lands, contained to limited reservations, and then prevented from practicing their traditional religions, dances, and medicines, Indians found themselves overwhelmed by the dramatically increasing white population through allotment of lands individually and then the famous land runs. Rights to the land, economic resources, and their own political systems had been systematically negated by the federal government with the Okmulgee convention, the Dawes Act, the Curtis Act, the Organic Acts, and the rejection of the state of Sequoyah. The formation of the state of Oklahoma was a culmination point for the disposition of Indigenous rights to lands, resources, and traditional political, religious, and medical systems. At the time of this juncture we find that the only assertive voice for Indigenous rights at the two major events founding the new nation-state were appeals by Peyotists for freedoms of religion and medicine.

The formation of the Native American Church is an example of the emergence of religious organizations that deliberately search for and create a sacred identity. As these emerge they adjust their fundamental beliefs and organizational principles to the larger nation-state's political and economic structure. In this process of adaptation, adjustment, and co-option they continue to articulate a powerful oppositional stance and resistance to the dominating and homogenizing nation-state. These emergent organizations respond at the local individual level of structural integration and cultural fragmentation by resisting the dominant worldview by presenting an alternative based on prior cultural traditions. These discourses at the juncture of the formation of the new state of Oklahoma juxtaposed the Indigenous worldview to a dominating and privileged worldview. Discourses during these critical events resulted in a reformulation and hybridization of the narratives used to justify identities and social and political structures leading to Peyotism being organized as the Native American Church in 1918 rather than as an ethno-medical health care system. Lechner contends that such hybridization and structural differentiation is a repeated process when cultural groups search for and attempt to restore an authentic sacred tradition within the political system imposed upon them.[80] This case shows that ethno-medical systems, which typically integrate spirituality and healing, are politically and legally forced to adopt the structure of a religious system at the juncture with the imposition of the nation-state.

Notes

This article is dedicated to Allen Dale, president of the Native American Church from 1946 to 1956 and founding president of the Native American Church of North America in 1955. Allen and his wife, Grace, devoted their lives to traveling the country defending the Native American Church and upholding Indigenous rights to medicine and religion. I presented a version of this article as an invited speaker at the Oklahoma Historical Society Indian Archives' seventy-fifth anniversary celebration on October

30, 2009. Special thanks to the library archives that provided access to documents and to the archivists who facilitated their location and use: Indian Archives at the Oklahoma Historical Society, Oklahoma City; Western History Collection at the University of Oklahoma, Norman; Omer Stewart Papers at the library of the University of Colorado, Boulder; and the Fort Sill Museum and Archives, Fort Sill, OK. Special gratitude goes to Martha Blaine and William Welgi of the Oklahoma Historical Society. Most importantly, to my wife, Felicia, who traveled with me along this road of life, encouraging and supporting my many research endeavors.

1. Minutes of the Senate Hearings on Mescal at the First Legislative Session of the State of Oklahoma, January 21, 1908, in Liquor, Peyote and Mescal Use, Cheyenne and Arapaho, Indian Archives, Oklahoma Historical Society (hereafter cited as IA, OHS).
2. Martin Terry et al., "Lower Pecos and Coahuila Peyote: New Radiocarbon Dates," *Journal of Archaeological Science* 33, no. 7 (2006): 1017–21.
3. American Indian Religious Freedom Act, Pub. L. No. 95–341, sec. 1, August 11, 1978, 92 Stat. 469.
4. American Indian Religious Freedom Act of 1994, Pub. L. No. 103–344, Laws of 103rd Cong., 2nd sess., October 6, 1994.
5. United Nations, *United Nations Declaration on the Rights of Indigenous Peoples*, September 13, 2007, http://www.un.org/esa/socdev/unpfii/en/declaration.html (accessed September 12, 2011).
6. Sidney Slotkin, *The Peyote Religion: A Study in Indian-White Relations* (Glencoe, IL: Free Press, 1956).
7. Omer Stewart, *Peyote Religion: A History* (Norman: University of Oklahoma Press, 1987).
8. Thomas C. Maroukis, *The Peyote Road: Religious Freedom and the Native American Church* (Norman: University of Oklahoma Press, 2010).
9. Donald Fixico, "Witness to Change: Fifty Years of Indian Activism and Tribal Politics," in *Beyond Red Power: American Indian Politics and Activism since 1900*, ed. D. Cobb and L. Fowler (Santa Fe: School of American Research, 2007), 2–15.
10. Dennis Wiedman, ed., *Ethnohistory: A Researcher's Guide*, Studies in Third World Societies, vol. 35 (Williamsburg, VA: College of William and Mary, 1986).
11. Immanuel Wallerstein, *The Modern World System III: The Second Era of Great Expansion of the Capitalist World-Economy, 1730–1840s* (New York: Academic Press, 1989).
12. Frank J. Lechner, "Global Fundamentalism," in *The Globalization Reader*, ed. Frank J. Lechner and John Boli (Oxford: Blackwell, 2004), 326–29.
13. Susan Lobo, Steve Talbot, and Traci Morris, *Native American Voices: A Reader*, 3rd ed. (Upper Saddle River, NJ: Prentice Hall, 2010); and Winona LaDuke, Recovering the Sacred: The Power of Naming and Claiming (Cambridge, MA: South End Press, 2005).
14. Annie Heloise Abel, "Proposals for an Indian State, 1778–1878," in *Annual Report of the American Historical Association*, 1908.

15. Charles J. Kappler, *Indian Affairs: Laws and Treaties*, vol. 2, *Treaties* (Washington, DC: Government Printing Office, 1904), http://digital.library.okstate.edu/kappler/Vol2/treaties/che0288.htm.
16. *Statutes at Large of the United States*, 8th Cong., 1st sess., 1804, 289.
17. Roy M. Gittinger, *The Formation of the State of Oklahoma, 1803–1906* (Norman: University of Oklahoma Press, 1939).
18. Treaty with the Western Cherokee, signed May 6 and proclaimed May 28, 1828, in Kappler, *Indian Affairs*, 2:288.
19. David W. Baird and Danney Goble, *The Story of Oklahoma* (Norman: University of Oklahoma Press, 1994), 322.
20. Arthur Lee Beckett, *Know Your Oklahoma* (Oklahoma City: Harlow Publishing, 1930).
21. Beckett, *Know Your Oklahoma*, 125.
22. Arrell Morgan Gibson, *Oklahoma: A History of Five Centuries* (Norman: University of Oklahoma Press, 1991), 194–96.
23. Baird and Goble, *The Story of Oklahoma*, 322.
24. Gaston Litton, *History of Oklahoma: At the Golden Anniversary of Statehood* (New York: Lewis Historical Publishing Co., 1957).
25. Irwin Hurst, *The 46th Star: A History of Oklahoma's Constitutional Convention and Early Statehood* (Oklahoma City: Semco Color Press, 1957).
26. William Chebahtah and Nancy McGown Minor, *Chevato: the Story of the Apache Warrior Who Captured Herman Lehman* (Lincoln: University of Nebraska Press, 2007).
27. Dennis Wiedman and C. Greene, "Early Kiowa Peyote Ritual and Symbolism: The 1891 Drawing Books of Silverhorn (Haungooah)," *American Indian Art Magazine* 13, no. 4 (1988): 32–41.
28. Dennis Wiedman, "Big and Little Moon Peyotism as Health Care Delivery Systems," *Medical Anthropology* 12, no. 4 (1990): 371–87.
29. Wiedman, "Big and Little Moon Peyotism"; Vincenzo Petrullo, *The Diabolic Root: A Study of Peyotism, the New Indian Religion, among the Delawares* (New York: Octagon Press, 1934).
30. Daniel Swan, "Early Osage Peyotism," *Plains Anthropologist* 43 (1998):51–71.
31. James Mooney, "The Mescal Plant and Ceremony," *Therapeutic Gazette* 12, no. 11 (1896): 7–11; Mooney, "The Kiowa Peyote Rite," Der Urquell 1 (1897): 329–33.
32. Stewart, *Peyote Religion*.
33. Order from the Special Agent in Charge to All Chiefs and Headmen of the Kiowa Agency, January 6, 1888, Liquor, Peyote and Mescal Use, Kiowa Agency, IA, OHS.
34. Thomas J. Morgan, Commissioner of Indian Affairs, to S. L. Patrick, Indian Agent, Sac and Fox Agency, Oklahoma, July 31, 1890, Liquor, Peyote and Mescal Use, Sac and Fox, IA, OHS.
35. H. Price, *Code of Indian Offenses and Rules Governing the Court of Indian Offenses* (Washington, DC: Department of the Interior, 1883), http://en.wikisource.org/wiki/Code_of_Indian_Offenses, accessed January 4, 2012.
36. "Capt. Woodson," *Hennessey Clipper*, May 21, 1896, 1.

37. A. E. Woodson, Report of Agent for Cheyenne and Arapaho Indian Agency, Darlington, Oklahoma, October 4, 1899, in *Annual Report of the Commissioner of Indian Affairs* (Washington, DC: Government Printing Office, 1899), 282–86.
38. "Oklahoma Laws List by Titles of Recent Session's Enacting: Bills and Resolutions," *Times Record* (Blackwell, OK), March 16, 1899, 1; "The House Today Passed the Following Measures," *El Reno* (OK) News, March 17, 1899, 2.
39. Territory of Oklahoma, *Session Laws of 1899* (Guthrie, OK: State Capital Printing Company, 1899), 122–23.
40. *Report of the Commissioner of Indian Affairs to the Secretary of the Interior* (Washington, DC: Government Printing Office, 1908).
41. William E. Johnson, Special Officer, Muskogee, Indian Territory, to Byron E. White, Superintendent of Indian School, Cantonment, Oklahoma, August 17, 1906, Liquor, Peyote and Mescal Use, Cheyenne and Arapaho, IA, OHS.
42. Hurst, *The 46th Star*.
43. Baird and Goble, *The Story of Oklahoma*, 322; Gibson, *Oklahoma*; Hurst, *The 46th Star*; Kathy Jekel, *The Original Constitution of the State of Oklahoma 1907 and the Road to Statehood* (Oklahoma City: Oklahoma Historical Society, 2007), 33.
44. *Proceedings and Debates of the Constitutional Convention of Oklahoma: November 20, 1906 to March 11, 1907*. Guthrie, OK: State of Oklahoma (Muskogee, OK: Muskogee Printing Co., 1907), 117.
45. "Red Men in Dreamland: Indians Are Happy to Learn They May Continue Use of 'Dope,'" *Daily Oklahoman*, January 23, 1906, 1, 3.
46. *Proceedings and Debates*, 117.
47. *Proceedings and Debates*.
48. Stewart, *Peyote Religion*, 136.
49. Jekel, *The Original Constitution*, 33.
50. "Red Men in Dreamland."
51. W. L. Fish, writing for Reuben Taylor, Cheyenne Indian, Kingfisher, Oklahoma, to Charles E. Shell, Superintendent of the Cheyenne and Arapaho Agency, Darlington, Oklahoma, January 11, 1907, Liquor, Peyote and Mescal Use, Cheyenne and Arapaho, IA, OHS.
52. Mildred Throckmorton, Kingfisher County Clerk, to James S. Slotkin, University of Chicago, August 3, 1955, Second Accession, 46—Chron. Files, 1945–55, Archives, Omer Stewart Papers, University of Colorado at Boulder Library.
53. Throckmorton to Slotkin.
54. Benedict Elder, *General Statutes of Oklahoma: A Compilation of All the Laws of a General Nature Including the Session Laws of 1907 Annotated to Volume 18 Oklahoma Reports, 96 Pacific Explorer, 76 Kansas Reports and 150 California Reports* (Kansas City, MO: Pipes-Reed Book Company, 1908), 152.
55. Baird and Goble, *The Story of Oklahoma*, 322.
56. Jekel, *The Original Constitution*, 33.

57. The three statutes of the new state of Oklahoma prohibiting Native American medicine and religion are on page 507 of the 1908 *General Statutes of Oklahoma*: "Section 1860. Medicine Men—It shall be unlawful for any so-called Indian Medicine Man to practice among the allotted Indians of the State, who is not legally authorized under existing statutes to do so, or to hold incantations over the sick, or to maltreat, or in any manner whatsoever abuse the sick, or to commit immoral practices among sick persons, or to demand payment for such services." "Section 1861. Mescal Beans—It shall be unlawful for any person to introduce on any Indian reservation or Indian allotment situated within this State, or to have in possession, barter, sell, give, or otherwise dispose of, any 'Mescal Bean,' or the product of any such drug, to any allotted Indian in this state: Provided, that nothing in this act shall prevent its use by any physician authorized under existing laws to practice his profession in this State." "Section 1862. Misdemeanor. Any person who shall violate the provisions of this act shall be guilty of a misdemeanor, and shall be fined in the sum not less than twenty-five nor more than two hundred dollars, or be confined in the county jail for not more than six months, or be assessed both such fine and imprisonment in the discretion of the court."
58. Elder, *General Statutes of Oklahoma*, 152.
59. "Quanah Parker Wants Beyoute: Will Go to Guthrie to Fight Proposed Mescal Bean Law," *Oklahoman*, December 18, 1907, 8.
60. Charles E. Shell, Superintendent and Special Agent, to Byron E. White, Superintendent, Cantonment, Oklahoma, December 31, 1907, Liquor, Peyote and Mescal Use, Cheyenne and Arapaho, IA, OHS.
61. Stewart, *Peyote Religion*, 138.
62. "Indians Claim Bill Prohibits Religion," *Daily Oklahoman*, January 21, 1908.
63. "Mescal Bean and Peyote Bill: Indian Religious Services—Peyote in Oklahoma City Times," *Weekly Times Journal*, January 24, 1908, 4. Wiedman: Upholding Indigenous Freedoms 245
64. Notes of a Hearing before a Committee of the House of Representatives, January 21, 1908, by Representative A. Frank Ross, Cheyenne and Arapaho Vices, IA, OHS.
65. Notes of a Hearing.
66. *Journal of the Proceedings of the Senate. Thirty-Sixth Day. Senate Chamber. Tuesday, January 21, 1908* (Guthrie: State of Oklahoma).
67. Minutes of the Senate Hearings on Mescal.
68. Minutes of the Senate Hearings on Mescal.
69. Minutes of the Senate Hearings on Mescal.
70. Minutes of the Senate Hearings on Mescal.
71. Minutes of the Senate Hearings on Mescal, 153.
72. Minutes of the Senate Hearings on Mescal, 186.
73. Lieutenant Governor George W. Bellamy to Indian Agent Charles E. Shell, Superintentendent of Cheyenne and Arapaho Agency, Darlington, Oklahoma, February 25, 1908, Liquor, Peyote and Mescal Use, Cheyenne and Araphaho, IA, OHS.

74. Slotkin, *The Peyote Religion*, 134–37; Weston La Barre, *The Peyote Cult* (New York: Crescent Moon Publishing, 2011).
75. Slotkin, *The Peyote Religion*, 58.
76. La Barre, *The Peyote Cult*, 168.
77. Mooney quoted in Slotkin, *The Peyote Religion*, 136.
78. Frederick E. Hoxie, *A Final Promise: The Campaign to Assimilate the Indians, 1880–1920* (Lincoln: University of Nebraska Press, 1984).
79. Hoxie, *A Final Promise*.
80. Lechner, "Global Fundamentalism."

Chapter Review

1. Explain Peyotism and the reaction against it.
2. Why do you think "Medicine Men" were considered suspect?
3. In what ways has Native American spirituality mixed with Native American politics?
4. How are alcohol and, in some cases, drugs used in other religious ceremonies? What makes Peyotism different?
5. Explain the emergence of the Native American Church.

Dennis Wiedman received his PhD in anthropology from the University of Oklahoma in 1979. His Native American research extends from the Miccosukee of South Florida, to the Delaware, Cherokee, and Plains Apache of Oklahoma, to the Tlingit, Alutiq, and Inupiat of Alaska. He specializes in Native American health issues, especially diabetes and the metabolic syndrome. He is an associate professor of anthropology in the Department of Global and Sociocultural Studies at Florida International University in Miami, Florida.

African Traditional Religions

By Mutombo Nkulu-N'Sengha

Liberation According to the "Bumuntu Paradigm" of Ancestral Religions

To those who subscribe to the economic, political, and civilizational orthodoxies of our time, African liberation theology may seem obnoxious, fallacious, or even blasphemous. And yet for the masses of Africans crushed by poverty, genocide, dictatorship, neocolonialism, economic exploitation, political oppression, and racism, much of the current "world order" is blasphemous. Over the last five centuries, African interaction with the outside world transformed the continent into a melting pot of different religious, moral, cultural, economic, political, and philosophical structures and worldviews which bequeathed to the people a "cross of humiliation and marginalization" amidst an ambivalent progress of modernity. Indeed, in the global context of geopolitics and market economy, Africa has remained since the fifteenth century poor, weak, and a battlefield of competing powers of domination and domestication.

Mutombo Nkulu-N'Sengha, "African Traditional Religions," *The Hope of Liberation in World Religions*, ed. Miguel A. De La Torre, pp. 217–238. Copyright © 2008 by Baylor University Press. Reprinted with permission.

At the same time it remains a continent of resilience and resistance par excellence, the land of Chaka zulu, "Jeanne d'arc du Congo," Patrice Lumumba, Kwame Nkrumah, Nelson Mandela, Desmond Tutu, or Wangari Maathai. In other words, Africa is a privileged locus of liberation theology. This chapter will articulate the basic tenets of such a liberation theology as it developed for centuries under the guidance of ancestral spirituality which has continued to work in new religions, be it Islam or Christianity. In so doing we shall address the question of "what Africa needs to be liberated from, and how." Traditional Africa referred to oppression with the concept of witchcraft (butshi, ndoki, buloji) which includes evil heart (mucima mubi), evil eye (diso dibi), poisonous tongue or evil speech (ludimi lubi), and greed (mwino). oppression is thus viewed as that which diminishes the vital force, brings about death, destroys life, destroys peace and harmony, creates chaos, anxiety, and insecurity, and hinders human flourishing. It is the opposite of a harmonious mode of existence.

As a "pursuit of unhappiness," oppression takes a myriad of forms. But for the sake of brevity, we can identify ten major categories of local and global forms of oppression which affect ten major dimensions of African existence: First and foremost we find cultural and racial oppression, which constitute the justification of other forms of oppression, notably economic, political, and religious oppression. To these types of oppression, we shall add gender oppression, biological oppression or "bioterrorism," environmental oppression, and artistic and aesthetic oppression. These forms of oppression are often grounded in the tenth category of epistemic violence or intellectual oppression which includes scientific, philosophical, and theological terrorism. Such intellectual oppression serves to rationalize oppression and to belittle African creative capacity and contribution to world civilization and thus world spiritual and moral values. In so doing it turns dehumanization into humanism and forms of oppression into pacification and liberation.

On the local level, oppression can be summarized into "seven deadly sins" which include the abusive use of divination (mwavi); tribalism; patriarchy, polygamy, and female circumcision; dictatorship; the manipulation of taboos and dietary regulations; the abusive use of the ideology of "divine kingship"; and moral vices in general (more notably greed, selfishness, envy, and libido dominandi). As for foreign forces of oppression, we could identify "ten plagues" that accompany the process of globalization since its inception: 1) "pauperisme anthropologique," 2) racism, 3) economic terrorism and "beggar thy neighbor" trade policies, 4) political terrorism, 5) military terrorism and arms trade folly, 6) cultural and linguistic terrorism, 7) religious, spiritual, and theological terrorism, 8) ecoterrorism, 9) bioterrorism, 10) sexual terrorism. A thorough analysis of such a catalog of oppression is beyond the scope of a succinct chapter such as this. We shall therefore limit ourselves to highlighting a few major categories of oppression in the local and global context.

We shall proceed in two major steps. First, in order to clarify our locus theologicus, we will articulate the basic beliefs of African traditional religions that constitute the foundation of traditional African liberation theology. Here we will focus on two basic notions, *Shaka-panga* (the supreme creator or God) and *Bumuntu* (the concept of a virtuous person). The notion of God as creator points to that of an ultimate judge of oppressive behaviors and an ultimate source of legitimacy for liberation struggle and resistance to oppressive rulers. The notion of genuine personhood (*Bumuntu*) establishes the sacredness of human dignity and thus delegitimizes oppression. Second we will analyze local and foreign or global forces of oppression and response of African liberation theology. For the sake of brevity we will focus on political, economic, cultural, intellectual, religious, and gender oppression.

The Basic Tenets of African Liberation Theology

African Traditional Religions and the Foundation of Liberation Theology

African liberation theology is based on the notion of the transcendence which constitutes the foundation of human dignity and the sacredness of the struggle for liberation from all forms of dehumanization. It is in reference to God and religious moral values that a behavior or institution is deemed oppressive or liberatory. Therefore a genuine understanding of the nature of African liberation theology requires a careful understanding of the fundamental beliefs of African traditional religions.

African traditional religions provide meaning of life to almost three hundred million people in Africa and in the Americas. This religious tradition is not a thing of the past but rather a living religion which entered a profound phase of revival with the collapse of colonial empires in the 1950s. African traditional religions originated more than twenty-eight thousand years ago[1] in the Bantu area that spans roughly from Nigeria to South Africa. Since the encounter between Europe and Africa in the fifteenth century, they progressively migrated to Europe and especially to the Americas where they found major centers of development, especially in Brazil, Haiti, Jamaica, Cuba, and the United States, where they are practiced in about ten different ways, including Vodun (prevalent in Haiti and Louisiana), Santeria or Lucumi (Cuba), the four types of Afro-Brazilian religions (Candom-ble, Macumba, Umbanda, Quimbanda), Kumina (of Jamaica), Shango (of Trinidad and Tobago), and Orisha or Yoruba religion. Some elements of African traditional religions can also be found to a lesser degree in Curanderismo and Espiritismo.

For centuries colonial scholarship denied any moral and spiritual value to African traditional religions. Theories and concepts such as "Deus otiosus," "anamarthesis," animism, ancestor worship, witchcraft, and magic contributed to turning African ancestral spiritual tradition into a religion of error, terror, and horror. We shall not dwell on this issue here; but suffice it to mention that although some of these colonial and racist fantasies still linger today, the process of decolonization of knowledge that began after World War II and intensified with the independence of most African nations in the 1970s and 1980s has led conscientious scholars to progressively acknowledge the spiritual and moral values of African traditional religions. Thus R. Bastide acknowledged that "among the Yoruba and Fon there is an entire civilization of spirituality comparable to that of the wood carvings and bronzes of Benin" (Zahan and Martin, 1983:126). Even Pope John Paul II acknowledged in 1994 that although Africa remains economically poor, "she is endowed with a wealth of cultural values and priceless human qualities which it can offer to the Churches and to humanity as a whole. ... Africans have a profound religious sense, a sense of the sacred, of the existence of God the Creator and of a spiritual world. The reality of sin in its individual and social forms is very much present in the consciousness of these peoples, as is also the need for rites of purification and expiation" (Browne, 1996:245).

Broadly speaking, African traditional religions encompass many of the beliefs common to traditional religions found in various regions of our planet, from Native American religions to Shintoism in Japan: the belief in a "Great Spirit," one supreme deity understood as the main source of all existence in the universe; the veneration of the ancestors, the veneration of nature as sacred and home to various spirits; the belief in the afterlife, the belief in communication with the world of the dead; the practice of divination; rituals of initiation, and rites of passage; the belief in goddesses and a greater role for women as priestesses and receptacles of deities; the practice of exorcism and a greater role of religion in the healing process; and a code of ethics based on solidarity, hospitality, harmony, and the notion of "pure heart" (*mucima muyample*). Worship includes incantations, prayers of various kind, purification rituals, libations, sacrifices, dance, trance, and observance of taboos, especially dietary regulations and rules pertaining to sexual behavior and bodily functions. It should be noted however that the goal of religion is ultimately to join the village of the ancestors safely and enjoy a blissful immortality. Hence the centrality of good character in African traditional religion, for as a Yoruba proverb has it, "Good character is the essence of religion" ("Iwa Lesin").

Thus the notion of God as Creator and the notion of Bumuntu as good character constitute the basic theological principles that guide liberation theology within the realm of African traditional religions. They serve as the criterion of distinction between good and evil, between oppression and liberation.

The Notion of God

The African conception of God is well articulated in creation myths, proverbs, praise songs and prayers, incantation formulas, and indeed the names by which the African people refer to God.[2] For the sake of brevity we shall not assess all the studies produced on the subject. Suffice it to mention that God is understood fundamentally as Creator of all life and Supreme Owner and Ruler of the universe; and in this capacity he is called the Ancestor of days (Hilolombi), the Bearer of the universe (Mebee), He who is everywhere and hears and sees everything (Nyi), and Father of all humans and things (Sha-Bantune-Bintu). In many creation myths God is spoken of as the Molder or the Potter who created the first human couple (male and female) by using clay. The Shilluk believe that God used clay of different colors in making men, which explains the diversity of human races. The Dogon explain racial differences by the fact that Amma who created all human beings used the light of the moon for the skin of Europeans and the sun for Africans. Thus contrary to an ingrained prejudice against the so-called tribal religions, Africa has the conception of a universal creator which led to an ethic that values the dignity of every human being and not merely that of the members of one's clan or ethnic group. The motherhood of God, another important point in African religion, constitutes the foundation of an African feminist theology.

Finally, God is referred to as "Vidye kadi katonye" (the blameless God). This belief in divine purity and goodness is enshrined in timeless cosmogonies. In their numerous creation myths, Africans have wrestled with the question of the origin of evil and suffering. The conclusion is that the source of evil is not God but rather the human heart. Because he abhors evil and punishes evildoers, God is not merely the fundamental source of morality but a God who abhors oppression. Africans say that God has long ears and is "the great eye," the Discerner of hearts, who sees both the inside and outside of human beings. As omnipotent, omniscient, pure, and wise, God is fundamentally against oppression and as such he remains the source of legitimacy for all forms of resistance and struggle for liberation.

Bumuntu: The Concept of Human Beingness

The fundamental question before us is "what makes somebody a good human being," a liberated person and a liberator, or an oppressor and an evil man. The African conception of the nature of human beings can be gleaned from African proverbs, creation myths, taboos, moral precepts, marriage and family institutions, kingship, and many other customs and traditions. The African vision of personhood is encompassed in ten key concepts (Muntu, Kintu, Bumuntu, Mucima Muyampe, Ludimi luyampe, Bilongwa biyampe, Fadenya, Badenya, Buya, Bubi) and ten key proverbs.

To the critical question of liberation theology, "what is a human being?" Africans respond with one word: *Bumuntu*.[3] The term stems from the lexicon of Bantu languages. A human being is referred to as a *Muntu* in Kiluba language (with *Bantu* for the plural). The concept of *Bumuntu* refers to the essence of being a human. The word *Bumuntu* comes from the Kiluba language, but it is widespread in regions that speak Bantu languages, from some areas of West Africa up to South Africa where *Bumuntu* has different linguistic variants such as *Ubuntu*. *Muntu* is not an ethnic concept but rather a generic term for every human being of any ethnicity, gender, or race. The opposite of a genuine *Muntu* is *Kintu* (a "thing"), a term that is used to refer to a human being without moral content, a person who has lost his *Bumuntu* through immoral conduct. *Bumuntu* is the African vision of a refined gentleperson, a holy person, a saint, a shun-tzu, a person of dao, a person of Buddha nature, an embodiment of Brahman, a genuine human being. The man or woman of *Bumuntu* is characterized by self-respect and respect for other human beings. Moreover he/she respects all life in the universe, he/she sees his or her dignity as inscribed in a triple relationship, with the transcendent beings (God, ancestors, spirits), with all other human beings, and with the natural world (flora and fauna). *Bumuntu* is the embodiment of all virtues, especially the virtues of hospitality and solidarity.

While compassion, generosity, solidarity, and hospitality are expected from family members, a genuine *Muntu* is expected to extend these virtues to the global village of the human race; the highest expression of *Bumuntu* is found in the treatment of those who cannot be expected to pay back favors: the strangers, children, and the most marginalized segments of society, especially the handicapped, the sick, poor, and beggars. In other words, one is genuinely human only when one honors humanity in every human being. Hence the belief among the Yoruba that prayers and invocations offered in Ile-Ife remain incomplete until prayers are offered for the people of the entire universe (Abimbola, 1990:138); this is why the Meru of Kenya believe that a genuine believer must pray not only for himself or herself but also for the welfare of all humanity, begging God to remove "the trouble of the other lands that I do not know" (Shorter, 1997:197–98).

This attitude of hospitality and solidarity is extended in a special way to the stranger, the poor, the weak, the defenseless, and people with disabilities. Thus the Bulsa treat strangers, orphaned, handicapped people, beggars, and lepers very well because of their belief that their ancestors visit them in these forms, and the Fang people of Gabon believe that an ancestor passes by in the person of a stranger, and therefore a stranger should be given a very kind and warm treatment (Olikenyi, 2001:105). The Fang are not an isolated case. As Moila rightly pointed out, generally in most African communities, it is believed that unexpected guests are the embodiment of ancestors; hence, they are given the ancestors' food (2002:3). Such a hospitality goes beyond simple courtesy. It is viewed as a way of communicating with the ancestors.

Such is the manifestation of *Bumuntu*, or the African understanding of "good character." This vision of *Bumuntu* is well expressed in the wisdom of proverbs. In West Africa, for example, an Akan proverb proclaims the divine origin of humans: "All human beings are children of God, no one is a child of the earth." Hence the centrality of good character on the path of becoming humane as the Yoruba put it explicitly, "Good character, good existence, is the adornment of a human being." Such goodness of character is inconceivable without hospitality and respect for the stranger and people with disabilities. Thus a Luba proverb commands to treat an alien guest with care and respect due to deities, for "your guest is your God." As for those with disabilities another Luba proverb warns: "Do not laugh at a crippled person, God is still creating." And to those proud of their knowledge a Luba proverb reminds them that the only true or worthwhile knowledge is to know how to live in harmony and loving relationship with our fellow human beings. In this African model of society, altruism and appreciation for the community are not viewed as antithetical to self-love, for as an Akan proverb has it, "If you do not let your neighbor have nine, you will not have ten." This vision of the humane mode of being is extended to political power. Thus a Luba proverb reminds the ruler who has a penchant for tyrannical behavior that "power is the people." Likewise in South Africa the tyrant is reminded that "one is a King only as long as he is acknowledged as such by the people." To those who suppress individuality, many proverbs remind them of the uniqueness and dignity of each individual in the eyes of the ancestors. "Human beings," says a Chewa proverb, "are like sand out of which one cannot make a mountain." Likewise the Baluba emphasize the value of individual privacy: "No one can put his arm into another person's heart not even when sharing the same bed."

One of the most striking aspects of this African theological anthropology is the distinction between a real or authentic human being and an empty human being that is regarded as a nonhuman. From West Africa to South Africa, there is the widespread belief that people of bad character are not truly human. In Nigeria, the Yoruba say: "He/she is not a person." In South Africa we find the expression "he is not human" or "he is a dead body walking." From an African standpoint a vicious dictator, for instance, is not merely regarded as a "bad ruler." He is viewed as a nonhuman altogether. The same is said about any person whose behavior is oppressive to others. The distinction between a good and a bad human being is well expressed in the *Mun-tu-Kintu* paradigm of Luba religion. According to Luba anthropology, every human being exists as a pendulum between two categories of being, *Muntu* and *Kintu*. A person of good thought, good speech, and good deeds is a genuine *Muntu*, a person of *Bumuntu*. The person of evil thought, evil speech, and evil deeds loses his humanity and falls into the *Kintu* category of things, as the following table shows:

BUYA (goodness)	BUBI (evil)
Mwikadilo Muyampe	Mwikadilo Mubi
mu-ntu (good human)	*ki-ntu* (a thing, worthless or evil person)
LIBERATOR	OPPRESSOR
mucima muyampe (good heart)	*mucima mubi* (evil thought)
ludimi luyampe (good speech)	*ludimi lubi* (evil speech)
diso diyampe (*good eye*)	*diso dibi* (evil eye)
bilongwa biyampe (*good deeds*)	*bilongwa bibi* (*evil actions*)

In African society, "the perfect person is the person with a good heart"; that is, one is human who has learned the art of living and promoting the essential harmonies of life. Such a person must have acquired fundamental *Bumuntu* virtues, and the whole traditional process of education in the African family and initiation in school consists of inculcating these virtues. The most important of these virtues are: respect for and protection of life, hospitality, solidarity, compassion, love, self-control, politeness, moderation, humility, friendship, goodness, and kindness. Such an ethical framework shows that the rejection of oppressive behavior toward other human beings occupies a pivotal role in African understanding of what it means to be a human being *(Bumuntu)*.

This openness to the other is part of the very nature of every human being as the "Fadenya-Badenya" paradigm teaches us. The African vision of personhood has a specific understanding of the individual and collective dimension of personhood which has an enlightening bearing on liberation theology. This vision of personhood was well captured in the Fadenya-Badenya paradigm to borrow the language of the Mande people. This anthropological paradigm points to a conception of the individual which is far from an "absolutized individualism," or a faceless token of the community. In the African worldview the *Muntu* is not a windowless monad. As the Mande well point out, each person is made up of two forces, Fadenya and Badenya, which explain the constant tension between individuality and respect for the community (Bird and Kendall, 1987:14–16).

Fadenya or "Father-childness" is the centrifugal force of individualism which paves the way to individual greatness. It orients people toward heroic actions and a defense of personal dignity and honor that stimulates resistance and rebellion against oppressive traditions, debilitating conventions, and status quo. But since the search for personal fame can easily lead to self-aggrandizing passions, selfish pursuit of self-interests, and antisocial behavior, Fadenya is feared as a force of social disequilibrium, a force of envy, jealousy, abuse of power, competition, and self-promotion. The individual can find equilibrium only with the intervention of a counterpower, the centripetal force known as Badenya or "mother-childness." This force pulls the child back home, back to the mother's womb. It is a conservative force of submission to authority, stability, cooperation, and dependency on others. From Badenya arises social solidarity, benevolence, altruism, and hospitality. Fadenya corresponds to the Promethean impulse within the being: restless, heroic, rebellious and revolutionary, individualistic, and innovative, eternally seeking freedom, autonomy, change, and novelty. Badenya, on the other hand, represents the Saturnian impulse: conservative, stabilizing, controlling, that seeks to contain, sustain, order, and repress (Tarnas, 1991:492). Fadenya and Badenya stand as two sides of the *Bumuntu* within every *Muntu*.

The Fadenya-Badenya paradigm indicates that a healthy mode of being requires a harmonious balance between the individualistic and altruistic tendencies of each human being. Fadenya is a revolutionary power that stimulates rebellion against all forces of oppression. It is an indispensable engine of the struggle for liberation. on the other hand the Badenya dimension of humanity curbs human's *libido dominandi*, i.e., the drive to exploit others and be a "proud oppressor."

In conclusion, African traditional religions bring to liberation theology the notion that oppression occurs at the level of thought, speech, and deeds. This means that an African liberation theology intends to liberate people who are victims of evil thought (especially epistemic violence in the form of scientific, philosophical, and theological terrorism), evil speech (the badmouthing of Africans in literature, science, philosophy, and comparative religions), and evil deeds (including slave trade, colonialism, problematic trade policies, inhumane wages, and excessive taxes). Most importantly, according to this African mode of thinking, in the "master-slave" dialectic it is the oppressor who is inferior and not the oppressed. Through thought and deeds that destroy humanity in other humans, the oppressor destroys his own humanity and becomes a *Kintu,* a thing, a nonhuman. Liberation theology, in this context, is not merely about a compassionate liberation of others. One liberates oneself from oppressive instincts, from a self-inflicted inhumanity, and increases one's own humanity by rejecting an oppressive mode of being and by struggling for the liberation of others. Such are the principles that have guided traditional African liberation theology. We shall now examine how these principles played out historically and how they apply to local and global forces of oppression.

Liberation from Local and Global Forces of Oppression

Liberation from Local Forces of Oppression

What are the local forms of oppression and how did liberation theology address such a challenge? Oppression takes a myriad of forms; however, for the sake of clarity we have identified in the introduction "seven mortal sins." These seven types of oppressive behaviors fall into two major categories that constitute the major forces of oppression: religion and the state government. For the sake of brevity we shall focus here on the response of traditional liberation theology to sociopolitical forms of oppression.

The liberation struggle for decency and full humanity is as old as Africa itself. Indeed, well before the arrival of Christianity and Islam, Africans have challenged their own rulers, abusive priests, and abusive religious customs. Africa, like any other society in human history, has produced virtuous people and institutions, as well as corrupt and vicious individuals and oppressive institutions. Even ancestral traditions could turn oppressive in the hands of unscrupulous individuals or rulers. A deep-seated patriarchy shaped proverbs and the traditional wisdom itself. Both colonialism and slave trade would not have been successful without the "collaboration" of some Africans. Likewise neocolonialism is led among others by those *dictateurs aux dents longues* that continue to loot their own countries and transfer wealth to Swiss banks and elsewhere while their population starves. Indeed, Africa has known about the human condition and the paradoxes of human nature. It identified evil or harmful impulses in human heart, thought, speech, and actions, and referred to it with the concepts of *Mucima Mubi* or *mucima wa nshikanyi* (evil heart), and *butshi* (sorcery). Most people today regard African politicians as "witches" and the very word "politics" has become a synonym of harm, trickery, and lie. They look upon this "independence of dictators" as a betrayal of the ancestral tradition of sage kings. Given its use of religion and its direct impact on all aspects of social life, political tyranny plays a crucial role in the grand scheme of oppression.

That political power is dangerous in the hands of unscrupulous individuals is a point well known in Africa. If African historical memory celebrates some rulers as sage kings, many others are remembered as monsters that brought misfortune and bad luck to people. In Luba empire, Nkongolo Mwamba is remembered as a paradigmatic tyrant. Even Ngoie Nsanza, who is celebrated for his reign of justice, is remembered for establishing an oppressive penal code which inflicted terrible forms of punishment to criminals, including mutilation: the cutting off of a hand to a thief, the upper lip to a liar, an eye or the nose to one guilty of adultery, and an ear to one who does not listen and disobeys constantly.

The question before us is: how did people react in the face of oppressive behaviors or institutions? Did they passively submit to oppression by accepting that the perpetrators acted according the will of the ancestors? Here African liberation theology found its most explicit expression in the traditional doctrine of "sage king," in political institutions created to control the power of the king and make sure that the ancestral sage king principle was followed, and finally in the numerous resistance movements by which people strived to liberate themselves from the yoke of tyrants.

A careful examination of African history shows that most oppressive actions were met with a liberatory reaction. This reaction begins with the power of the word. At the core of African social life we find the institution of palaver, a legitimate discussion and debate which indicates that the will of the ancestor was not left to the canonical interpretation of kings, priests, or the privileged class of noble people. Indeed, Africans have agreed to disagree on the interpretation of the *Kishila-kya-bankambo* (the will of God and the will of the ancestors). The manipulation of religion and tradition by the powerful did not go unchallenged. Quite often it was rejected as a betrayal of the will of the ancestors. And indeed rebellion flourished whenever people had enough power to ascertain their resistance. A king was considered divine only insofar as his rule followed the will of God and the ancestors. Like in the Chinese doctrine of the Mandate of Heaven, once a king became oppressor to his people, he was *ipso facto* considered as a being abandoned by the ancestors and therefore a candidate to impeachment and even execution. Thus the Asante people destooled several of their kings. King Osei Kwame, for instance, was destooled in 1799 for absenting himself from the capital Kumasi and endangering the security of the nation in failing to perform his religious duties. Karikari was impeached in 1874 for extravagance, among other failings, and Mensa Bonsu for excessively taxing the Asante people. And the Asante were not an exception in that regard. Although the Zanj people of East Africa considered their ruler as a "supreme Lord" they never hesitated to depose and execute him in case he departed from the rule of equity (Davidson, 1994:36). In Africa as in other parts of the world, resistance against tyranny remains the first article of people's conception of political power. As the Luba proverb "Bulohwe I Bantu" put it, power is for the people and a ruler who tyrannizes the people *ipso facto* delegitimizes his authority and forfeits his right to rule. Throughout sub-Saharan Africa we find similar examples.

By glorifying for centuries sage kings at the expense of tyrants, African myths and popular traditions translate the peculiar aspiration of the African people to a good government and a radical rejection of despotism as immoral. Well before the United States declared independence from England, Africans overthrew many kings. Even Hegel who held African politics in extreme contempt declared that "when the Negroes are discontented with their king they express their dissatisfaction and warn him by sending parrots' eggs or a deputation, and finally when there is no change they depose and execute him" (Hegel, 1994:208).

What is most important is not merely rebellion against tyranny. African traditional religions produced a powerful antidote to tyranny, a political theology of good governance, enshrined in proverbs and investiture speeches. This doctrine begins with a distinction between a legitimate and an illegitimate ruler. The Baluba who make a distinction between Mulohwe (sage king) and Kilohwe (an inhuman tyrant) remind the ruler who has a penchant for tyrannical behavior that *bulohwe* is *Bantu* (power is the people). Likewise in South Africa where a clear distinction is made between the *Morena-Inkosi* (a king of the people) and the *Morena wa Mekopu* (the king of pumpkins), the tyrant is reminded that *Morena Ke Morena Ka Batho* (one is a king only when and as long as he is acknowledged by the people). It is significant to note that kings became kings during their investiture, often preceded by a divination which has to guarantee the legitimacy of the new ruler by confirming his acceptance by the ancestors.

Investiture happened after days of the rite of passage during which the future king had to symbolically die to his "ordinary nature" in order to be born as a new being capable of carrying the heavy duty of government with honesty, fairness, and passion for the common good. The criterion was that the will of the ancestors was to foster happiness and guarantee justice and the protection of the people. This vision is widespread in Africa as can be seen in the case of a Tswana Chief, who under pressure from his courtiers to act in an obviously prejudiced manner against another, retorted: "I cannot do that! How shall I face my fathers if I do so?" (Setiloane, 1993:148).

Finally and most importantly, African political theology of the sage king found its best articulation in investiture speeches. The investiture speech of the Ashanti, for example, stipulates that the king should not disclose the origin (ethnicity) of any person, should not curse people, should not be greedy or violent, should not call people "fools," and should never act without following the advice of his people (Ayit-tey, 1992:57). The investiture speech of the Asanti people of Bekwai warns the new king against the danger of drinking and other shameful behaviors and prohibits him from making civil wars and "gambling with the people." Everywhere rulers are told that they must listen to the advice and the wish of the people.

In conclusion, traditional religions generated a liberation theology based on five basic principles that constitute the traditional "pentagon of power."

1. African traditional religions built their political theology on the notion that life is the central gift from the ancestors and the creator. In virtue of its transcendent origin, life was regarded as sacred and the fundamental ethical criterion for distinguishing virtues from vices, good rulers from bad ones, liberation from oppression.

2. African traditional religions maintained that the *raison d'etre* of government is to ensure the welfare of all the people, by protecting life and being sure that people are not stripped of adequate means of existence.
3. African tradition acknowledges civil authority as vice regent of the Divinity on earth, however it does not view any individual civil authority as absolute.
4. A ruler is accepted as ruler only in so far as he conforms himself to the will of the ancestors and the creator, who established civil authority for the good ordering of society, and for the transmission of life and beneficence of the Divinity to the people.
5. When a civil authority ceases to be the transmitter of the graces and benefits of Divinity, i.e., to execute what has been entrusted to it, it forfeits its validity. At this level a "bellum justum" component emerges in traditional liberation theology. According to African traditional religion, such a forfeiture of validity by the king means an extrication of the people from his authority and rule. If the illegitimate government refuses to resign, then it becomes the "abomination of desolation" standing in the ancestral shrine, a hindrance to people's access to the Divinity, hence the foundation of the legitimacy of uprising and resistance to the evil rule. It is then believed that it is against the will of the ancestors to fail to strike an evil regime, be it local or that of a foreign occupier. This is the foundation of Africa resistance to slave trade, colonialism, African dictators, and some ambiguous powers of globalization. This leads to the analysis of forces of foreign oppression.

Liberation from Outside Forces of Oppression

The fact that foreign forces, using a superior military might directly or indirectly seize control of African political and economic life implied not a greater prosperity for Africa but rather *ipso facto* African loss of freedom and various human rights. It implied slave labor, ridiculous salaries, heavy taxes, an unfair judicial system, appointment of token African rulers, transfer of wealth from Africa to Europe, and fake elections. Pseudodemocratic regimes ruled from Paris, Brussels, London, or Washington. African response came instantly by way of resistance movements. In 1891, when the British, who were trying to turn Ghana (then the Gold Coast) into their protectorate, told the king Prempeh I of Asante that the Queen of England wanted to "protect" him and his kingdom, he replied: "The suggestion that Asante in its present state should come and enjoy the protection of Her Majesty the Queen and Empress of India I may say is a matter of very serious consideration, and which I am happy to say we have arrived at this conclusion, that my kingdom of Asante will never commit itself to any such policy. Asante must remain as of old at the same time to remain friendly with all white men" (Boahen, 1990:1). In 1895 Wobogo, the Moro Naba or King of Mosi (in modern Burkina Faso) told the French Captain Destenave: "I know the whites wish to kill me in order to take my country, and yet you claim that they will help me to organize my country. But

I find my country good just as it is. I have no need of them. I know what is necessary for me and what I want: I have my own merchants; also consider yourself fortunate that I do not order your head to be cut off. Go away now, and above all, never come back" (Boahen, 1990:1).

Similar reaction is reported from Lat Dior, the Damel of Cayor (in modern Senegal) in 1883; from King Machemba of the Yao in modern Tanzania in 1890; from Hendrik Witbooi, a king in southwest Africa; and many other regions. In Central Africa, between 1885 and 1905, more than a dozen groups revolted in the Congo alone. Likewise a series of enlightened "sage kings" emerged in various parts of Africa challenging slave trade. In 1526, Affonso, King of Kongo, sent a letter of protest to the King of Portugal (Dom Joao). The letter first describes in detail the evils of the slave trade and then concludes with a decision to abolish it:

> To the most powerful and excellent prince Dom Joao, King our Brother
>
> Sir your Highness (of Portugal) should know how our Kingdom is being lost in so many ways. ... so great, Sir, is the corruption and licentiousness that our country is being completely depopulated, and Your Highness should not agree with this nor accept it as in your service. ... That is why we beg of Your Highness to help and assist us in this matter, commanding your factors that they should not send here either merchants or wares, because it is our will that in these Kingdoms there should not be any trade of slaves nor outlet for them. (Davidson, 1991:223–24)

Affonso's analysis of the impact of slave trade on Kongo contradicts also the argument often used by some scholars who claim that the kingdoms of black Africa flourished because of the wealth gained by African kings through slave trade. But this phenomenon of enlightened kings is not unique to Central Africa. Another notorious case is reported in West Africa in the eighteenth century by the Swedish traveler Wadstrom. In a report to the British Privy Council Committee of 1789 on the political chaos caused by the slave trade in Africa, Wadstrom evokes the case of the enlightened king of Almammy who in 1787 enacted a law stating that no slave whatever should be marched throughout his territories. This same passion for moral correctness led the Asantehene of Ashanti (Ghana) to reject a European demand for enslaving people. In 1819 he replied to a European visitor that it was not his practice "to make war to catch slaves in the bush like a thief."

This resistance to the injustices of the global trade and global politics was deeply rooted in the traditional religious sense of dignity and justice. The few examples quoted above do not constitute a treatise of liberation theology. But they do wonderfully reflect the effects of a spirit of liberation theology at work, for those kings were influenced by a specific worldview steeped in ancestral spirituality. Indeed, traditional religions and their priests and diviners played a crucial role in formulating a liberation theology that provided moral legitimacy to resistance and even outright wars of liberation. The role of African traditional religions in liberation theology was twofold: First religion established the principle of just cause thus providing legitimacy and a powerful motivation for struggle against oppression. Secondly it established the principle of divine and ancestor assistance during wars of liberation. Such assistance was materialized in the "blessed water ritual" by which the ancestors bestowed strength, invulnerability, and even invisibility upon the warriors on the battlefield.

Thus, traditional religion, Africanized Christianity and Africanized Islam, spearheaded the "art of resistance" against slave trade and colonial oppression. Various "prophets" and "prophetesses" emerged on the political scene, preaching a kind of "social gospel," a "liberation theology." The Maji Maji uprising resorted to African traditional religion and the power of its "magic." In so doing it became the most serious challenge to colonial British rule in East Africa.

Germans too faced in their colony of Tanganyika the powerful prophet Kinjikitile Ngwale who resorted to traditional religious practices and worldview to preach that the war of liberation was ordained by God, and that the ancestors would return to life to assist the African people in this war. God and the ancestors, he added, want the unity and freedom of all the African people and want them to fight the German oppressors. The war raged for more than two years, from July 1905 to August 1907. Although Kinjikitile himself was captured early on and hanged by the Germans, his brother picked up his mantle, assumed the title of "Nyamguni," one of the three divinities in the region, and continued to administer the "Maji," a religiously blessed water aimed at rendering the warrior invulnerable (Mwanzi, 1990:80). This practice of blessed water is widespread in Africa. Among the Baluba it is referred to as "koya kizaba" (taking a bath in a magical water, blessed by the ancestors to gain extraordinary strength and invulnerability on the battlefield).

The traditional role played by women in African traditional religions brought them to the forefront in resistance movements. In the Zambezi valley, the Shona mediums instigated the famous rebellions of 1897, 1901, and 1904. In the Congo the notorious case remains that of the Christian independent church of Dona Beatrice: Kimpa Vita's struggle for freedom in the Kongo kingdom was so passionate that historians have called her "Jeanne d'Arc du Congo" in reference to the spirit of French Revolution. In Congo-Brazaville, the priestess Maria Nkoie instigated the Ikaya rebellion which lasted for five years, until 1921. And many other women have played a crucial role in the struggle for freedom. Almost all wars waged against Western conquest were backed by religious belief in justice and just cause. Enslaved Africans crossed the Atlantic carrying with them a liberation theology that was to have a global repercussion in the famous Haitian revolution and various slave rebellions in the United States and in Latin America.

The spirit of traditional religions impacted various charismatic figures converted to Christianity, such as Simon Kimbangu, and led them to challenge not only colonial governments but also the colonial Christianity that lent moral and spiritual legitimacy to foreign tyranny. Indeed, well before the rise of African theology and its process of Africanization of Christianity, and almost 250 years before the rise of the civil rights movement and the ensuing Afrocentric paradigm in the United States, Kimpa Vita, a young Congolese girl nicknamed "Jeanne d'Arc du Congo," after initiation in both traditional religions and Christianity, set up a radical movement to reform both religions. Preaching against some traditional customs, she also challenged the Portuguese slave traders and their understanding of Christianity and articulated her own version of Christian theology. Disgusted by racism within the sanctuary of Christianity, she taught her followers that Christ appeared to her as a black man in São Salvador and that all his apostles were black. She argued that Jesus identified himself with the oppressed black Africans and opposed the white exploiters and oppressors. She also created a Christian creed adapted to the African situation.

Persecuted by the Portuguese missionaries she was burned at the stake, but her liberation theology and her doctrine of the Africanization of Christianity was to continue in subsequent generations of new prophets. Beatrice Kimpa Vita did not only attack the structure of the global market of that time but also its religious foundation in a colonial version of Christianity. She was also capable of transcending the colonial mask to appreciate the values of Christianity, thus exhibiting that fundamental African spirit of religious tolerance and appreciation of the spiritual values and truth inherent in other religions. Her critical evaluation of African traditional religions and customs also exemplifies that traditional African power of self-criticism so relevant to issues of liberation theology.

This is the traditional spirit that had instigated the impeachment of many traditional kings and recently the democratic movements against African dictators. It is also to this traditional liberation theology that African Christian theologians have turned in their effort to Africanize Christianity and articulate a Christian theology that takes into account the well-being of the African people. The theme of the Africanization of Christianity is important for understanding the impact of traditional religious worldview on Christian liberation theology that is now dominant in Africa. It stems from the failure of Western Christianity to adequately address the needs of Africans. This brings us to one of the crucial issues of religious oppression.

Religious Oppression

It is widely acknowledged, by Christian and Muslim scholars alike, that in Africa the traditional religions, not Christianity or Islam, offer a great tradition of tolerance. According to the Catholic theologian Benezet Bujo, religious wars were unknown in African traditional society (1992:55). Summarizing the Islamic view, Ali Mazrui, a Muslim scholar, is more explicit:

> Of the three principal religious legacies of Africa (indigenous, Islamic, and Christian), the most tolerant on record must be the indigenous tradition. One might even argue that Africa did not have religious wars before Christianity and Islam arrived, for indigenous religions were neither universalist (seeking to convert the whole of the human race) nor competitive (in bitter rivalry

against other creeds). ... Like Hinduism and modern Judaism—and unlike Christianity and Islam—indigenous African traditions have not sought to convert the whole of humanity. The Yoruba do not seek to convert the Ibo to the Yoruba religion—or *vice versa*—and neither the Yoruba nor the Ibo compete with each other for the souls of a third group, such as the Hausa. Because they are not proselytizing religions, indigenous African creeds have not fought with each other. Over the centuries, Africans have waged many kinds of wars with each other, but they were rarely religious ones before the universalist creeds arrived. (1999:77)

Writing from the perspective of the Yoruba religion of Nigeria, Abimbola observed that the Yoruba religion starts with myths of creation that maintain the idea of a universal common descent of all human beings from the same God creator, Obatala (Abimbola, 1990:138). Thus arises the African belief in the necessity of respect for all the religious traditions of humankind, as a condition for a peaceful coexistence among people and nations. Although in recent decades religious conflicts have erupted in Nigeria and the Soudan, religious crusades were alien to traditional religious spirit. This traditional spirit of religious tolerance epitomized by the extraordinary harmonious coexistence between Christians and Muslims in Senegal, and some other countries as well, constitutes in this era of rising fundamentalism one of the most important contributions of Africa to the liberation of the world from religious extremism and "sacred" violence.

Gender Oppression

African feminist philosophers and theologians such as Mercy Amba Oduyoye and many others have abundantly challenged the sexism inherent in African traditions and traditional religions. I also have elsewhere analyzed in detail the oppressive nature of African patriarchy (Nkulu-N'Sengha, 2001:69–108). In light of growing modern forms of sexism (including grotesque pornography, "leisure industry" or "sexual tourism," the global trade of women for prostitution, and the exclusion of women from priesthood) women are now turning toward ancestral notions of womanhood and dignity to combat the alienation generated by a modernity that purports to be essentially a force of liberation.

CONCLUSION: THE WISDOM OF THE POOR

"Wisdom," says Ecclesiastes, "is better than strength; Nevertheless the poor man's wisdom is despised; and his words are not heard" (9:14–16). As a poor continent, Africa has been largely conceptualized as the unwise land of oppressive ancestral traditions awaiting for foreign liberators. Such a perception is in itself one of the major oppressive forces that not only Africa but the outside world needs to be liberated from. The wisdom of African liberation theology begins with faith in the self-liberation capacity of the African tradition. Such a tradition is grounded in ancestral spirituality. Africa has indeed a long tradition of ancestral wisdom which enabled life to thrive by constantly overcoming local and foreign structures of oppression. As Jacques Maquet (and Georges Balandier) pointed out in their classical *Dictionary of Black African Civilization*, "African wisdom is not merely a convenient expression; it is something that exists. It is a collection of unique precepts that enable the people of traditional Africa to settle as harmoniously as possible the disputes that mar human relationships" (Balandier and Maquet, 1974:336).

Overlooked and despised during the colonial era, this wisdom is being increasingly acknowledged as indispensable for solving many of the problems that Africa faces in modern times. This wisdom is well encapsulated in the key notion of Bumuntu that has shaped the African idea of genuine humanity and authentic mode of being, from the Nile to the Niger, from the Congo river to the Zambezi. For millennia, this Bumuntu wisdom of "the good life" has guided the African sense of good and evil, and the African understanding of oppression and liberation.

The effort to rediscover African traditional values is in itself a liberatory act. It takes the first step in the articulation of a genuine liberation theology. I have remarked that although 80 percent of Africans have converted to Christianity and Islam, traditional religions still remain the foundation of African identity and African spirituality and the soul and heart of African civilization, so much so that in Africa even Christianity and Islam are deeply shaped by a traditional worldview. This traditional spirit enables African Christians to challenge the oppressive nature of colonial and neocolonial Christianity. It is indeed the traditional spirit of Bumuntu wisdom that led the children of Soweto to face the machine guns of the apartheid regimes and elsewhere animated adult and school children to challenge the tyranny of Bokassa, Idi Amin, or Mobutu Sese Seko, and other ubuesque dictators. It is the same spirit of Bumuntu that produced Kimpa Vita and Wangari Mathai, Nelson Mandela and Desmond Tutu, Kwame Nkru-mah and Patrice Lumumba. The same spirit led Sarawiwa to face the tyranny of oil companies such as Shell.

Although African ancestors did not produce a written treatise of a systematic liberation theology, such a theology existed in oral tradition and is well expressed in countless African resistance movements to local and foreign oppression. Nowadays such a theology exists in African independent movements as well as in writings by some Christian theologians who make extensive use of traditional religions and ancestral values in their articulation of the Africanization of Christianity which is perceived as a *sine qua non* condition for African spiritual liberation. It is a theology that repudiates religious patriotism, religious fanaticism, and religious imperialism. It is also a theology deeply grounded in the notion of human dignity we have referred to as Bumuntu. African liberation theology moves beyond the Cartesian "Cogito ergo sum" into an epistemology of solidarity and hospitality which maintains that "I am because we are; and since we are, therefore I am" as John Mbiti put it beautifully.

CHAPTER REVIEW

1. Describe the African conception of God.
2. What is Bumuntu?
3. Describe dualism in an ATR.
4. What are the five basic principles that constitute the traditional ATR "pentagon of power"?
5. In what ways have ATR's been different from Christianity and Islam with regard to evangelization?

Hinduism

By James Chiriyankandath

INTRODUCTION: THE UNIQUENESS OF HINDUISM

As a religion Hinduism stands out. Of all the great world faiths, Hinduism is the one that is the most geographically focused, both in terms of its sacred topography and the concentration of its adherents in the Indian subcontinent. All the sacred sites of Hinduism are located within the subcontinent as are over 98 percent of Hindus (O'Brien and Palmer 1993:24–25). In this respect it is profoundly unlike the great monotheist and universal faiths of Semitic origin, Christianity and Islam. Yet it also does not possess either the singularity of their precursor, Judaism, with which it shares the sense of a specific sacred homeland, or its geographical dispersion (the majority of the world's Jews continue to live outside Israel).

In claiming no single founder and possessing no scriptural canon, Hinduism is different from Zoroastrianism, the other living religion of Indo-Aryan origins, as well as later Indic religions founded

James Chiriyankandath, "Hinduism," *Routledge Handbook of Religion and Politics*, ed. Jeffrey Haynes, pp. 79–91. Copyright © 2009 by Taylor & Francis Group LLC. Reprinted with permission.

by great teachers or *gurus*—Buddhism, Jainism and Sikhism—or the religious traditions associated with Taoism or Confucianism. While it might resemble traditional African, American, Australian and other aboriginal belief systems in its variety, it is set apart by factors such as its written traditions and the overarching sub-continental unity imparted by the hierarchically complex social institution of caste. In this sense it is not so much a religion as a body of philosophy, ritual and social practice that has evolved in a particular geographical region and come to be interpreted in a world of religions as one.

An important distinction between Hinduism and the other contemporary world religions is what has variously been described as its 'inclusiveness' (Lannoy 1971:227) or its uniquely 'capacious' character (Sen 2005:49). This uniqueness is significant in considering the relationship of Hinduism to politics because it endows it with features that are peculiar to the Indian situation. On the one hand, its bewildering variety can make the political influence of Hinduism seem pervasive. Yet, paradoxically, its very plurality appears to limit its capacity to dominate politics. The modern politics of 'Hindutva' (Hindu-ness) can thus be seen as an attempt to overcome the historically well-established 'broad and generous' Hinduism (Sen 2005: 49) that has been seen as an obstruction to the kind of unilinear social and institutional development witnessed in the West (Lannoy 1971: 227; Saberwal 1996:3).

This chapter shall explore the changing political role of Hinduism. It will begin by examining how it came to be recognised as a religion and its significance in pre-colonial India. Subsequent sections will consider the use of 'Hindu' identity in post-independence India, the impact it has had on contemporary Indian politics and the future for Hinduism in politics.

THE CONSTRUCTION OF 'HINDUISM'

Hinduism may be defined and understood as denoting the spiritual beliefs and rituals associated with the Indian subcontinent rather than as a singular, organised religious system. While its origins predated the Indo-Aryan invasion of the Indus Valley in the northwest early in the second millennium BCE, it was Aryan religion that imparted to it the characteristics now most distinctly associated with what the philosopher Sarvepalli Radhakrishnan, the second President of the Republic of India, called the 'Idea of Hinduism' (Radhakrishnan 1937: 256). The *Rig Veda*, the oldest of the four main *Vedas* (from the Sanskrit *vid*, to know), or collections of most sacred knowledge in the Indic tradition, was composed more than a millennium before the time of Christ. It is therefore the oldest of the religious scriptures of any living religious tradition, a point of pride for contemporary Hindu nationalists.

The *Upanishads* followed the *Vedas* and are therefore also known as *Vedanta*—the end of the *Vedas*. Numbering over a hundred texts concerned with the ultimate dual search for the eternal self (atman) and the eternal universe (brahman), they represented the end of the sruti, literally hearing (the eternal word heard by the sages of antiquity) and were followed by the more amorphous *smrti*, or texts of memory. The latter include the philosophic *Sutras*, books on *dharma* (maintaining the natural order of the universe), the *Puranas* (mythologies extolling one or other great deity) and the well-known epics of the *Mahabharatha* and the *Ramayana*. The *Mahabharatha* relates the story of the victory of the Pandavas over the Kauravas in a struggle involving all of India and includes the *Bhagavad Gita* (Lord's Song), a dialogue on righteous action between Arjuna, the Pandava warrior, and Krishna, his charioteer and the incarnation of the Vedic god Vishnu. The *Ramayana* narrates the story of Ram, the righteous heir to the throne of the kingdom of Ayodhya who in the Sanskrit rendition of Valmiki heroically rescues his kidnapped wife Sita and defeats Ravana, the demon king of Lanka, to return to his kingdom in triumph.

The responsibility of the ruler to protect the *dharma* became central to the Indian idea of kingship—an idea until very recent preserved in neighbouring Nepal where the 1990 Constitution defined it as a Hindu kingdom of which the monarch is 'an adherent of Aryan culture and the Hindu religion' (http://www.nepalgov.gov.np/sambhidan/6.pdf). Indeed, scholars such as K.M. Panikkar discern in the dualism between *dharma* and *artha* (worldly wisdom) the basis for a Hindu conception of 'a purely secular theory of state of which the sole basis is power' (Panikkar quoted in Murty 1967: 136). Yet in India in the past century the phrase Ram rajya (the rule of Ram) has acquired a religious connotation, being widely used in politics—from Mahatma Gandhi in the campaign for Indian independence to Hindu nationalists today—to denote just and righteous government. (That the Ram story retains a powerful resonance was dramatically illustrated in the 1980s and 1990s by the political reverberations set off by the campaign to construct a Ram temple at his legendary birthplace in Ayodhya, and the 1991 general election manifesto of the Hindu nationalist Bharatiya Janata Party (BJP) was entitled 'Towards Ram Rajya'.)

Nevertheless, the alternative versions of the *Ramayana* that exist emphasise the plural character of Hinduism, a feature that has inhibited its utility as a basis for modern Hindu nationalism. This is not to gainsay the crucial role played by the Indic religious tradition in imparting a sense of unity to the subcontinent, one particularly notable from the perspective of the Brahmanical Hinduism associated with Shankara, the ninth-century CE religious teacher who founded the school of *Advaita* [non-dualist or monist] *Vedanta* and the four great *mathas* (seminaries), each headed by a Shankaracharya who continues to command widespread respect and authority. Significant in embedding that authority has been the social institution that India is best known for: caste.

Even though the hierarchical ancient Aryan Vedic classification of Indian society was based on *varna* (Sanskrit—colour), it was the Portuguese who, from the fifteenth century CE, applied the Spanish-Portuguese word *casta* (pure or chaste), used by the Spanish to refer to race, to describe the social divisions encountered on the subcontinent. Over the past five hundred years the idea of caste has changed. It has acquired new meanings and significance and shed old connotations.

Two related concepts that are central to unravelling caste are *varna* and *jati*. The Vedic division of society into four *varnas* first encountered in the *Rig Veda*—Brahmins (priests), *Kshatriyas* (warriors/rulers), *Vaisyas* (merchants) and *Sudras* (cultivators)—reflects a notional ideal typology. What actually operates locally throughout the subcontinent is *jati* (Hindi—birth group) and there are thousands of endogamous *jatis*, based on a variety of elements, most notably kinship and occupation. The position of the latter is not static—*jatis* can move up and down the *varna* hierarchy over time, depending on wealth and control over resources (especially land), and through the process the sociologist M.N. Srinivas called 'Sanskritisation', achieving upward mobility by changing ritual and social practices (1969: 6). The intensification of spatial communications (roads, railways etc.), and the spread of a sub-continental administrative system, helped consolidate local *jatis* into regional *jatis*, usually based on linguistic areas. The most important element in bringing this about was the British colonial preoccupation with classifying and ordering *jatis*, a concern that matched the stress laid on differentiating between followers of different religions and manifested in ethnographical surveys, census reports and administrative classifications. In post-independence India the role of caste as the basis for political mobilisation has been further reinforced by the conjunction of mass democratic politics with the official recognition accorded it in terms of the reservation of seats in legislatures, administrative jobs and educational places for historically disadvantaged low castes.

In many ways it was the European 'discovery' of Hinduism that created the modern idea of it as one religious tradition to be interpreted and understood as such—'a Hinduism in their own image' (Marshall 1970: 43). This perception influenced subsequent Indian thinkers but they were also more aware of the difference between the legacy of Hinduism and that of the great monotheist religions. For instance, Radhakrishnan not only interpreted Jainism, Buddhism and Sikhism as reform movements 'from within the fold of Hinduism' but added that 'Zoroastrianism, Islam, and Christianity have been so long in the country that they have become native to the soil and are deeply influenced by the atmosphere of Hinduism' (Radhakrishnan 1937: 259). The fact that the perception and operation of caste is found in some form among people of almost all religious backgrounds in India is the most striking testimony to this.

Paradoxically, the persistence, prevalence and mutation of caste represent a formidable obstacle to the attempt to create a singular Hindu nationalism on the basis of Hinduism. It might even be argued that it is the overarching phenomenon of caste that has made possible the modern Indian adaptation of liberal-democratic government. It has provided a common frame of reference for social groups right across the hierarchy, from the Brahmins at the apex to the so-called Untouchables (now commonly referred to as *Dalits*) at the bottom, to progressively mobilise to access the novel institutions of democracy. So, despite its intrinsically anti-democratic nature, the history and consciousness of caste created a shared sense of a bounded social universe within which people from competing groups competed to appropriate the democratic institutions to their needs and purposes. The six decades since India's independence have thus seen the country's democracy undergo a messy process of democratisation—a 'silent revolution' in the making, transferring power from upper-caste elites to the traditionally underprivileged (Jaffrelot 2003: 494).

'HINDU' IDENTITY AND MODERN POLITICS

The idea of Hinduism developed in parallel with that of nationalism in India through the nineteenth and twentieth centuries. The Hindu social reform movements that arose in British India, beginning with Raja Ram Mohun Roy's Brahmo Samaj founded in Bengal in 1828, helped form the intellectual climate in which a nascent western-educated predominantly upper caste and urban middle class began to inculcate notions of national political identity and self-government. One movement that gave this process a more militant edge was the Arya Samaj, founded by Dayanand Saraswati in Punjab in 1875, less than two decades after the 1857 uprising against the spread of British dominion. Unlike the Brahmo Samaj, which derived much of its inspiration from combining Christian ethics and rationalist ideas with the philosophy contained in the *Upanishads*, the latter aggressively asserted the need to return to the *Vedas* to create a rejuvenated Hinduism free of alien accretions, able to effectively counter Christian and Muslim proselytisation and yet modern in its organisation, methods and commitment to education.

The overlap of Hindu reform and nascent Indian nationalism was visible in the membership and leadership of the Indian National Congress that held its first meeting in Bombay in 1885. Leading personalities in the pre-First World War Congress such as Mahadev Ranade and Gopal Krishna Gokhale in the Bombay Presidency, the Brahmo Samajist Bipin Chandra Pal in Bengal and the Arya Samajist Lala Lajpat Rai in Punjab all began their public careers as social reformers. Others, most notably Bal Gangadhar Tilak in Bombay, combined a robust defence of what they perceived as orthodox Hindu *sanatana dharma* (eternal religion)—the caste system, child marriage and *purdah* (the seclusion of women)—with militant nationalism. However, the lines of political divisions did not necessarily coincide with social attitudes. For instance, when Congress temporarily split between 'Moderates' and 'Extremists', Chandra Pal and Lajpat Rai were found together with Tilak in the latter camp, the consequence, at least in part, of the regional social and political differences between western India and Punjab and Bengal.

The way in which religious sentiment imbued the more radical manifestations of Indian nationalism was seen in the adoption of *Vande Mataram* (Hymn to the Mother), a poem composed by Bankim Chandra Chatterjee and first published in his novel *Anandamath* in 1881, as the political cry of the movement against the British partition of Bengal in 1905. After independence the Indian Constituent Assembly eventually made it the national song. That it did not become the national anthem—Rabindranath Tagore's 'Jana gana mana' was preferred—was due to the longstanding objections of many Muslims and others that its evocation of India as motherland was idolatrous and distinctly Hindu in tenor:

> In the arm thou art might, O Mother,
> In the heart, O Mother, thou art love and faith,
> It is thy image we raise in every temple.
> For thou art [the goddess] Durga holding her ten weapons of war.
> (Bhattacharya 2003: 101)

The poem continues to stir political passions. In 1998 the general election manifesto of the BJP highlighted *Vande Mataram* in deprecating what it described as the post-independence tendency to reject pre-independence values and symbols based on ancient Indian wisdom as 'unsecular and unacceptable' (BJP 1998). Shortly afterwards the BJP state government in Uttar Pradesh issued a directive, later withdrawn after public protests, requiring the daily recitation of the poem in government-aided schools.

With the rise of Mahatma Gandhi to the leadership of Congress in the years immediately after the First World War, the connection between religion and Indian nationalism found its most striking embodiment. The transformation of Congress into much more of a mass movement over the next decades was marked by his use of the language and symbolism of religion to imbue it with a popular character. While this was not exclusively Hindu (Congress under Gandhi adopted the Indian Muslim Khilafat movement to defend the status of the Ottoman Caliph in 1920–22), it came to be widely perceived as predominantly so, especially by Muslims. Gandhi's own proclaimed personal commitment to the equality of all religions (Gandhi 1980: 84)—he regularly read texts from the Bible, the Koran and the Sikh Granth Sahib, as well as from the *Bhagavad Gita*, in the daily prayer meetings held in his ashram—and the fact that his close followers included people from diverse religious backgrounds, could not dispel this impression.

The Gandhian approach to politics and religion was actively opposed by radical campaigners against the oppression and discrimination of the caste system such as Dr B.R. Ambedkar, for nearly three decades the leading champion of the cause of the outcaste Untouchables who constituted close to an eighth of the population, and Ramaswamy Naicker, who launched the anti-Brahmin Dravidian (Tamil) Self-Respect Movement in south India in 1925. While Gandhi himself vigorously opposed the stigmatisation and discrimination associated with the observance of caste distinctions, calling the Untouchables '*Harijans*', or people of God, he nevertheless accepted the fourfold *Varnashrama dharma* as Vedic and 'inherent in human nature' (Gandhi 1980: 15). Another perspective from which the Gandhian position came under criticism was from secular modernisers such as Jawaharlal Nehru, independent India's first prime minister from 1947 to 1964, who felt that organised religion produced 'narrowness and intolerance, credulity and superstition, emotionalism and irrationalism' (Nehru 1961: 513).

Nehru was conscious that his was a minority viewpoint not only within the country but also within Congress, where Gandhians and Hindu majoritarians of various shades were far more common. But the most uncompromising Hindu chauvinists were found outside the capacious folds of the Congress cloak. Two organisations in particular sought to promote a distinctly Hindu nationalism. The first was the *Hindu Mahasabha*, initiated mainly by Punjabi Arya Samajists in 1915 and including among its early leaders prominent Congressmen like Lajpat Rai and Madan Mohan Malaviya. Its chief ideologist was Veer Damodar Savarkar, its president from 1937 to 1943. A onetime follower of Tilak, in 1923, while exiled by the British to a penal colony in the Andaman Islands, he published *Hindutva: Who Is a Hindu* which defined a Hindu as a person who 'looks upon the land that extends ... from the Indus to the Seas ... as his Fatherland (*Pitribhu*) ... as his Holyland (*Punyabhu*), as the land of his prophets and seers, of his godmen and gurus, the land of piety and pilgrimage' (Savarkar quoted in Gottlob 2003: 154–155). Politically no match for the National Congress, the Mahasabha was banned after the assassination of Gandhi in 1948 by a onetime member, Nathuram Godse. Despite the subsequent acquittal of Savarkar of complicity, it then effectively disappeared as a political force with many of its members joining the Bharatiya Jana Sangh (Indian People's Organisation) founded in 1951.

The second organisation, the *Rashtriya Swayamsevak Sangh* (National Volunteer Organisation) (RSS), was started in 1925 in Nagpur in what is now the state of Maharashtra in western India and proved more resilient and significant. Founded by K.B. Hedgewar, a Brahmin doctor, and led for more than three decades during its formative phase by his successor, M.S. Golwalkar, known as *Guruji* (teacher), it concentrated on a wide spread of cultural and social activity and what it saw as building up a distinct, strong, martial Hindu ethos closely associated with the Mahasabha in the 1930s and 1940s, it was not uncommon to find men, like Gandhi's assassin, who had been members of both. However, while also temporarily banned in 1948–49, the distance it kept from direct involvement in party politics facilitated its steady growth into what by the 1980s was a formidable force in Indian public life. At the beginning of the 1990s it claimed over three million members, organised in thousands of *shakhas* (branches) across India guided in each region by *pracharaks* (celibate full-time propagandists), as well as a network of linked organisations known collectively as the *sangh parivar* (organisational family). The latter included the second biggest national students and labour federations, as well as a multiplicity of political, religious cultural, intellectual, social service, cooperative, peasants and women's bodies.

The independence of India in 1947, in the wake of the traumatic partition of the subcontinent and the creation of Pakistan as a separate homeland for Muslims, left aspirations for a distinctly Hindu nationhood unrealised. Despite the Hindu sympathies of many congressmen, the 1950 constitution was, in large measure, couched in secular terms, notwithstanding features such as statutory provisions reserving seats in legislatures and shares in public jobs and educational institutions for low-caste people, and empowering the state to open all Hindu religious institutions to all classes of Hindus. It was against this backdrop that the Jana Sangh was launched in 1951 with the object of 'the rebuilding of Bharat [India] on the basis of Bharatiya "*Sanskriti*" [culture] and "*Maryada*" [rectitude]' (Graham 1993: 51).

RSS activists formed the bulk of the leadership and activists of the new party and over the next twenty years it was mainly in the Hindi-speaking states of central and northern India, where the RSS and the Hindu Mahasabha had a history of strength, that it made the greatest electoral inroads, campaigning on issues such as the banning of the slaughter of cows, sacred to Hindus, the promotion of Hindi as India's sole official language, the appeasement of minorities and the Indian claim to Kashmir. The Jana Sangh registered a high-water mark of 35 of 520 parliamentary seats and 9.4 percent of the vote in the 1967 general election (Graham 1993: 261–262). In 1977 it merged with a broad range of other non-communist opposition parties opposed to form a *Janata* (People's) coalition that defeated the Congress Party but the merger was short-lived with controversy over the RSS connection resulting, following the Janata defeat in 1980, in the exit of most of the erstwhile Jana Sangh group to form the new BJP.

Hindu nationalism in India since 1980

The BJP faced the same challenge as its predecessor—how to translate the notional overwhelming Hindu majority in India into the electoral basis for a Hindu nationalist takeover of the state? According to the 2001 census, 80.5 percent of the more than a billion Indians were Hindu, 13.4 percent Muslim, 2.3 percent Christian, 1.9 percent Sikh, 0.8 percent Buddhist and 1.1 percent others. Hindus are not in the majority in only 6 of the 28 states and only in 6 others do non-Hindus even constitute as much as a quarter of the population. Yet despite a century of effort at developing a distinct Hindu political identity, Indians remain stubbornly plural in their political, religious and social identities.

Not only are Hindus differentiated by language, region and attachment to particular local deities, as well as by other significant social markers such as class and education, the Indian Constitution actually recognises a third of Hindus separately as belonging to the Scheduled Castes—the erstwhile Untouchables or *Dalits* (oppressed) (16 percent of the total population) or Scheduled Tribes (8 percent). The remainder can also be variously grouped as upper caste (17 percent) or Other Backward Classes (OBC), another administratively recognised category (43 percent) (Mandal 1980). When taken together with the complex system of locally or regionally discrete *jatis*, this represents a formidable obstacle to the creation of a singular Hindu political identity. However, in the space of less than a decade the BJP succeeded in moving from the political periphery to becoming the main party in a coalition government that ruled India for six years. This section shall discuss how it was able to do so and what this tells us about the contemporary political significance of Hinduism.

Several factors made the theme of giving a more distinctly 'Hindu' hue to national identity central to Indian politics in the 1980s and 1990s. First, there was, after Indira Gandhi's return to power in 1980, the increasing exploitation by the Congress Party of the ambiguity of Indian secularism for the political use of religion, especially in the form of populist invocations of a majority Hindu identity. This was manifested in the use of the mass media, particularly television, to cultivate a more homogenised national ethos—a Hinduism redefined as 'an ideology for modernization' (Thapar 1989: 23). The trend continued under Mrs Gandhi's son and successor, Rajiv Gandhi. Most strikingly, in 1988 and 1989, Doordarshan, the state television network, broadcast hugely popular soap operas based on essentially Brahminical versions of the Hindu epics of the *Ramayana* and *Mahabharatha*.

One reason for the movement away from the more secular attitude espoused by Mrs Gandhi's father, Jawaharlal Nehru, lay in the steady decline of Congress as a mass political institution at a time when its authority was under increasing challenge not only from the Hindu right but also low-caste and regional parties—the outcome of the process of the steady 'democratisation' of the Indian polity previously referred to, with the rise of social groups and regions hitherto not directly represented in the political arena. The political and personal insecurity, which had pushed Mrs Gandhi towards reforming Congress into a personality-based vote-gathering machine, facilitated such a shift. One factor was the increasingly strident, even violent, separatist demands on the part of some non-Hindus in peripheral regions, which culminated in the descent into effective civil war of border states like Assam, Punjab and Kashmir. This was itself to some degree the consequence of short-term Congress stratagems involving the exploitation of communal divisions. For instance, in Punjab Congress leaders initially promoted the radical Sikh preacher and inspiration for the Khalistani separatists, Sant Jarnail Singh Bhindranwale, in order to undermine its chief rival, the Akali Dal, the Sikh regional party.

Another element fostering the growth of Hindu nationalism at this stage in India's development was the liberalisation of the economy, initiated in half-hearted fashion in the 1980s and adopted more wholeheartedly by the minority Congress government of P.V. Narasimha Rao in the wake of the balance of payments crisis of 1991. Some of the repercussions of the economic changes initiated by liberalization facilitated the growing appeal of a kind of 'syndicated Hinduism' (Thapar 1990: 31) upon which Hindu nationalism could draw, especially among the burgeoning sector of urban middle-class consumers who have been the primary beneficiaries of India's recent economic growth. As one commentator put it, the 'overlap between the narratives of communal and consumer identity formation' (Rajgopal 1996: 341), together with the rapid expansion of electronic communication (the proliferation of satellite television channels, TV advertising and the spread of the internet) allowed for the emergence of a kind of retail Hindu identity that the Hindu nationalists were able to turn into a valuable political resource. At times, such as during the explosion of anti-Muslim violence in Gujarat in early 2002, it could become a powerfully malign force:

> For the first time, persons of middle class background, including women, well dressed and driving from bazaar to bazaar, cooperated in the looting of Muslim-owned shops and businesses, providing cover for those breaking open television stores and cloth shops to take goods away. Revealed suddenly was the expanding urban middle class base for the majoritarian definition of the nation.
>
> (Frankel 2005: 744)

It was the unprecedented mass mobilisation of Hindus in a movement launched in 1984 to construct a temple on the disputed site of a disused sixteenth-century mosque, the Babri Masjid, claimed as the legendary birthplace of the Ram in Ayodhya in the northern state of Uttar Pradesh, that was the most important factor in highlighting the appeal of Hindu nationalism. After having spent the first half of the 1980s in the political doldrums, the preparedness of the BJP to exploit the movement catapulted the party to centre stage. Despite being the product of the ructions in the shortlived Janata coalition over the association of the Jana Sangh group with the RSS, the BJP had begun as a party apparently less closely tied to the apron strings of the *sangh parivar*. It initially adopted the deliberately ill-defined concept of 'Gandhian Socialism' as its guiding philosophy but, following a dismal performance in the 1984 general election when it won just two of 542 parliamentary seats, this was effectively jettisoned. Under Lal Krishan Advani, who succeeded Atal Bihari Vajpayee as party president in 1986, the party drew closer to the RSS.

Before the 1989 general election the party's National Executive endorsed the Ram Janmabhoomi (Ram's birthplace) campaign, launched five years earlier by the Vishwa Hindu Parishad (VHP; the World Council of Hindus). (The VHP had been founded in 1964 on the initiative of the RSS's *Sarsanghchalak* (Supreme Guide), M.S. Golwalkar, in order to organise religious leaders to consolidate and strengthen Hindu society.) Advani and other BJP leaders attended Ram *shila pujas*, ritual ceremonies held across India to consecrate bricks to be used in building the Ram temple. On the eve of the November 1989 general election, a foundation-laying ceremony took place in Ayodhya. The communally vitiated atmosphere engendered by the Ram *shila* processions, together with widespread disenchantment with the congress government and an electoral accommodation reached by the BJP with the other main non-communist opposition party, the Janata Dal, played a significant role in contributing to the remarkable advance recorded by the party.

It won 86 seats and 11.5 percent of the popular vote, increasing this to 120 seats and 20.1 percent in the subsequent midterm poll in 1991 when the BJP assumed the position of the official opposition to the ruling congress. In between the two polls Advani undertook a six-week, 10,000-kilometre Ram *rath yatra* (chariot journey) to Ayodhya in a van decorated in the style of the chariot of Arjuna in the *Mahabharatha* television serial. As with the Ram *shila* processions, the *rath yatra* sparked off an epidemic of communal rioting in which hundreds died. Again there was a striking correlation between where the BJP enjoyed greatest electoral success and the spread of communal violence (Chiriyankandath 1992: 68–69, 73).

The Ayodhya campaign sought to transcend caste and regional distinctions in emphasising a common Hindu, indeed national, objective. The BJP's 1991 manifesto, entitled *Towards Ram Rajya*, affirmed the construction of the Ram temple as a 'vindication [sic] of our cultural heritage and national self respect'. Yet the continuing significance of caste in Indian public life was highlighted by another controversy that came to a head in 1990. The shortlived National Front government of Prime Minister V.P. Siṅgh adopted the 1980 Report of the Backward Classes Commission chaired by B.P. Mandal which had recommended the reservation of more than a quarter of all public service jobs for the OBC, the numerically large low castes not included in the Scheduled Castes and Tribes categories already guaranteed reserved jobs through constitutional provisions. This was strongly opposed by people from other castes, especially educated youth, who feared the impact on their own job prospects, and there was a wave of public protest including a rash of self-immolations by youths. Advani's *rath yatra* was designed in part to deflect the potential for embarrassment for the BJP in how to respond to Mandal without alienating either its bedrock support among upper-caste, educated, urban Hindus or the OBC who represented the single largest category of Hindus.

Communal tensions reached a fever pitch in December 1992 when Hindu militants unrestrained by the BJP state government of Uttar Pradesh, and in the presence of party leaders including Advani, destroyed the Babri Masjid. The nationwide communal violence that followed was the worst since partition, claiming at least two thousand lives, and led to both the RSS and VHP being temporarily banned. Although the intensity of the passion whipped up by the Ayodhya confrontation had hitherto paid rich political dividends for the BJP, in the years that followed the BJP's political strategy, recognising the logic of India's political demography, shifted steadily towards building a network of alliances with regional parties. This aimed at outflanking Congress by gaining strength in areas of the country, notably the south and east, where Hindu nationalism remained a peripheral force. The strategy proved remarkably successful. Despite continuing to trail Congress in the popular vote, adding merely 5 percent to its share—still only a quarter of the electorate, it emerged as the largest single party in parliament in three successive elections (1996, 1998 and 1999), with 183 of 543 seats by 1999. This provided the platform for six years of BJP-led coalition government (the 1999–2004 National Democratic Alliance was supported by as many as 24 parties) from 1998 until its unexpected defeat at the hands of a rival Congress-led combination in 2004.

In government, the BJP under Prime Minister A.B. Vajpayee, like Advani a veteran of the RSS and a founder-member of the Jana Sangh, proved much more restrained than their rhetoric and agitational strategy of the early 1990s might have led observers to expect (Adeney and Saez 2005). For instance, controversial longstanding party manifesto commitments such as those to do away with separate Muslim and Christian personal law in favour of a uniform civil code, the pledge to build the Ram temple at Ayodhya and to revoke the special constitutional status of Jammu and Kashmir, were not acted upon. In addition, although early in the NDA's period of office there was a spate of attacks on Christian churches and missionaries by Hindu extremists and the BJP state government in Gujarat was widely censured for permitting a veritable anti-Muslim pogrom to take place in March 2002 in which some two thousand people died, much of India did not witness the kind of communal violence seen in the early 1990s. This apparent moderation may in part be ascribed to the need to retain the support of its regional coalition partners, many of which were sensitive to the reaction of their Muslim and other supporters. A desire not to alienate moderate voters, as well as foreign investors and business interests, by embarking on controversial policies that risked jeopardising both social stability and India's healthy economic growth may also be surmised to have played a role.

However, there were areas of policy where the Hindu nationalist agenda did make an impression on government policy. Most dramatic was India's public emergence as a nuclear power with the underground tests carried out in May 1998, just weeks after the BJP-led government had taken office (Chiriyankandath and Wyatt 2005). This represented the realisation of a long-held aim of the BJP and its precursor, the Jana Sangh, considered by the chief RSS ideologue, M.S. Golwalkar, to be a national imperative (Golwalkar

1980: 429). Yet, Vajpayee, after appearing to lead the country to the brink of war with Pakistan over cross-border attacks by Kashmiri Muslim militants in 2001 and 2002, ended his premiership by initiating a peace process with Pakistan.

Domestically, the main focus of Hindu nationalist attempts to bring about significant change came in the field of education under the direction of Murli Manohar Joshi, like Advani and Vajpayee a former president of the BJP who had been a member of the RSS since before independence. RSS members or sympathisers were appointed to leading positions in many national educational institutions and a wide-ranging programme of revising school textbooks, especially in history and the social sciences, in line with the Hindu nationalist narrative was attempted (Lall 2005). That it made only limited progress was not for want of trying but down to the difficulties of imposing such changes from the centre in the face of resolute opposition from the majority of state governments controlled by parties opposed to the Hindu nationalist agenda.

The 2004 defeat of the BJP-led coalition government was partly the consequence of its perceived indifference to people, especially among India's rural majority, who felt left out of the rapid growth of India's liberalised economy (the NDA's ill-advised campaign slogan, 'India Shining' appeared to reflect this indifference). As one observer pithily put it, 'Among these "ordinary" citizens, the notion of "India Shining" only illuminated the darkness in which they lived' (Frankel 2005: 783). In the months after its election defeat the BJP demonstrated little of the discipline or cohesion associated with the RSS. Its veteran leaders, Vajpayee and Advani, both came under attack from more militant Hindu chauvinists and in 2005 Advani, who had succeeded Vajpayee as parliamentary leader and party president after the election, resigned from the latter post. This followed outspoken attacks on him by VHP and RSS leaders after a visit to Pakistan during which he controversially praised a 1947 speech in which Mohammed Ali Jinnah, the founder of Pakistan, had upheld secular principles. Although Advani remains the BJP's leader in parliament, and therefore its projected prime ministerial candidate in the next general elections, he is now (2008) already over 80 and the party lacks any younger leaders of national stature with a significant power base except for Narendra Modi, the controversial Chief Minister of Gujarat who presided over the 2002 massacre of Muslims in the state.

The future of Hinduism in politics

The political salience of Hindu nationalism and the rise of the BJP in the 1980s and 1990s belied the image of Hinduism as tolerant and pluralistic. Yet the latter perception of Hinduism was always based on a superficial grasp of the nature of Hindu religion. In pointing out Hinduism's 'ability to encapsulate almost any religious or cultural entity without admitting any genuine dialogue or possibility of interaction' (Embree 1990: 25), Ainslie Embree touched upon an aspect that modern Hindu nationalist discourse exploited in its endeavour to transform the bewildering variety of Hindu beliefs and deities into a supple political resource for the creation of a sub-continental ethno-religious nationalism.

Still, the BJP's failure to significantly expand its electoral base, after an initial surge in the early 1990s, underscored the difficulties inherent in trying to reconcile the hierarchy and amorphousness of Hindu religion with a modern ideology of nationalism. This was especially the case within a context of deepening mass democracy. While religious groups that possessed a distinct non-Hindu identity were, understandably, strongly antipathetic to the Hindu nationalist project, newly politically mobilised people belonging to low castes were also profoundly suspicious of what they saw as its Brahminical Hindu bias. Both factors go a long way towards explaining the limits of the Hindu nationalist advance and in 2007 contributed to the upset election victory of the Bahujan Samaj Party (BSP) led by a *Dalit* woman, Mayawati, in state elections in India's most populous state, Uttar Pradesh, which saw the BJP relegated to a distant third place in a state that they had ruled until 2002. The fact that nearly a third of the winning BSP candidates were Brahmins or other upper-caste people was also significant, indicating the waning appeal of Hindu nationalism even among its traditional supporters.

There can be little doubt that Hinduism, broadly defined as the distinctive culture of Indian religion and encompassing deeply entrenched social institutions like caste, will continue to influence Indian politics. With the BJP having now been one of the two major political parties in India for the best part of two decades, Hindu nationalism as an organised political force remains powerful enough to be a serious contender for power at the national level at the head of another coalition government after the next general election, due in 2009. However, although over the past century the evolving ideology and praxis of Hindu nationalism has left a deep imprint on Indian public life, the spread of the Hindu nationalist project appears likely to continue to be delimited by Hinduism's most significant legacy to contemporary Indian politics—the potency of caste. In this sense the diversity and plurality of Hinduism has proved an effective antidote to the attempt, through the ideology of 'Hindutva', to make all Hindus embrace a singular political identity.

Bibliography

Adeney, K. and Saez, L. (eds) (2005) *Coalition Politics and Hindu Nationalism*, London: Routledge.
Bayly, S. (1999) *Caste, Society and Politics in India: From the Eighteenth Century to the Modern Age*, Cambridge: Cambridge University Press.
Bhattacharya, S. (2003) *Vande Mataram: The Biography of a Song*, New Delhi: Penguin.
BJP (1998) *BJP Election Manifesto '98*. Available at http://www.bjp.org/manifes.html, accessed 23 March 2000.

Chiriyankandath, J. (1992) 'Tricolour and Saffron: Congress and the Neo-Hindu Challenge', in S.K. Mitra and J. Chiriyankandath (eds), *Electoral Politics in India: A Changing Landscape*, New Delhi: Segment, pp. 55–79.

Chiriyankandath, J. and Wyatt, A. (2005) 'The NDA and Indian Foreign Policy', in K. Adeney and L. Saez (eds), *Coalition Politics and Hindu Nationalism*, London: Routledge, pp. 193–211.

Dumont, L. (1980) *Homo Hierarchicus: The Caste System and Its Implications*, Chicago: University of Chicago Press.

Embree, A.T. (1990) *Utopias in Conflict. Religion and Nationalism in Modern India*, Berkeley: University of California Press.

Frankel, F. (2005) *India's Political Economy 1947–2004*, 2nd edn, New Delhi: Oxford University Press.

Gandhi, M.K. (1980) *The Spirit of Hinduism*, New Delhi: Pankaj Publications.

Golwalkar, M.S. (1980) *Bunch of Thoughts*, Bangalore: Jagarana Prakashana.

Graham, B. (1993) *Hindu Nationalism and Indian Politics*, Cambridge: Cambridge University Press.

Hansen, Blom T. (1999) *The Saffron Wave: Democracy and Hindu Nationalism in Modern India*, Princeton: Princeton University Press.

Jaffrelot, C. (1996) *The Hindu Nationalist Movement: 1925 to the 1990s*, London: Hurst & Co.

Jaffrelot, C. (2003) *India's Silent Revolution: The Rise of the Lower Castes in North India*, London: Hurst & Co.

Lall, M. (2005) 'Indian Education Policy under the NDA Government', in K. Adeney and L. Saez (eds), *Coalition Politics and Hindu Nationalism*, London: Routledge, pp. 153–170.

Lannoy, R. (1971) *The Speaking Tree: A Study of Indian Culture and Society*. Oxford: Oxford University Press.

Mandal, B.P. (1980) *Report of the Backward Classes Commission*, New Delhi: Government of India Press.

Marshall, P.J. (1970) 'Introduction', in P.J. Marshall (ed.), *The British Discovery of Hinduism in the Eighteenth Century*, Cambridge: Cambridge University Press, pp. 1–44.

Nehru, J. (1961) *The Discovery of India*, Bombay: Asia Publishing House.

O'Brien, J. and Palmer, M. (1993) *The State of Religion Atlas*, New York: Simon & Schuster.

Panikkar, K.M. (1967) 'The Hindu Conception of the State' (from The State and the Citizen, Bombay, Asia Publishing House), in K. Satchidananda Murty, *Readings in India History, Politics and Philosophy*, London: George Allen & Unwin, pp. 135–138.

Radhakrishnan, S. (1937) 'Hinduism', in G.T. Garratt (ed.), *The Legacy of India*, Oxford: Oxford University Press, pp. 256–286.

Rajagopal, A. (1996) 'Communalism and the Consuming Subject', *Economic and Political Weekly*, 10 February, pp. 341–347.

Saberwal, S. (1996) 'Enlargement of Scales, Plural Traditions, and Rule of Law', *Review of Development & Change*, 1(1), pp. 1–19.

Savarkar, V.D. (2003) 'Hindutva' (from Hindutva: Who is a Hindu?, 6th edn, Delhi, Bharti Sahitya Sadan, 1989), in M. Gottlob (ed.), *Historical Thinking in South Asia: A Handbook of Sources from Colonial Times to the Present*, New Delhi: Oxford University Press, pp. 153–157.

Sen, A. (2005) *The Argumentative Indian: Writings on Indian Culture, History and Identity*, London: Penguin Books.

Srinivas, M.N. (1969) *Social Change in Modern India*, Berkeley: University of California Press.

Thapar, R. (1989) 'Epic and History: Tradition, Dissent and Politics in India', *Past and Present*, 125 (November), pp. 3–26.

Thapar, R. (1990) 'The Politics of Religious Communities', *Seminar*, 365 (Jan.), pp. 27–32.

Zaehner, R.C. (1962) Hinduism, Oxford: Oxford University Press. Zavos, J. (2003) *The Emergence of Hindu Nationalism in India*, Delhi: Oxford University Press.

CHAPTER REVIEW

1. Comment on the Hindu caste system.
2. Describe the role Ghandi played in Hinduism.
3. Differentiate between the *Vedas* and the *Upanishads*.
4. How was 1947 a pivotal year for Hinduism?
5. Discuss in what ways Hinduism reflects Indian politics.

Buddhism and Jainism

By Eugene F. Gorski

Hinduism Challenged

In India in the late fifth century BCE, a spiritual vacuum arouse out of a complex matrix of factors that challenged Hinduism and give rise to Buddhism and Jainism. The first factor was that of a spiritual malaise. By this time, the doctrines of *karma* and *samsara*, which had been controversial at the time of Yajnavalkya, were universally accepted by the people.[1] "Bad" karma meant that individuals would be reborn as slaves, animals, or plants. "Good" karma would ensure their rebirth as kings or gods. But this was not a fortunate occurrence: even gods would exhaust this beneficent karma, die, and be reborn in a less exalted state on Earth. As this teaching took hold, the mood of India changed, and many people became depressed with the fear of being doomed to one transient life after another. Not even good karma could save them. As they reflected on their community, they could see only pain and suffering. Wealth

Eugene F. Gorski, "Buddhism and Jainism," *Theology of Religions: A Sourcebook for Interreligious Study*, pp. 105–130. Copyright © 2008 by Paulist Press. Reprinted with permission.

and material pleasure were darkened with the grim reality of old age and mortality. As this gloom became more and more intense people sought to find a way out.

People became increasingly unsatisfied with the old Vedic rituals that could not provide a solution to this problem. The very best these rituals could do was provide a rebirth in the domain of the gods, but this could be only a temporary release from the relentless and suffering-producing cycle of samsara. Some even rejected the spirituality of the *Upanishads*, which was not for everyone. It was a full-time task, demanding hours of effort each day, and it was incompatible with the duties of a householder. And at this time the revolution that produced bhakti devotion as the universally accessible means to salvation had not yet taken place. So, because of the prevailing malaise of doom and despair, many people in India were looking for a spiritual solution and longing for a *jina*, a spiritual conqueror or a Buddha, an enlightened one who had woken up to a different dimension of existence.

Social, Political, and Economic Change

In addition to the spiritual malaise of this time, there was a social crisis. The people of northern India were undergoing major political and economic changes. The Vedic system had been the spirituality that supported a highly mobile society, constantly engaged in migration. But the peoples of sixth and fifth centuries were settling down in increasingly larger communities that were focused on agricultural production. There was also political development. The small chiefdoms had been absorbed into the larger units of kingdoms. As a result, the *Kshatriya* kingly warrior class had become more prominent. The new kingdoms stimulated trade in the Ganges basin. This generated more wealth, which the kings could spend on luxury goods, on their armies, and on the new cities that were becoming centers of trade and industry.

This new urbanization was another blow for Vedic spirituality, which was not well suited to urban culture and civilization. The kings began to shrug off control of the priests, and the urban republics tended to ignore the Brahmin class altogether and put a limit on the traditional sacrifices. The lavish sacrifices had been designed to impress the gods and enhance the prestige of the patrons. By the fifth century, the eastern peoples realized that their trade and culture brought much more wealth and status than the Vedic sacrifice rites. Instead of conforming to the old traditional ways, the new cities encouraged personal initiative and innovation; individualism was replacing tribal, community identity; the lower classes of the Vedic system were acquiring wealth and status that once would have been inconceivable.

These massive social changes brought about by urbanization were unsettling and left many people feeling disoriented or lost. The tensions were especially acute in the east, where urbanization was more advanced and where the next phase of the Indian Axial Age began. Here, life probably was experienced as particularly ephemeral, transient, plagued by disease and anomie, confirming the new well-established belief that life was *dukka*, suffering. The urban class was ambitious and powerful, but the gambling, theater, prostitution, and spirited tavern life of the towns seemed disarming to the people who still trusted in the older values.

Radical Dissent

Life was becoming more and more aggressive than before, in strong contrast to the older ideal of *ahimsa* that had become so crucial in north India. In the kingdoms there was infighting and civil strife. The economy was moved by greed and rugged competition. Life was experienced as even more violent and terrifying than when cattle rustling had been the backbone of the economy. The Vedic religion impressed people as increasingly out of touch with the violence of contemporary public life. People needed a different religious situation.

These ideas of radical dissent, along with the spiritual malaise and social, economic, and political crisis of the time, formed the complex matrix from which Buddhism and Jainism emerged during the Axial Age to vex the course of Hinduism. The founders of these religions, Siddhattha Gotama and Mahavira, provided alternative solutions to what had become the central problem of Indian life: how to find self-transcendence and salvation from the continual cycle of rebirths in the frightening and suffering-producing world. The Buddhists and Jains, of the warrior tribes and the *Kshatriya* caste, were more than ready to contest the Brahmins' claim to cultural control. They did not appreciate either the social or the religious implications of the Brahmins' teaching. Among the ranks of the Buddhists and Jains there were persons of brilliant mind for whom the costly sacrifices prescribed by the priests were not satisfactory. They and others like them had no interest in priestly sacrifices that did not immediately give them solace or fulfill their spiritual needs; they sought near-at-hand practical modes of release from their growing sense of the essential misery of existence. Like the authors of the *Upanishads*, they considered the world flawed and a cause of suffering. So they rejected the religion controlled by the Brahmins as being ineffectual for souls inwardly pained. Their radicalism was in their rejection of the sacrificial system of the *Bramanas* as well as their refusal to give the Brahmins first place of prescriptive rights in their urgent search for ways to liberation from the plight of suffering and the cycle of rebirths.

BUDDHISM

Buddhism emerged from the complex matrix of radical dissent, spiritual malaise, and the social, economic, and political crisis of the Indian Axial Age. About its founder, the Buddha, historians are confident of a few key facts. He was born into the family of King Shuddhodana and Queen Maya about the year 566 BCE in a region of the Indian subcontinent that now lies in southern Nepal. This date has been questioned recently by a group of historians who place his birth in the fifth century BCE. Most scholars now think that the Buddha in fact lived around 490 to 410. He was a member of the Shakya tribe, his clan name being Gotama, his given name Siddhattha. It is common to refer to him as *Siddhattha Gotama* or, more commonly as *Shakyamuni,* "The Sage of the Shakya Tribe." He was one among the thousands of brave individuals who searched in the northeastern forests of India to end samsara, the transmigration of life, during the Axial Age. Like many others, Gotama had become convinced that conquering the suffering of samsaric existence was the highest aspiration of life. Nothing else was of equal importance. And like others, he willingly gave up everything to attain that goal.

He departed from his princely existence and began his search for salvation as a wandering mendicant. For six years following his departure from palace life, he made serious efforts to attain his spiritual goal. As he engaged in this quest, he came to the conclusion that the philosophy of the Brahmins was unacceptable and their claims unsubstantiated. He also denied the saving efficacy of the *Vedas* and the ritual observances based on them. But he did take up the options available to him for practicing the ascetic and contemplative disciplines. Quickly he mastered the extreme ascetic method for reaching union with Brahman but found it did not bring him what he was looking for. After many years of frustrating searching, he decided to abandon the well-trodden spiritual paths passed on to him by his teachers and to devise his own path. Within a short time after this decision, he went to a nearby river, cleansed himself of the dust that had accumulated on his body for many months, and then ate a bowl of milk rice. According to his new, self-taught approach to the spiritual journey, he would have to care for his body because physical well-being was necessary to pursue liberation from samsara. The traditional harsh forms of self-mortification he had followed previously had to be abandoned. Shortly later, on the evening of the full moon in the month of Vesakha (which is between April and May) he sat beneath the *bodhi* tree near the village of Bodhgaya in the present Indian state of Bihar. Resting in the shade of that tree released an old memory of sitting under a rose-apple tree as a child during a clan agricultural festival. Gotama recalled that as his father was engaged in a ceremonial plowing action, he became restless and bored. And with nothing else to do, he began to pay close attention to his breath. In those moments, he experienced a heightened sense of awareneness and a pervasive serenity that diminished his boredom and restlessness. Remembering that time of his childhood, Siddhattha thought that this gentle practice of awareness meditation might be useful for the spiritual practices he wanted to devise for himself.

This form of meditation was different from the practices of his teachers in that it emphasized the quality of *mindfulness.* While the goal of other meditations was to become absorbed in exceptional states of mind, *his* mindfulness meditation aimed at attaining a heightened awareness of the immediate present moment, so that one became attentive to what was occurring in the mind, the body, and the external environment and observing these processes without judgment. By putting aside goals and releasing preconceptions and judgments, the Buddha believed the mind would become more open to insight into the nature of the world and self. Gotama sat beneath the huge tree, practicing his meditation, and vowed not to leave the spot until he realized the liberating knowledge he had sought for so many years.

In his mindfulness he scrutinized his behavior, carefully noting the ebb and flow of his feelings and sensations as well as the fluctuations of his consciousness. He made himself aware of the constant stream of desires, irritations, and ideas that coursed thorough his mind in the space of a single hour. By this introspection, he was becoming acquainted with the working of his mind and body in order to exploit their capacities and use them to best advantage. Finally, at dawn, he was convinced that he had attained the knowledge that liberates and conquers samsara. At this moment Gotama earned the title, the *Buddha*, which means the "awakened one."

For forty-nine days, the Buddha enjoyed his liberation. He then decided to teach others the knowledge with which he had been enlightened. He found five former disciples and delivered to them a discourse that is sometimes called the "Buddha's First Discourse and Turning the Wheel of Dhamma." This formal talk consisted of a concise formulation of the insights that he had received under the bodhi tree. It contained what the Buddhist tradition calls the "Four Noble Truths," considered by many to be the essence of Buddhism. Most of the Buddha's subsequent teachings might be considered explanations or amplifications of these basic points. As the four truths are discussed here, other teachings in the Pali scriptures will be used to clarify them.

The First Noble Truth: Suffering

The first noble truth is that life is *dukka*—suffering—and that craving for things of the world is responsible for suffering. It was not only the traumas of old age, sickness, and death that made life so unsatisfactory. "Human existence was filled with countless frustrations, disappointments, and its nature was impermanent. Pain, grief and despair are *dukka*," he explained. "Being forced into proximity with what we hate is suffering; being separated from what we love is suffering; not getting what we want is suffering."[2] Suffering includes a whole range of human experiences from the usual events of getting sick, growing old and dying, to not getting what we want and getting what we do not want. Suffering is the fundamental quality of the whole of existence. The very makeup of human existence is entangled in suffering. The whole of human life—not only certain occasions—is suffering. In his mindfulness he also observed how one craving after another took hold of him, how he was ceaselessly yearning to become something else, go somewhere else, and get something he did not have.

We might ask, Why did the Buddha teach that suffering is comprehensive and constant and not simply episodic in human life? Mark W. Muesse suggests the reason the Buddha taught this "is because we do not fully appreciate the extent to which we suffer or feel the unsatisfactoriness of existence."[3] The First Noble Truth is not a statement of a self-evident fact of life; rather, for individuals it is a challenge to discover for themselves the depth and breadth of *dukka* by the means of introspection and observation. The Buddha himself hinted at much when he said, "'This Dhamma that I have attained is profound, hard to see and hard to understand, peaceful and sublime, unattainable by mere reasoning, subtle, to be experienced by the wise.'"[4] Muesse adds, "I would even go so far as to say that one cannot realize the nature and extent of *dukka* until the moment of complete awakening, as the Buddha himself did on the full moon of Vesakha. The true depth of suffering can only be seen from the perspective of the enlightened mind."[5] Recognizing that suffering is manifested not only in particular experiences, but in the whole of existence requires persistent and attentive awareness.

The Second Noble Truth: The Cause of Suffering

In the Second Noble Truth, the Buddha states that the root of suffering is desire, or craving. This aspect of the Buddha's teaching distinguishes it the most from other religious perspectives.

The cause of suffering is *tanha*, desire. Desires are problematic when they are self-centered and become intense craving: that is, when an object of desiring becomes a matter of necessity, as if our lives depended on it. Or when we already possess what we desire and believe that losing it would be devastating to our existence. And such craving can lead to the point where relationships to objects, people, values, beliefs, ideas, power, status, experience, and sensation have the nature of attachments or clinging. The problem is not with the objects of attachment themselves, but with the nature of a person's relationships to them, which can become addictions. Since everything in the world is of constant change, nothing can support a person's attachments; all things to which we become attached are subject to change, and this causes suffering. To allay this suffering we seek something else to cling to, but the more we try to secure happiness through acquisition the more we suffer. Attachment can also include an aversion to an object or situation, causing a negative relationship that is just as difficult to relinquish as an attachment. Both Hinduism and Buddhism recognize attachments as mechanisms that lead to samsara and suffering. The Buddha's answer to the dual dangers of attachments and aversion is equanimity, the Middle Way between the two extremes.

Now that the effects of *tanha* and attachments have been discussed, we ask in turn about their antecedent causes. What makes us have desires that become attachments? The cause is ignorance: ignorance of the true nature of ourselves and the world. We develop strong desires and attachments when we are ignorant of the fact that the world and self are really impermanent; they are not things, they are only processes. In the mind of the Buddha, change and impermanence are constant, persistent. Even solid objects are in constant flux. The Buddha viewed the cosmos as a complex arrangement of processes rather than a set of things. It is not only that things change, but that change is the only thing there is. Unlike the Vedanta tradition of Hinduism, the Buddha held that the soul or true self of the human person is impermanent.

No-Self Anatta

On his spiritual journey, the Buddha eventually became convinced that the ultimate cause of his suffering and unfulfilled longing was delusion about himself. He failed to see that he was selfless. The human person as "me" or "I" forms a distorting lens through which the world takes on a false character. In that lens the universe is misinterpreted as structured around "me," and the world process is accordingly experienced as a stream of objects of my desires and aversions, hopes, and fears that give rise to grasping. This covetousness expresses itself in egotism, injustice, and cruelty, in a pervasive self-regarding anxiety in face of life's uncertainties, in the inevitability of final decay and death—all of which comprehensively constitute the "suffering of human existence," *dukka*. The salvation Siddhattha searched for was liberation from the suffering caused by the powerful illusion of "me" or "self." It involved the recognition of his having *no* self: his selflessness. Being liberated from the illusory and falsely evaluating "me" was for him to exchange the realm of ego-infected consciousness for the sublime freedom of *nirvana*.

What the Buddha came to perceive and teach his followers about selflessness is called *anatta* in Pali. However, the Sanskrit term, *anatman* ("no-self") makes it evident that the Buddha denies the reality of the *atman*, the Hindu concept of the permanent, immortal, substantial soul or true self. Most interpreters of Buddhism hold that *anatta* was meant to be a doctrine or concept or an ontological statement-theory about the nonexistence of the conscious subject. But it is perhaps more appropriate to hold that it was intended to refer to an *anti-concept* as well as an *axiological or value-oriented, realistic prescription for a certain kind of moral practice*. It is more a denial of what humans ordinarily believe themselves to be. Let us develop this position, first focusing on *anatta* as an anti-concept.

Anatta *as Anti-Concept and Axiological Prescription*

The Buddha held that the concept of the self can promote fruitless speculation and contribute to humankind's suffering. Instead of putting forth another view of self, the Buddha simply indicates that the concept of the self is an inept way of thinking about human beings. While it is permitted to refer to the self reflexively, as in talking about ourselves, the Buddha insisted that we should never consider that it refers to anything substantial or permanent. However, one should not think that the Buddha denies human existence or suggests that human life is unreal or an illusion. *Anatta* means essentially that human beings do not exist in the way they think they do, that is, as separate, substantial selves. To hold this is to hold to an illusion, an unsubstantiated belief in the same way a rainbow is an optical illusion, created by the convergence of various conditions.[6] To the Buddha, atman is an illusion supported by changing conditions. That is why no one is able to identify or pinpoint the soul or essential self. The Buddha taught that the problems of human beings arise when they ascribe reality to this illusion. Belief in a permanent, substantial self is the origin of suffering; it sets into motion a series of thoughts, words, and actions that bring on anguish and disappointment. The so-called self is not a thing; it is no-thing, nothing; it is insubstantial; it lacks permanence and immortality. The Buddha's denial of self states that no concept is able to express the reality of who we are. His intention is merely to attempt to disrupt human beings' old habits about who they are.

Instead of viewing individuals as immortal souls in perishable bodies, the Buddha saw the human person as a complex of interconnected and ever-in-flux energies or forces that he called the "Five Aggregates of Being." These are (1) matter, one's physical makeup; (2) sensation or feeling, the way one judges experiences as pleasant, unpleasant, or neutral (such judgments condition one's tendencies of attachment and aversion); (3) perception and apperception; (4) mental formations, the sources of desire, craving, and intention; mental formations are, in the Buddha's thinking, the sources of karma; therefore as long as there is craving, there will be rebirth; (5) consciousness, the process of awareness. There is nothing about these components that endures. All of them are in flux. Neither is there a permanent agent of subject that underlies these processes.

The Buddha's teaching, then, about *anatta* is an anti-concept. Furthermore, it is appropriate to understand it also as an axiological or value-oriented and practical ethical prescription about how one should direct his or her life in order to attain salvation. A person should live in a way that is selfless, that is, without being attached to the notion of "my self"—and this is truly a way of being that is "authentically myself." It is the distinctive and famous path to axial self-transcendence that Gotama personally chose to follow. It led to the overturning of the delusion of self and discovering nirvana, the Place of Peace, of inner freedom and the extinction of suffering.

The Third Noble Truth: The Cessation of Suffering

The Buddha's good news for humanity can be found in the Third and Fourth Noble Truths. The Third Noble Truth is direct and clear: "Now this, bhikkus, is the noble truth of the cessation of suffering: it is the remainderless fading away and cessation of the same craving, the giving up and relinquishing of it, freedom from it, non-reliance on it."[7] One does not have to suffer. If *tanha*, thirst or craving, is the cause of suffering, then clearly the solution is to cease from craving, and when persons end craving, attachments dissolve, and they are liberated from the cycle of suffering and rebirth. The reason to end craving is *nibbana*, in Pali, or *nirvana* in Sanskrit. *Nirvana* means the eradication of desire, the cessation of thirst, and the destruction of the illusion that one is a separate, substantial self. It is the end of suffering, the point where a person ceases craving for reality to be other than that what it is, radically accepting the way the world and the self truly are. The *method* for quenching thirst is set forth in the Fourth Noble Truth. But before we focus about the way to the goal, let us discuss the goal itself.

Nirvana is experienced at death, but a form of it can be realized in one's historical lifetime. One who achieves this is called an *arahant*: he or she has fully realized the truth of the Buddha's vision and is free from craving, aversion, and ignorance. *Arahants* continue to experience physical pain and other forms of old karma. However, even with physical pain, one does not suffer. Suffering is distinguished from pain; pain is a bodily sensation, while suffering pertains to the mental anguish that comes from resisting pain or merely resisting the way things are. The *arahant* does not generate new karmas but still must experience effects of the old ones. When at death nirvana is experienced, all karmic forces that sustain existence are dissipated, and the *arahant* is released from rebirth. The image that is frequently associated with final nirvana is a candle, the flame of which has gone out because the fuel and the oxygen have been exhausted. In a parallel fashion, without karma to perpetuate rebirth, the flame of the candle belonging to the *arahant* "goes out."

The Buddha's disciples, of course, were strongly interested in what occurs at final nirvana. One of the central issues of the Axial Age, as we have seen, was the matter of an individual's destiny after death. So the disciples were curious: whether an *arahant* exists after death or does not exist after death; or both exists and does not exist after death; or neither exists nor does not exist after death. But the Buddha refused to respond because knowing the answer was not essential to seeing nirvana, and dwelling on such questions was an obstacle to the goal. The Buddha was generally reticent about issues that were not essential to the termination of suffering.

It should be noted that, for the Buddha, freedom from suffering was not received as a grace or gift from God. Like the path of knowledge in Hinduism, the Buddha's Middle Way required great effort and discipline because human beings are the cause of their own suffering and only they themselves can find freedom from it. The Buddha only shows the way to that freedom.

The Fourth Noble Truth: The Eightfold Path to Enlightenment

In this final truth, the Buddha shows the way to enlightenment with an outline of what the discipline involves. "Now this, bhikkus, is the noble truth of the way leading to the cessation of suffering: It is this Noble Eightfold Path that is right understanding, right intention, right speech, right action, right livelihood, right mindfulness and right concentration."[8] The Noble Eightfold Path the Buddha followed and taught was in the middle between simply giving in to the sensual, vulgar desires of an ordinary foolish person and depriving oneself of even the very necessities of existence. Traditionally, the eight components of the plan of action have been divined into three sections: *conduct,* or developing ethical behavior; *concentration,* or developing the mind by meditation; and *study,* or cultivating the wisdom that enabled persons to see themselves and all things as they truly are. For this reason the Noble Path is sometimes called the "Triple Practice." By following his middle path and thus avoiding the two extremes, Gotama achieved, at Bodhgaya in Bihar, the enlightenment for which he passionately searched.

Right Understanding

The Buddha recognized that to begin engaging in the Eightfold Path requires some initial understanding of his teaching about the Middle Way and the Four Noble Truths, and that this understanding is achieved by study, discussion, and reflection. The result of such study and reflection is, however, only a glimmer of the truth that the practitioner sees that prompts him or her to take the path at the outset.

Right Intention

The interior motive bridges right understanding and the next division of the triple practice, developing moral conduct. Right intention involves the determination to practice specific virtues that neutralize the conditioned tendencies of individuals toward greed, hatred, and harming. The virtues that exert the counteracting effect are nonattachment, goodwill, and harmlessness.

Right Speech-Action-Livelihood

Developing moral conduct, the second part of the triple practice, is the chief part of the Buddha's path. This moral behavior is not commanded either by a god or by the Buddha. It is rooted, the Buddha believed, in the very nature of human beings. He also held that karma is generated only by intentional acts; the source of karma is the aggregate of mental formations, the idea of desire and intention. An appropriate way to discuss the moral dimension of the Buddha's teaching is to start with what he called the "Five Precepts":

1. "I will refrain from harming sentient beings."
2. "I will refrain from taking what is not offered"; that is, one promises not to steal or to covet.
3. "I will refrain from sexual misconduct."
4. "I will refrain from false speech"; not only lying and slandering, but also gossiping, cursing, loud talk, idle chatter.
5. "I will refrain from stupefying drink"; intoxicants.[9]

Right Mindfulness-Concentration

Virtuous moral behavior is central to the holy life, but the Buddha considered it equally important to discipline the mind. As self-absorbed habits hinder the basic compassion of the human heart, so misled habits of the thinking mind obstruct the ability to understand the world and the self as they truly are. For the Buddha, the mind meant the complex of thoughts, sensations, feeling, and consciousness that in each moment arise and fall away. The mind has great power and potential; however, in its unenlightened condition it is out of control, unruly and undisciplined. And to bring it under control requires skill, persistent training, and patience.

Right concentration involves the practice of meditation to strengthen the virtues of attentiveness and nonattachment. The Buddha intended the practice of meditation to heighten consciousness of the world and self by being attentive to the events of ordinary life in the present moment. The fundamental meditative practice, based on the Buddha's own experiences, involved attending to the breath and observing without judgment the coming and going of thoughts, sensations, feeling, and perceptions. As these phenomena come to awareness, the subject notes them and allows them to fall away without dwelling on them. Simply by being observant of the mind, the body, and the surrounding world, the Buddha held it was possible to gain an insight into the true essence of the world and the self, and on the basis of such insight to act and think accordingly. He believed this meditative practice would disclose the illusionary nature of self and the origin of suffering in the mind's tendency to thirst for new pleasures and to avoid unpleasant experiences. He also held that meditation could hold back the mind's inclination to make spontaneous judgments and to become absorbed in thoughts about the future and the past, all of which were considered to be unwholesome habits.

In the development of mindfulness and the practice of contemplation, the Buddha also fostered the skillful states of a lucid, conscious mind, completely alert, filled with compassion and loving welfare for all beings.[10] By performing these mental exercises at sufficient depth, they could, he was convinced, transform the restless and destructive tendencies of his conscious and unconscious mind. At each stage of his journey into the depths of his mind, he intentionally evoked the emotion of love and directed it to the four corners of the Earth without omitting a single plant, animal, friend, or foe from its embrace. This outpouring of loving kindness was a fourfold program. First, he developed an attitude of friendship for everything and for everybody. Next, he cultivated an empathy with their pain and suffering. In the third stage of his mindfulness, he evoked a "sympathetic joy" that rejoiced in the happiness of others, without envy or a sense of personal diminishment. Finally, he aspired to an attitude of complete equanimity toward others, feeling neither attraction nor antipathy.

This expression of universal love was a difficult challenge because it involved Gotama's turning away completely from the egotism that always is concerned with how other people and things might benefit or detract from the self. He was learning to surrender his entire being to others, and thus to transcend the ego in compassion and loving kindness for all creatures.[11]

Enlightenment

In the Buddhist tradition there are two levels of understanding. The first is attained by mere reasoning. The second form is the understanding that occurs in enlightenment; it is the content of enlightened experience. Gotama's great experience of enlightenment was the first most significant event in the history of Buddhism. His followers who follow his Eightfold Path aspire to achieve that same enlightened experience. When they arrive at this goal, then in light of the eternal reality of being itself—the transcendent stream of Universal Being—they see themselves and the world around them, as he himself saw, as passing, unsubstantial expressions of the Absolute. This is seeing reality as it is, unfettered by expectation, belief, or defilement of any kind. In this form of comprehension, one knows for certain the authenticity of the Four Noble Truths without reliance on authorities other than one's own experience. To comprehend the Buddha's teaching at this level means to live one's life in accord with the truth. One no longer seeks for or aspires to nirvana. Nirvana has been seen.

In written accounts of the Buddha's enlightenment, he is described as rapt in ecstatic joy, imbued with a compassionate love of all sentient beings, "as a mother toward the only child," and endowed with the equanimity of a perfectly liberated person. In monastic commentaries, this state of even-mindedness is described as the opposite of three kinds of experience: the pleasure that comes with attachment, the displeasure due to aversion, and an ignorant kind of indifference. What the Buddha experienced was nirvana: It transformed his life.

Nirvana

What was nirvana? It was the extinguishing of the fires of greed, hatred, and delusion, the elimination of the craving, hatred, and ignorance that subjugate humanity. And even though the Buddha was still subject to physical ailments and other vicissitudes, nothing could cause him serious mental pain or diminish his inner peace of complete selflessness. The Buddha would continue to suffer; he would grow old and sick like everybody else; but by following his Noble Eightfold Path, he had found the inner haven that enables a person to live with suffering, take possession of it, affirm it, and experience in its midst a profound serenity.

The Buddha was convinced that nirvana was a transcendent state because it lay beyond the capacities of those who had not achieved the inner awakening of enlightenment. And while no words could adequately describe it, in mundane terms it could be called "Nothing" since it corresponded to no recognizable reality. But those who had been able to find this sacred peace realized that they lived a limitlessly richer life.[12] Later monotheists would speak about God in similar terms, claiming that God was "nothing" because "he" was not another being; and that it was more precise to state that he did not exist because human notions of existence were too limited to apply to the divine reality.[13] They would also state that a selfless, compassionate life would bring people into God's presence.

But, like other Indian sages and mystics, the Buddha found the idea of a personalized deity too limiting. He always denied the existence of a supreme being because such a deity would become another block to enlightenment. The Buddhist Pali texts never mention Brahman. Gotama's rejection of God was a calm and measured posture. He simply put the notion serenely out of his mind.

When Gotama made an effort to give his disciples a hint of what nirvana was like, he used both negative and positive terms. Nirvana was the "extinction of greed, hatred and delusion"; it was "taintless," "unweakening," "undisintegrating," "inviolable," "non-distress," "unhostility," and "deathless." Nirvana was "the Truth," "the Subtle," "the Other Shore," "Peace," "the Everlasting," "the Supreme Goal," "Purity, Freedom, Independence, the Island, the Shelter, the Harbor, the Refuge, the Beyond."[14] It was the supreme goal of humans and gods, an incomprehensible serenity, an utterly safe refuge. Many of these images are suggestive of words later used by monotheists to describe their experiences of the ineffable God.

The Buddha as Teacher

After the important event of his enlightenment, for nearly a half-century the Buddha traveled the Gangetic basin teaching his doctrine and building a community of followers. After his initial enlightenment at Bodhgaya, the second most significant occurrence in the history of Buddhism is Gotama's first sermon, which was given at Sarnath. In this presentation to his first five followers, he began to expound the Middle Path and the Four Noble Truths as the kernel of his awakening experience. The principle conception of his teaching was the doctrine of *anatta*, "No Self," and the invitation to his listeners to a way of life that leads to the Axial ideals of self-transcendence and salvation from the suffering and dissatisfaction that is part and parcel of human existence.

At the age of eighty, the Buddha peacefully died and passed into final nirvana. After his death, the Sangha or Buddhist community continued his teaching, and with grand success. They gathered together to consider how to preserve the Buddha's teaching. Early Buddhist councils led to the creation of authoritative texts and to the discussion of important doctrinal issues. This ultimately divided the community into several sects. Of the eighteen different varieties of Buddhist schools, only the Theravada school remains, making it the oldest extant Buddhist tradition. It probably represents the form closest to the way Buddhism was practiced around the time of the Buddha.

Around the first century CE the Mahayana form of Buddhism began to take shape in northwestern India; it added a substantially different dimension and new views about the Buddha and his role in making salvation accessible to humanity. New narratives were created that ascribed to the Buddha divine, godlike status. Mahayana developed the idea of the *bodhisattva*, an enlightened being who remained in the samsaric circle or in the heavenly domain in order to help others attain enlightenment and salvation. Mahayana was carried to China, Korea, and Japan. It eventually became the most popular form of Buddhism but has also fragmented over time into new schools. Out of the Mahayana emerged the third major form of Buddhism, the Vajrayana, practiced for centuries in Tibet and Mongolia.

Gotama's doctrine of "No Self" is at the heart of both the Theravada and the Mahayana schools of Buddhism. In Theravada there is a psychological realization of *anatta* which is the loss of "conceit of I am." This constitutes the attainment of the state of enlightenment, the state of be an *arahant*. In Mahayana the same concept of liberation from self applies, but here the aim is not to become an *arahant* but a *bodhisattva*, an enlightened person whose openness to the Transcendent is expressed in unlimited compassion for all sentient beings. For to live as a "self" is to seek happiness for oneself. But transcending the ego, becoming a manifestation of the universal Buddha nature, is to seek the happiness of all.

Today there are a total of approximately 329 million Buddhists in many areas of the world, including Sri Lanka, Burma, Thailand, Cambodia, Laos, China, Korea, Japan, Tibet, Mongolia, Europe, and the United States. One hundred twenty-four million Buddhists are of the Theravada branch; 20 million are

Jainism

Almost all estimates indicate that there are 350 million Buddhists in the world today and fewer than 5 million Jains, almost all of them in India, mostly in Mumbai and other large urban centers.[16] While they account for less than 5 percent of the Indian population, their influence on the religious, social, political, and economic life of India has been, and is, quite out of proportion to their numbers. In Europe, largely in the United Kingdom, there are presently estimated to be 25,000 Jains. Some estimates suggest a similar number may be found in North America. There is a vast disparity in the number of Buddhists and Jains, but the two traditions share similar histories, beliefs, and practices. Both reject the authority of the *Vedas*, and both accept rebirth and karma and aspire to release from samsara.

Modern history specifies the origins of Jainism in the same cultural environment that gave rise to Hinduism and Buddhism. Jainism grew from the struggle for enlightenment of its main figure, Vardhamana Jnatrputra (c. 497–425 BCE), called the *Jina* ("Conqueror") or *Mahavira* ("Great Hero"). Sometimes he is referred to by outsiders as the founder of Jainism, but Jains themselves see their religion as a tradition going back dozens of generations before Mahavira. Devout adherents of Jainism insist that their religious tradition is eternal, based on truths that have no beginning in time. At certain moments in the universal life cycle, these truths have been forgotten and lost, but then rediscovered and reintroduced to humanity. When an Axial Age sage named Vardhamana Mahavira began to teach the doctrines of Jainism, he was only communicating a religion that had been taught many times before by others. Each of these former teachers was a *Tirkanthara*, a word that means "bridge builder" ("those who find a ford over the river of suffering"). The *Tirthankaras* were exceptional individuals who showed the way to salvation by their words and example. In the last turn of the universal cycle, there have been twenty-four *Tirthankaras*. The most recent was Vardhamana, portrayed mythically as being of supernatural birth and the twenty-third and last in a long line of *Tirthankaras*. He is not considered to be the founder of Jainism, only its reformer and reviver. It should be noted that there is no historical evidence to support the existence of the first twenty-two *Tirthankaras*.

Modern scholarship locates the origins of Jainism in the person of Vardhamana Mahavira of the Axial Age, who according to tradition was born into the *Kshatriya* in 599 BCE. Both Buddhist and Jain texts indicate that the Buddha and Mahavira were contemporaries living in the same region of northeastern India, in Bihar state. The texts indicate that they knew of each other but never actually met. However, if the Buddha in fact lived around 490 to 410, as most scholars now think, then the traditional dates of Mahavira would be inaccurate.

After the death of his parents, at the age of thirty Mahavira gave up his princely life and became a wondering monk in search of liberation from death and rebirth, following a harsh lifestyle as a *samana*, a renouncer of wealth and life in society. For the next twelve years, he practiced intense asceticism, including fasting for long periods of time, mortification of the flesh, meditation, and the practice of silence. He scrupulously avoided harming other living beings, including animals and plants. By dedication to these austere practices he merited a title given to him by his admirers, the *Mahavira*, meaning the "Great Hero." At the age of forty-two, after twelve years of uncompromising dedication to self-discipline, he believed he was simply the latest in a long line of *jinas* who achieved complete victory over his body and the desires that bound him to the world of matter and sin; he had crossed the river of *dukka* (suffering) to find access to liberation and enlightenment. In his enlightened state he attained a transcendent knowledge that gave him a unique perspective of the world. He was able to perceive all levels of reality simultaneously, in every dimension of time and space, as though he were a god. In fact, for Mahavira, God was simply a creature who had accomplished supreme knowledge by perceiving and respecting the single divine transcendent soul that existed in every single creature. This state of mind could not be described, because it entirely transcended ordinary consciousness. It was a state of absolute friendliness with all creatures, however lowly. He had crossed the river of *dukka* to find access to liberation and enlightenment.

For the next thirty years he roamed around the Ganges region teaching others his principles and practices for achieving liberation from samsara, for which he used both the terms *moksha* and *nirvana*. Like the Buddha, he drew men and women and children from all social strata. His followers were called "Jainas," or now, according to a more modern pronunciation, "Jains," because they were disciples of the *jina*. Some legends indicate that at one point Mahavira had gathered more than 400,000 disciples. He organized his followers into an order of monks, nuns, and laypersons. To attain liberation, one had to become a monk because of the austere discipline required to achieve it. Laypersons expected to strive for *moksha* in a future lifetime when circumstances were more favorable for such a pursuit. His teaching became the basis of the *Agam Sutras*, one of the most important scriptures in Jainism. According to tradition, Mahavira died and attained final nirvana at the age of seventy-two, after thirty years of successful teaching and organizing. He is now, according to all Jain sects, at the top of the universe, where all perfect ones go, enjoying complete self-transcendent bliss in a state no longer subject to rebirth. After his death, the Jains would develop an elaborate prehistory, claiming that in previous eras there had been twenty-four of these ford makers who had discovered the bridge to salvation.

Mahavira taught his followers in conformity with this vision. Like Buddhists and Hindus, he appropriated many of the basic assumptions and beliefs circulating in the Ganges basin in the early Indian Axial Age, but he reinterpreted them to fit his particular enlightened view of the world. We now explore how Mahavira understood these concepts, including his idea of time, the structure of the world, the nature of the soul, karma, and the path to salvation.

Time

Mahavira was of the belief that the world was never created and will never be destroyed. Cosmic time, therefore, is infinite, but it does conform to a cyclical pattern. Each cycle has two half-segments, a period of decline and a period of ascendancy. Each segment is further divided into six unequal parts. The half-cycles are incalculably long. One half-cycle is a time of decline. During the first part of this period, people are very tall and live lives that are very long. They are exceedingly happy, wise, and virtuous, with no need of religion or ethics. All of their needs are provided by wish-granting trees. As the cycle proceeds, conditions become progressively worse. The world and life are gradually tainted with corruption and deterioration; ethics and religion are then introduced; writing is invented, since peoples' memories begin to fail. During these times the *Tirthankaras* appear. When the lowest point of the cycle of decline is reached, people will be only about three feet tall and live twenty years. Like animals, they will live in caves and pursue all sorts of immoral activity.

But as time reaches its lowest point, it begins to ascend, and the world becomes increasingly better. People then start to live longer, healthier lives, to conduct themselves in more compassionate ways, and to experience greater happiness. When this cycle reaches its apex, time begins again its downward motion. The pattern is repeated over and over again, forever. According to Jain belief, we are presently in the fifth stage of the cycle of descent, a period when things are bad and will become even worse. The current era began a little over 2,500 years ago and will continue for a total of 21,000 years. When this period ends, Jainism will be lost and will be reintroduced by the next *Tirthankaras* after the half-cycle of ascent commences again.

Structure of the World

According to the teaching of Mahavira, the physical world is made up of three levels: the underworld; the surface of the world, or the middle realm; and the heavens. In the underworld are a series of seven or eight hell realms, and each of these is colder than the next. The hell realms are for the punishment of the wicked as a means of purifying negative karma. The Jain hells are more like a purgatory than a location of ultimate condemnation. When souls have suffered sufficiently for their sins, they may be reborn in another realm. The middle level is the place of life; it is known by the name of *Jambudvipa*, or the island of the rose-apple tree. It is a name used also by Buddhists and Hindus. The upper level of the world is the realm of the gods. It has sixteen heavens and fourteen celestial abodes. And then, above the ceiling of the universe is a crescent-shaped structure where the *Tirthankaras* and the completely liberated souls dwell. This is the ultimate goal and destination of those who attain *moksha*.

Nature of the Soul

Mahavira, like the sages who wrote the *Upanishads*, believed that the soul was real, not illusionary as the Buddha thought. Mahavira considered the soul to be a living, luminous, and intelligent entity within the material body; it was unchanging in essence, but its characteristics were subject to change. It was also his conviction that there were an infinite number of souls, each an actual, separate individual. Therefore, Mahavira would not have accepted the Vedantic idea that soul and ultimate reality are consubstantial, since that view denies individuality. Furthermore, all souls are of equal value; one is no better than another. Souls may be embodied in gods and in humans, as well as in animals and plants, and even, according to some, stones, minerals, bodies of water, fire, and the winds. By the karmas of former lives they had been brought to their present existence. Therefore, all beings share the same nature and must be treated with equal respect and care that persons would want to receive themselves.[17]

Karma

In its pure state, the soul enjoys perception, knowledge, happiness, power, all of which are perfect. However, at the present time, all souls, with the exception of the completely liberated ones, are defiled because they are embodied and tainted with karma. The Jain understanding of karma is of a fine, material substance that clings to and stains the soul. Karmas are invisible particles, floating throughout the world. When a soul commits a karmic act, it attracts these fine articles, which adhere to the soul and weigh it down. These karmas accumulate and, in due course, color the soul. We cannot see a soul because of our defiled state; but if we could, we could with ease detect a soul's moral and spiritual quality. The souls that are worse are stained black, and the purest are white. And in between, from bad to good, the soul may be blue, gray, red, lotus-pink, or yellow. Like in Buddhism and Hinduism, karma determines persons' future births and keeps them bound to the material, samsaric world.

Since they are imprisoned in matter, souls do not enjoy omniscience as they do in their pure state. Karmic stains cause our perceptions to be distorted and our knowledge of the world limited. These distortions urge the soul to seek pleasure in material possessions and fleeting enjoyments, which further lead to self-absorbed thoughts and anger, hatred, greed, and other states of the mind. These, in turn, bring about the further accumulation of karma. Consequently, the cycle is a vicious one.

The limitations that result from karmic defilement also mean that we are unable to understand the great richness and complexity of reality. The Jains propose that reality is many sided; this means that the world is made up of an infinite number of material and spiritual substances, each with an infinite number of qualities and manifestations. Since the universe is complex and our knowledge is limited, all claims of truth must be tentative. The Jains refer to the principle as "non-absolutism," which means making no categorical or unconditional statements.

Path to Liberation

In Mahavira's teaching, liberation meant the release of one's true self from the constraints of body and thus the achievement of salvation, inner control, and transcendent peace of mind, enlightenment, all being the great values of the Axial Age. The path to liberation is simple. At first, preventing the flow of new karma and then, second, eliminating the old karmas that have already accumulated and weigh the soul down.

To attain the first goal, Mahavira urged his followers to fulfill five Great Vows. The first and foremost of these vows is *ahimsa*, to avoid harming any living beings. The Jains take this rule further than the Buddhists, who drew the line at sentient life, not at life itself. The Jains are convinced that even unintentionally injuring another creature causes negative karma. In line with these beliefs, Jains are vegetarians and refuse to use leather or other animal products. Most avoid agriculture, because the plow might inadvertently damage a worm, and other kinds of occupations that might cause harm to other forms of life. Some, especially the monks, use a cloth to cover a glass when they drink so as to strain out insects that may have fallen into the liquid; and they sweep the pathways before them to avoid stepping on bugs. *Ahimsa*, however, means more than avoiding physical injury to life. It also involves what the Jains call *ahimsa* of the mind and *ahimsa* of speech. The former is the practice of right thought. Evil thoughts are held to generate negative karma. The latter is speaking in a nonhurtful way, using kind, compassionate language.

Achieving salvation is centered on not harming one's fellow creatures. Until persons had acquired this empathetic view of the world, they could not attain salvation. Consequently, nonviolence was a strict religious duty. All other ethical and religious practices were useless without *ahimsa*, and this could not be achieved until the Jain had acquired a state of empathy, an attitude of positive benevolence, with every single creature. All living creatures should be of support and assistance to one another. They should relate to every single human being, animal, plant, insect, or pebble with friendship, goodwill, patience, and gentleness.

The other four vows are connected to *ahimsa* and the cessation of karmic accumulation. They are always to speak the truth; not to steal or take what is not given; chastity, which is understood as celibacy for the monks, and faithfulness in marriage for the laypeople; and last, nonattachment to people and material things.

Preventing new karmas from staining the soul is the first step to liberation; purification of the stains of old karmas is the next. Good deeds and asceticism are the principle means of eliminating the accumulation of karmas. Those who desired to attain perfect enlightenment must, like Mahavira, practice fasting, engage in certain types of meditation, penance, yoga, study, and recitation of the scriptures. These acts purge the soul of its karmic deposit. They lead to transcendence over one's own physical state and to a trance state marked by complete disassociation from the outer world. This trance state is believed to be like the one Mahavira entered into in the thirteenth year of his seeking and assured him of his final liberation.

The ultimate ascetic observance, assumed by many throughout history, is fasting to death. The fast is the symbol and producer of absolute renunciation. Before this point, the ascetic has abstained from all but food and water. And then in a profound meditative state, food and water are given up, ending for good all attachments to samsara. This fast is not considered an act of violence, but a gesture of compassion, because there is no anger or pain associated with it.

The purging of all karmas restores the soul to its pure, undefiled state. It then has perfect knowledge, perfect perception and power. It is no longer weighed down by the burden of its karma, so it ascends to the very ceiling of the universe, where it enjoys the bliss of nirvana in the company of other liberated beings.

Similar to the Buddha and the Upanishadic sages, Mahavira taught a path of self-salvation. Since each individual soul is responsible for its own karmas, only the individual person is able to reverse the karmic accumulations. The purpose of the monastic community was to provide a supportive context for the pursuit of nirvana. Because the Jain search for nirvana required a more austere asceticism than the Buddha's Middle Way, taking on the life of a monk or nun was more vital to the realization of nirvana in Jainism than in Buddhism. The monks were also responsible for safeguarding the Mahavira's teaching, first in oral tradition and then in writing.

Although there are in Jainism differences of doctrine and practice, they should not be overemphasized. According to the contemporary Jains scholar, Nathmal Tatia, all Jains agree on the central message of Jainism, which is nonviolence, non-absolutism, and nonattachment.[18] These basic observances are the elements in the Jain quest for personal liberation from samsara and the communitarian goal of peace throughout the world.

NOTES

1. Thomas J. Hopkins, *The Hindu Religious Tradition* (Encino, CA, and Belmont, CA: Dickenson, 1971), 50–51.
2. *Vinaya: Mahavagga* 16. This text is part of the *Vinaya Pitaka*, the *Book of Monastic Discipline*, which codifies the rule of the Buddhist order. Cited in Karen Armstrong, *The Great Transformation: The Beginning of Our Religious Traditions* (New York/Toronto: Knopf, 2006), 278.
3. Mark W. Muesse, *Religions of the Axial Age: An Approach to the World's Religions* (Chantilly, VA: Teaching Company, 2007), part 1, 175.
4. Ibid.
5. Ibid.
6. Ibid., part 2, 16.
7. Cited in Ibid., part 2, 23.
8. Ibid., 26.
9. Ibid., 28–29.

10. *Majjhima Nikaya* (MN) 38. Cited in Armstrong, *The Great Transformation*, 278. The Pali scriptures include four collections of the Buddha's sermons (*Majjhima Nikaya, Digha Nikaya, Anguttara Nikaya,* and *Samyutta Nikaya*) and an anthology of minor works, which include *Udana,* a collection of the Buddha's maxims, and the *Jataka*, stories about the past lives of the Buddha and his companions.
11. Hermann Oldenberg, *Buddha: His Life, His Doctrine, His Order* (London and Edinburgh: Williams & Norgate, 1882), 299–302.
12. Muesse, *Religions of the Axial Age,* part I, 97–98.
13. Karen Armstrong, *A History of God: The 4000-Year Quest of Judaism, Christianity and Islam* (New York: Knopf, 1993).
14. *Sutta-Nipata* 43:1–43; cited in Armstrong, *Great Transformation,* 282. The *Sutta-Nipata* is an anthology of early Buddhist poetry.
15. Major Religions of the World Ranked by Number of Adherents. Available at: http://www.adherents.com/adh_branches.html.
16. Ibid.
17. Muesse, *Religions of the Axial Age,* part 2, 59–62.
18. *That Which Is: Tattvartha Sutra,* trans. Nathmal Tatia (San Francisco: HarperCollins, 1994).

CHAPTER REVIEW

1. Explain how both Buddhism and Jainism can be said to be protests against Hinduism.
2. How did Mahavira explain the soul?
3. What type of person might be attracted to Jainism?
4. Explain the Middle path.
5. Describe the Buddhist path to enlightenment.

Sikh Dharam

Pashaura Singh

By Sushil Mittal and Gene Thursby

THE TRADITION DEFINED

Sikh religion originated in the Punjab ('five rivers') region of northwest India five centuries ago. It is a monotheistic faith that stresses the ideal of achieving spiritual liberation within a person's lifetime through meditation on the divine Name. It is also oriented toward action, encouraging the dignity of regular labor as part of spiritual discipline. Family life and social responsibility are important aspects of Sikh teachings. Notably, the Sikh tradition is the youngest of the indigenous religions of India where the Sikhs constitute about 2 percent of India's 1 billion people. What makes Sikhs significant in India is not their numbers but their contribution in the political and economic spheres. The global Sikh population is approximately 23 million; that is more than the worldwide total of Jewish people. About 18 million Sikhs live in the state of Punjab, while the rest have settled in other parts of India and elsewhere, including substantial communities established through successive waves of emigration in South-east Asia, East

Pashaura Singh, "Sikh Dharam," *Religions of South Asia: An Introduction*, ed. Sushil Mittal and Gene Thursby, pp. 131–148. Copyright © 2006 by Taylor & Francis Group LLC. Reprinted with permission.

Africa, the United Kingdom, and North America. In the last century, about a quarter of a million Sikhs immigrated to the United States of America.

Cosmos and history

Origins of the tradition

The Sikh tradition is rooted in a particular religious experience, piety, and culture and is informed by a unique inner revelation of its founder, Guru Nānak (1469–1539), who declared his independence from the other thought forms of his day. He tried to kindle the fire of autonomy and courage in those who claimed to be his disciples (*sikh*, 'learner'). Notwithstanding the influences he absorbed from his contemporary religious environment, that is, the devotional tradition of the medieval *sants* (poet-saints) of North India with whom he shared certain similarities and differences, Guru Nānak laid down the foundation of 'true teaching, practice, and community' from the standpoint of his own religious ideals. Among the religious figures of North India, he had a strong sense of mission that compelled him to proclaim his message for the ultimate benefit of his audience and to promote socially responsible living.

Nānak was born to an upper-caste professional Hindu family in the village of Talwandī, present-day Nankana Sāhib in Pakistan. Much of the material concerning his life comes from hagiographical *janam-sākhīs* (birth narratives). His life may be divided into three distinct phases: his early contemplative years, the enlightenment experience accompanied by extensive travels, and a foundational climax that resulted in the establishment of the first Sikh community in western Punjab. In one of his own hymns he proclaimed, 'I was a minstrel out of work, the Lord assigned me the task of singing the divine Word. He summoned me to his court and bestowed on me the robe of honoring him and singing his praise. On me he bestowed the divine nectar (*amrit*) in a cup, the nectar of his true and holy Name' (*Ādi Granth* p.150). This hymn is intensely autobiographical, explicitly pointing out Guru Nānak's own understanding of his divine mission, and it marked the beginning of his ministry. He was then thirty years of age, had been married to Sulkhani for more than a decade, and was the father of two young sons, Sri Chand and Lakhmi Dās. He set out on a series of journeys to both Hindu and Muslim places of pilgrimage in India and elsewhere. During his travels he came into contact with the leaders of different religious persuasions and tested the veracity of his own ideas in religious dialogues.

At the end of his travels, in the 1520s, Guru Nānak purchased a piece of land on the right bank of the Rāvī River in West Punjab and founded the village of Kartarpur ('Creator's Abode'; today in Pakistan). There he lived for the rest of his life as the 'Spiritual Guide' of a newly emerging religious community. His attractive personality and teaching won him many disciples who received the message of liberation through religious hymns of unique genius and notable beauty. They began to use these hymns in devotional singing (*kīrtan*) as a part of congregational worship. Indeed, the first Sikh families who gathered around Guru Nānak in the early decades of the sixteenth century at Kartarpur formed the nucleus of a rudimentary organization of the Nānak-Panth, the 'path of Nānak,' the community constituted by the Sikhs who followed Guru Nānak's path of liberation. In his role as what the sociologist Max Weber dubbed an 'ethical prophet,' Guru Nānak called for a decisive break with existing formulations and laid the foundation of a new, rational model of normative behavior based on divine authority. Throughout his writings he conceived of his work as divinely commissioned, and he demanded the obedience of his audience as an ethical duty.

Guru Nānak prescribed the daily routine, along with agricultural activity for sustenance, for the Kartarpur community. He defined the ideal person as a Gurmukh ('one oriented toward the Guru'), who practiced the threefold discipline of 'the divine Name, charity, and purity' (*nām-dān-iśnān*). Indeed, these three features, *nām* (relation with the Divine), *dān* (relation with the society), and *iśnān* (relation with the self) provided a balanced approach for the development of the individual and the society. They corresponded to the cognitive, the communal, and the personal aspects of the evolving Sikh identity. For Guru Nānak the true spiritual life required that 'one should live on what one has earned through hard work and that one should share with others the fruit of one's exertion' (*Ādi Granth* p. 1,245). In addition, service (*sevā*), self-respect (*pati*), truthful living (*sach achār*), humility, sweetness of the tongue, and taking only one's rightful share (*haq halāl*) were regarded as highly prized ethical virtues in pursuit of liberation. At Kartarpur, Guru Nānak gave practical expression to the ideals that had matured during the period of his travels, and he combined a life of disciplined devotion with worldly activities set in the context of normal family life. As part of Sikh liturgy, Guru Nānak's *Japjī* (Meditation) was recited in the early hours of the morning and *So Dar* (That Door) and *Ārti* (Adoration) were sung in the evening.

Guru Nānak's spiritual message found expression at Kartarpur through key institutions: the *sangat* ('holy fellowship') where all felt that they belonged to one large spiritual fraternity; the *dharamsala*, the original form of the Sikh place of worship that developed later into the *gurdwārā*; and the establishment of the *langar*, the interdining convention which required people of all castes to sit in status-free lines (*pangat*) to share a common meal. The institution of *langar* promoted the spirit of unity and mutual belonging and struck at a major aspect of caste, thereby advancing the process of defining a distinctive Sikh identity. Finally, Guru Nānak created the institution of the Guru ('Preceptor'), who became the central authority in community life. Before he passed away in 1539, he designated one of his disciples, Lehnā, as his successor by renaming him Angad, meaning 'my own limb.' Thus, a lineage was established, and a legitimate succession was maintained intact from the appointment of Guru Angad (1504–52) to the death of Guru Gobind Siṅgh (1666–1708), the tenth and the last human Guru of the Sikhs.

Successors of Guru Nānak

The early Sikh Gurus followed a policy of both innovation and preservation. The second Guru, Angad, consolidated the nascent Sikh Panth in the face of the challenge offered by Guru Nānak's eldest son, Sri Chand, the founder of the ascetic Udāsī sect. Guru Angad further refined the Gurmukhi script for recording the compilation of the Guru's hymns (*bāni*). The original Gurmukhi script was a systematization of the business shorthands (*landelmahājani*) of the type Guru Nānak doubtless used professionally as a young man. This was an emphatic rejection of the superiority of the Devanagri and Arabic scripts (along with Sanskrit and the Arabic and Persian languages) and of the hegemonic authority they represented in the scholarly and religious circles of the time. The use of the Gurmukhi script added an element of demarcation and self-identity to the Sikh tradition. In fact, language became the single most important factor in the preservation of Sikh culture and identity and the cornerstone of the religious distinctiveness that is part and parcel of the Sikh cultural heritage.

A major institutional development took place during the time of the third Guru, Amar Dās (1479–1574), who introduced a variety of innovations to provide greater cohesion and unity to the ever-growing Sikh Panth. These included the establishment of the city of Goindval, the biannual festivals of Dīvālī and Baisākhī that provided an opportunity for the growing community to get together and meet the Guru, a missionary system (*mañjīs*) for attracting new converts, and the preparation of the Goindval *pothīs*, collections of the compositions of the Gurus and some of the medieval poet-saints.

The fourth Guru, Ram Dās (1534–81), founded the city of Rāmdāspur, where he constructed a large pool for the purpose of bathing. The city was named Amritsar, meaning 'the nectar of immortality.' To build an independent economic base, the Guru appointed deputies (*masand*) to collect tithes and other contributions from loyal Sikhs. In addition to a large body of sacred verse, he composed the wedding hymn (*lāvān*) for the solemnization of a Sikh marriage. Indeed, it was Guru Rām Dās who for the first time explicitly responded to the question 'Who is a Sikh?' with the following definition: 'He who calls himself Sikh, a follower of the true Guru, should meditate on the divine Name after rising and bathing and recite *Japjī* from memory, thus driving away all evil deeds and vices. As day unfolds he sings *gurbānī* (utterances of the Gurus); sitting or rising he meditates on the divine Name. He who repeats the divine Name with every breath and bite is indeed a true Sikh (*gursikh*) who gives pleasure to the Guru' (*Ādi Granth* pp. 305–306). Thus, the liturgical requirements of the reciting and singing of the sacred word became part of the very definition of being a Sikh. The most significant development was related to the self-image of Sikhs, who perceived themselves as unique and distinct from the other religious communities of North India.

The period of the fifth Guru, Arjan (1563–1606), was marked by a number of far-reaching institutional developments. First, at Amritsar he built the Harimandir, later known as the Golden Temple, which acquired prominence as the central place of Sikh worship. Second, he compiled the first canonical scripture, the *Ādi Granth* (Original Book), in 1604. Third, Guru Arjan established the rule of justice and humility (*halemi rāj*) in the town of Rāmdāspur, where everyone lived in comfort (*Ādi Granth* p. 74). He proclaimed, 'The divine rule prevails in Rāmdāspur due to the grace of the Guru. No tax (*jizyah*) is levied, nor any fine; there is no collector of taxes' (*Ādi Granth* pp. 430, 817). The administration of the town was evidently in the hands of Guru Arjan, although in a certain sense Rāmdāspur was an autonomous town within the context and the framework of the Mughal rule of Emperor Akbar. Fourth, by the end of the sixteenth century the Sikh Panth had developed a strong sense of independent identity, which is evident from Guru Arjan's assertion 'We are neither Hindu nor Musalman' (*Ādi Granth* p.1,136).

Fifth, dissentions within the ranks of the Sikh Panth became the source of serious conflict. A great number of the Guru's compositions focus on the issue of dealing with the problems created by 'slanderers' (*nindak*), who were rival claimants to the office of the Guruship. The Udāsīs and Bhallās (Guru Amar Dās' eldest son, Bābā Mohan, and his followers) had already established parallel seats of authority and had paved the way for competing views of Sikh identity. The rivalry of these dissenters was heightened when Guru Arjan was designated for the throne of Guru Naanak in preference to the former's eldest brother, Prithi Chand, who even approached the local Mughal administrators to claim the position of his father. At some point Prithī Chand and his followers were branded *minās* ('dissembling rogues').

Finally, the author of *Dabistān-i-Mazāhib* (The School of Religions), a mid-seventeenth-century work in Persian, testifies that the number of Sikhs had rapidly increased during Guru Arjan's period and that 'there were not many cities in the inhabited countries where some Sikhs were not to be found.' In fact, the growing strength of the Sikh movement attracted the unfavorable attention of the ruling authorities because of the reaction of Muslim revivalists of the Naqshbandiyyah Order in Mughal India. There is clear evidence in the compositions of Guru Arjan that a series of complaints were made against him to the functionaries of the Mughal state, giving them an excuse to watch the activities of the Sikhs. The liberal policy of Akbar may have sheltered the Guru and his followers for a time, but in May 1606, within eight months of Akbar's death, Guru Arjan, under torture by the orders of the new emperor, Jahangīr, was executed. The Sikh community perceived his death as the first martyrdom, which became a turning point in the history of the Sikh tradition.

Indeed, a radical reshaping of the Sikh Panth took place after Guru Arjan's martyrdom. The sixth Guru, Hargobind (1595–1644), signaled the formal process when he traditionally donned two swords symbolizing the spiritual (*pīrī*) as well as the temporal (*mīrī*) investiture. He also built the Akal Takhat (Throne of the Timeless One) facing the Harimandir, which represented the newly assumed role of temporal authority. Under his direct leadership the Sikh Panth took up arms in order to protect itself from Mughal hostility. From the Sikh perspective this new development was not taken at the cost of abandoning the original spiritual base. Rather, it was meant to achieve a balance between temporal and spiritual concerns. A Sikh theologian of the period, Bhai Gurdas, defended this martial response as 'hedging the orchard of the Sikh faith with the hardy and thorny *kikar* tree.' After four skirmishes with Mughal troops, Guru Hargobind withdrew to the Sivalik Hills, and Kiratpur became the new center of the mainline Sikh tradition. Amritsar fell into the hands of the *minās*, who established a parallel line of Guruship with the support of the Mughal authorities.

During the time of the seventh and eighth Gurus, Har Rai (1630–61) and Har Krishan (1656–64), the emphasis on armed conflict with the Mughal authorities receded, but the Gurus held court and kept a regular force of Sikh horsemen. During the period of the ninth Guru, Tegh Bahadur (1621–75), however, the increasing strength of the Sikh movement in rural areas again attracted Mughal attention. Guru Tegh Bahadur's ideas of a just society inspired a spirit of fearlessness among his followers: 'He who holds none in fear, nor is afraid of anyone, Naanak, acknowledge him alone as a man of true wisdom' (*Ādi Granth* p. 1,427). Such ideas posed a direct challenge to the increasingly restrictive policies of the Mughal emperor, Aurangzīb (r. 1658–1707), who had imposed Islamic laws and taxes and ordered the replacement of Hindu temples by mosques. Not surprisingly, Guru Tegh Bahadur was summoned to Delhi by the orders of the emperor, and on his refusal to embrace Islam he was publicly executed in Chāndnī Chowk on November 11, 1675. The Sikhs perceived his death as the second martyrdom, which involved larger issues of human rights and freedom of conscience.

Tradition holds that the Sikhs who were present at the scene of Guru Tegh Bahadur's execution shrank from recognition, concealing their identity for fear they might suffer a similar fate. In order to respond to this new situation, the tenth Guru, Gobind Siṅgh, resolved to impose on his followers an outward form that would make them instantly recognizable. He restructured the Sikh Panth and instituted the Khālsā ('pure'), an order of loyal Sikhs bound by a common identity and discipline. On Baisākhī Day 1699 at Anandpur, Guru Gobind Siṅgh initiated the first 'Cherished Five' (*pañj piare*), who formed the nucleus of the new order of the Khālsā. The five volunteers who responded to the Guru's call for loyalty, and who came from different castes and regions of India, received the initiation through a ceremony that involved sweetened water (*amrit*) stirred with a two-edged sword and sanctified by the recitation of five liturgical prayers.

The inauguration of the Khālsā was the culmination of the canonical period in the development of Sikhism. The most visible symbols of Sikhism known as the five Ks—namely, uncut hair (*keś*), a comb for topknot (*kaṅghā*), a short sword (*kirpan*), a wrist ring (*karā*), and breeches (*kachh*)—are mandatory to the Khālsā. Guru Gobind Siṅgh also closed the Sikh canon by adding a collection of the works of his father, Guru Tegh Bahadur, to the original compilation of the *Ādi Granth*. Before he passed away in 1708, he terminated the line of personal Gurus and installed the *Ādi Granth* as the eternal Guru for Sikhs. Thereafter, the authority of the Guru was invested together in the scripture (*Guru Granth*) and in the corporate community (Guru Panth).

Evolution of the Panth

The historical development of the Sikh Panth took place in response to four main elements. The first of these was the ideology based on religious and cultural innovations of Guru Nānak and his nine successors. This was the principal motivating factor in the evolution of the Sikh Panth.

The second was the rural base of the Punjabi society. Guru Nānak founded the village of Kartarpur to sustain an agricultural-based community. Its location on the bank of the river Rāvī, provides extremely fertile soil for agriculture. Guru Nānak's father, Kālū Bedī, and his father-in-law, Mula Chona, were village revenue officials (*patvāri*) who must have been instrumental in acquiring a parcel of land at Kartarpur. Since the Mughal law recognized Guru Nānak's sons as the rightful owners of their father's properties, Guru Angad had to establish a new Sikh center at Khadur. It confirmed an organizational principle that the communal establishment at Kartarpur could not be considered a unique institution but rather a model that could be cloned and imitated elsewhere. Similarly, Guru Amar Daas founded the city of Goindval. Interestingly, the location of Goindval on the right bank of the Beās River was close to the point where the Mājhā, Mālvā, and Doāba areas converge. This may help account for the spread of the Panth's influence in all three regions of the Punjab. Guru Rām Dās founded the city of Rāmdāspur (Amritsar). During the period of Guru Arjan the founding of the villages of Taran Taran, Sri Hargobindpur, and Kartarpur (Punjab) in the rural areas saw a large number of converts from local Jāt peasantry. Further, Guru Tegh Bahadur's influence in the rural areas attracted more Jāts from the Mālvā region, and most of them became Khālsā during Guru Gobind Siṅgh's period. It may have been the militant traditions of the Jāts that brought the Sikh Panth into increasing conflict with the Mughals, a conflict that shaped the future direction of the Sikh movement.

The third factor was the conflict created within the Sikh community by dissidents, which originally worked to counter and then, paradoxically, to enhance the process of the crystallization of the Sikh tradition. Guru Nānak's son, Sri Chand, was the first dissident who lived a life of celibacy. Although he failed to attract much support from early Sikhs, he created his own sect of Udāsīs (renunciants). This group was closer to the Nātha Yogīs in its beliefs and practices. Similarly, the followers of Mohan (Guru Amar Dās' elder son), Prithī Chand (*minā*), Dhir Mal (Guru Har Rai's elder brother, who established his seat at Kartarpur, Jalandhar), and Rām Rai (Guru Har Krishan's elder brother, who established his seat at Dehrā Dūn) posed a challenge to the mainline Sikh tradition. All these dissidents enjoyed Mughal patronage in the form of revenue-free grants (*madad-i-māsh*). Their proestablishment stance triggered the mainline tradition to strengthen its own resources.

Finally, the fourth element was the period of Punjab history from the seventeenth to the eighteenth centuries in which the Sikh Panth evolved in tension with Mughals and Afghans. All four elements combined to produce the mutual interaction between ideology and environment that came to characterize the historical development of Sikhism.

Worldview

The nature of the Ultimate Reality in Sikh doctrine is succinctly expressed in the Mūl Mantar ('seed formula'), the preamble to the Sikh scripture. The basic theological statement reads as follows: 'There is one Supreme Being ('1' Oankar), the Eternal Reality, the Creator, without fear and devoid of enmity, immortal, never incarnated, self-existent, known by grace through the Guru. The Eternal One, from the beginning, through all time, present now, the Everlasting Reality' (Ādi Granth p. 1). The numeral '1' at the beginning of the original Punjabi text represents the unity of Akāl Purakh (the 'Timeless One,' God), a concept that Guru Nānak interpreted in monotheistic terms. It affirms that Akāl Purakh is one without a second, the source as well as the goal of all that exists. He has 'no relatives, no mother, no father, no wife, no son, no rival who may become a potential contender' (Ādi Granth p. 597). The Sikh Gurus were fiercely opposed to any anthropomorphic conceptions of the divine. As the creator and sustainer of the universe, Akāl Purakh lovingly watches over it. As a father figure, he runs the world with justice and destroys evil and supports good (Ādi Granth p. 1,028). As a mother figure, the Supreme Being is the source of love and grace and responds to the devotion of her humblest followers. By addressing the One as 'Father, Mother, Friend, and Brother' simultaneously, Guru Arjan stressed that Akāl Purakh is without gender (Ādi Granth p. 103). Paradoxically, Akāl Purakh is both transcendent (*nirguna*, 'without attributes') and immanent (*saguna*, 'with attributes'). Only in personal experience can he be truly known. Despite the stress laid on *nirguna* discourse within the Sikh tradition, which directs the devotee to worship a nonincarnate, universal God, in Sikh doctrine God is partially embodied in the divine Name (*nām*) and in the collective Words (*bānī*) and the person of the Guru and the saints.

Guru Nānak's cosmology hymn in *Māru Rag* addresses the basic questions about the genesis of the universe: 'For endless eons, there was only darkness. Nothing except the divine Order (*hukam*) existed. No day or night, no moon or sun. The Creator alone was absorbed in a primal state of contemplation. ... When the Creator so willed, creation came into being. ... The Un-manifested One revealed itself in the creation' (Ādi Granth pp. 1,035–36). Guru Nānak maintained that the universe 'comes into being by the divine Order' (Ādi Granth p. 1). He further says: 'From the True One came air and from air came water; from water he created the three worlds and infused in every heart his own light' (Ādi Granth p. 19). Guru Nānak employed the well-known Indic ideas of creation through five basic elements of air, water, ether, fire, and earth. As the creation of Ak Ādi Granth l Purakh, the physical universe is real but subject to constant change. It is a lush green garden (*jagg vari*), where human beings participate in its colorful beauty and fragrance (Ādi Granth p. 118). For Guru Nānak the world was divinely inspired. It is a place that provides human beings with an opportunity to perform their duty and achieve union with Ak Ādi Granth l Purakh. Thus, actions performed in earthly existence are important because 'all of us carry the fruits of our deeds' (Ādi Granth p. 4).

For the Gurus, human life is the most delightful experience that one can have with the gift of a beautiful body (*Ādi Granth* p. 966). It is a 'precious jewel' (*Ādi Granth* p. 156). Indeed, the human being has been called the epitome of creation: 'All other creation is subject to you, [O Man/Woman!], you reign supreme on this earth' (*Ādi Granth* p. 374). Guru Arjan further proclaimed that human life provides an individual with the opportunity to remember the divine Name and ultimately to join with Akāl Purakh (*Ādi Granth* p.15). But rare are the ones who seek the divine Beloved while participating in worldly actions and delights.

The notions of *karma* (actions) and *sarnsāra* (rebirth or transmigration) are central to all religious traditions originating in India. *Karma* is popularly understood in Indian thought as the principle of cause and effect. This principle of *karma* is logical and inexorable, but *karma* is also understood as a predisposition that safeguards the notion of free choice. In Sikh doctrine, however, the notion of *karma* undergoes a radical change. For the Sikh Gurus, the law of *karma* is not inexorable. In the context of the Guru Nānak's theology, *karma* is subject to the higher principle of the 'divine order' (*hukam*), an 'all-embracing principle' which is the sum total of all divinely instituted laws in the cosmos. The law of *karma* is replaced by Akāl Purakh's *hukam*, which is no longer an impersonal causal phenomenon but falls within the sphere of Akāl Purakh's omnipotence and justice. In fact, the primacy of divine grace over the law of *karma* is always maintained in the Sikh teachings, and divine grace even breaks the chain of adverse *karma*.

Sacred life and literature

Sacred life

The Sikh view of sacred life is intimately linked with the understanding of the nature of *gurmat* ('Guru's view or doctrine') whereby one follows the teachings of the Gurus. Guru Nānak employed the following key terms to describe the nature of divine revelation in its totality: *nām* (divine Name), *śabad* (divine Word), and *guru* (divine Preceptor). The *nām* reflects the manifestation of divine presence everywhere around us and within us, yet the people fail to perceive it due to their *haumai* or self-centeredness. The Punjabi term '*haumai*' ('I, I') signifies the powerful impulse to succumb to personal gratification so that a person is separated from Akāl Purakh and thus continues to suffer within the cycle of rebirth (*samnsara*). Akāl Purakh, however, looks graciously upon the suffering of people. He reveals himself through the Guru by uttering the *śabad* (divine Word) that communicates a sufficient understanding of the *nam* (divine Name) to those who are able to 'hear' it. The *śabad* is the actual 'utterance,' and in 'hearing' it a person awakens to the reality of the divine Name, immanent in all that lies around and within.

The institution of the Guru carries spiritual authority in the Sikh tradition. In most of the Indian religious traditions the term 'Guru' stands for a human teacher who communicates divine knowledge and provides his disciples with a cognitive map for liberation. In Sikhism, however, its meaning has evolved in a cluster of doctrines over a period of time. There are four focal points of spiritual authority, each acknowledged within the Sikh tradition as Guru: doctrine of eternal Guru; doctrine of personal Guru; doctrine of Guru Granth; and doctrine of Guru Panth. First, Guru Nānak uses the term 'Guru' in three basic senses: the Guru is Akāl Purakh; the Guru is the voice of Akāl Purakh; and the Guru is the Word, the Truth of Akāl Purakh. To experience the eternal Guru is to experience divine guidance. In Sikh usage, therefore, the Guru is the voice of Akāl Purakh, mystically uttered within human heart, mind, and soul (*man*).

Second, the personal Guru functions as the channel through whom the voice of Akāl Purakh becomes audible. Nānak became the embodiment of the eternal Guru only when he received the divine Word and conveyed it to his disciples. The same spirit manifested itself successively in his successors. In Sikh doctrine, a theory of spiritual succession was advanced in the form of 'the unity of Guruship' in which there was no difference between the founder and the successors. Thus they all represented one and the same light (*jot*) as a single flame ignites a series of torches.

Third, in Sikh usage, the *Ādi Granth* is normally referred to as the *Guru Granth Sāhib*, which implies a confession of faith in the scripture as Guru. As such, the *Guru Granth Sāhib* carries the same status and authority as did the ten personal Gurus from Guru Nānak through Guru Gobind Siṅgh, and therefore, it must be viewed as the source of ultimate authority within the Sikh Panth. In actual practice, it performs the role of Guru in the personal piety and corporate identity of the Sikh community. It has provided a framework for the shaping of the Sikh Panth and has been a decisive factor in shaping a distinctive Sikh identity. The *Ādi Granth* occupies a central position in all Sikh ceremonies, and its oral/aural experience has provided the Sikh tradition with a living presence of the divine Guru. Indeed, the *Guru Granth Sāhib* has given Sikhs a sacred focus for reflection and for discovering the meaning of life. It has functioned as a supratextual source of authority within the Sikh tradition. In a certain sense Sikhs have taken their conception of sacred scripture farther than other people of the Book such as Jews and Muslims.

Finally, the key term Guru Panth is normally employed in two senses: first, the Panth of the Guru, referring to the Sikh community; and second, the Panth as the Guru, referring to the doctrine of Guru Panth. This doctrine fully developed from the earlier idea that 'the Guru is mystically present in the congregation.' At the inauguration of the Khālsā in 1699 Guru Gobind Siṅgh symbolically transferred his authority to the Cherished Five when he received initiation from their hands. Thus the elite corps of the Khālsā has always claimed to speak authoritatively on behalf of the whole Sikh Panth, although at times non-Khālsā Sikhs interpret the doctrine of Guru Panth as conferring authority on a community more broadly defined. As a practical matter, consensus within the Sikh community is achieved by following democratic traditions.

In order to achieve a state of spiritual liberation within one's lifetime one must transcend the unregenerate condition created by the influence of *haumai*. In fact, *haumai* is the source of five evil impulses traditionally known as lust (*kām*), anger (*krodh*), covetousness (*lobh*), attachment to worldly things (*moh*), and pride (*hankār*). Under the influence of *haumai* a person becomes 'self-willed' (*manmukh*), one who is so attached to his passions for worldly pleasures that he forgets the divine Name and wastes his entire life in evil and suffering. This unregenerate condition can be transcended by means of the strictly interior discipline of *nām simaran* or 'remembering the divine Name.' This threefold process ranges from the repetition of a sacred word, usually Vahigurū (Praise to the Eternal Guru), through the devotional singing of hymns with the congregation to sophisticated meditation on the nature of Akāl Purakh. The first and the third levels of this practice relate to private devotions, while the second refers to corporate sense. On the whole the discipline of *nām simaran* is designed to bring a person into harmony with the divine order (*hukam*). The person thus gains the experience of ever-growing wonder (*vismād*) in spiritual life and achieves the ultimate condition of blissful 'equanimity' (*sahaj*) when the spirit ascends to the 'realm of Truth' (*sach khand*), the fifth and the last of the spiritual stages, in which the soul finds mystical union with Akāl Purakh.

The primacy of divine grace over personal effort is fundamental to Guru Nānak's theology. There is, however, neither fatalism nor any kind of passive acceptance of a predestined future in his view of life. He proclaimed, 'With your own hands carve out your own destiny' (*Ādi Granth* p.474). Indeed, personal effort in the form of good actions has a place in Guru Nānak's view of life. His idea of 'divine free choice,' on the one hand, and his emphasis on the 'life of activism' based on human freedom, on the other, reflect his ability to hold in tension seemingly opposed elements. Guru Nānak explicitly saw this balancing of opposed tendencies, which avoids rigid predestination theories and yet enables people to see their own 'free' will as a part of Akāl Purakh's will, as allowing Sikhs the opportunity to create their own destinies, a feature stereotypically associated with Sikh enterprise throughout the world. Sikhism thus stresses the dignity of regular labor as an integral part of spiritual discipline. This is summed up in the following triple commandment: engage in honest labor (*kirat karanī*) for a living, adore the divine Name (*nām japan*), and share the fruit of labor with others (*vand chhakanā*). The formula stresses both the centrality of meditative worship and the necessity of righteous living in the world.

Scriptures and other literature

The *Ādi Granth* is the primary scripture of the Sikhs. It contains the works of the first five and the ninth Sikh Gurus, four bards (Sattā, Balvand, Sundar, and Mardānā), eleven Bhatts (eulogists associated with the Sikh court), and fifteen Bhagats ('devotees' such as Kabīr, Nāmdev, Ravidās, Shaikh Farid, and other medieval poets of *sant*, *sūfī*, and *bhakti* origin). Its standard version contains a total of 1,430 pages, and each copy corresponds exactly in terms of the material printed on individual pages. The text of the *Ādi*

Granth is divided into three major sections. The introductory section includes three liturgical prayers. The middle section, which contains the bulk of the material, is divided into thirty-one major *rāgs* or musical patterns. The final section includes an epilogue consisting of miscellaneous works that could not be accommodated in the middle section.

The second sacred collection, the *Dasam Granth* is attributed to the tenth Guru, Gobind Siṅgh, but it must have extended beyond his time to include the writings of others as well. Mani Siṅgh, who died in 1734, compiled the collection early in the eighteenth century. Its modern standard version of 1,428 pages consists of four major types of compositions: devotional texts, autobiographical works, miscellaneous writings, and a collection of mythical narratives and popular anecdotes.

The works of two early Sikhs, Bhāī Gurdās (1551–1637) and Bhāī Nand Lāl Goyā (1633–1715), make up the third category of sacred literature. Along with the sacred compositions of the Gurus, their works are approved in the official manual of the *Sikh Rahit Maryādā* (Sikh Code of Conduct) for singing in the *gurdwārās*.

The last category of Sikh literature includes three distinct genres: the *janam-sākhīs* (birth narratives), the *rahit-nāmās* (manuals of code of conduct), and the *gur-bilās* (splendor of the Guru) literature. The *janam-sākhīs* are hagiographical accounts of Guru Nānak's life, produced by the Sikh community in the seventeenth century. The *rahit-nāmās* provide rare insight into the evolving nature of the Khālsā code in the eighteenth and nineteenth centuries. The *gur-bilās* mainly focus on the mighty deeds of two warrior Gurus, Hargobind and particularly Gobind Siṅgh.

Institutions and Practices

The Khalsa and the Rahit

From the perspective of ritual studies, three significant issues were linked with the first *amrit* ceremony. First, all who chose to join the order of the Khālsā through the ceremony were understood to have been 'reborn' in the house of the Guru and thus to have assumed a new identity. The male members were given the surname Siṅgh ('lion'), and female members were given the surname Kaur ('princess'), with the intention of creating a parallel system of aristocratic titles in relation to the Rājput hill chiefs of the surrounding areas of Anandpur. Second, the Guru symbolically transferred his spiritual authority to the Cherished Five when he himself received the nectar of the double-edged sword from their hands and thus became a part of the Khālsā Panth and subject to its collective will. In this way he not only paved the way for the termination of a personal Guruship but also abolished the institution of the *masands*, which was becoming increasingly disruptive. Several of the *masands* had refused to forward collections to the Guru, creating factionalism in the Sikh Panth. In addition, Guru Gobind Siṅgh removed the threat posed by the competing seats of authority when he declared that the Khālsā should have no dealings with the followers of Prithī Chand (*minā*), Dhir Mal, and Rām Rai. Finally, Guru Gobind Siṅgh delivered the nucleus of the Sikh Rahit (Code of Conduct) at the inauguration of the Khālsā. By sanctifying the hair with *amrit*, he made it 'the official seal of the Guru,' and the cutting of bodily hair was thus strictly prohibited. The Guru further imposed a rigorous ban on smoking.

All Sikhs initiated into the order of the Khālsā must observe the Rahit as enunciated by Guru Gobind Siṅgh and subsequently elaborated. The most significant part of the code is the enjoinder to wear five visible symbols of identity, known from their Punjabi names as the five Ks (*pañj kakke*). These are unshorn hair (*kes*), symbolizing spirituality and saintliness; a wooden comb (*kaṅghā*), signifying order and discipline in life; a miniature sword (*kirpan*), symbolizing divine grace, dignity, and courage; a steel 'wrist ring' (*karā*), signifying responsibility and allegiance to the Guru; and a pair of short breeches (*kachh*), symbolizing moral restraint. Among Sikhs the five Ks are outer symbols of the divine Word, implying a direct correlation between *bānī* ('divine utterance') and *bānā* ('Khālsā dress'). The five Ks, along with a turban for male Sikhs, symbolize that the Khālsā Sikhs, while reciting prayers, are dressed in the word of God. Their minds are thus purified and inspired, and their bodies are girded to do battle with the day's temptations. In addition, Khālsā Sikhs are prohibited from the four cardinal sins (*chār kurahit*): 'cutting the hair, using tobacco, committing adultery, and eating meat that has not come from an animal killed with a single blow.'

Worship, practices, and lifecycle rituals

The daily routine of a devout Sikh begins with the practice of meditation upon the divine Name. This occurs during the *amritvelā*, the 'ambrosial hours' (that is, the last watch of the night, between 3 and 6 a.m.), immediately after rising and bathing. Meditation is followed by the recitation of five liturgical prayers, which include the *Japjī* of Guru Nānak. In most cases the early morning devotion concludes in the presence of the *Guru Granth Sāhib*, in which the whole family gathers to receive the divine command (*vāk lainā* or 'taking God's Word') by reading a passage selected at random. Similarly, a collection of hymns, *Sodar Rahiras* (Supplication at That Door), is prescribed for the evening prayers, and the *Kīrtan Sohila* (Song of Praise) is recited before retiring for the night.

Congregational worship takes place in the *gurdwārā*, where the main focus is upon the *Guru Granth Sāhib*, installed ceremoniously every morning. Worship consists mainly of the singing of scriptural passages set to music, with the accompaniment of instruments. The singing of hymns (*kīrtan*) in a congregational setting is the heart of the Sikh devotional experience. Through such *kīrtan* the devotees attune themselves to vibrate in harmony with the divine Word, which has the power to transform and unify their consciousness. The exposition of the scriptures, known as *kathā* ('homily'), may be delivered at an appropriate time during the service by the *granthī* ('reader') of the *gurdwārā* or by the traditional Sikh scholar (*gyanī*). At the conclusion of the service all who are present join in reciting the *Ardās* ('Petition,' or Sikh Prayer), which invokes divine grace and recalls the rich common heritage of the community. Then follows the reading of the *vak* (divine command) and the distribution of *karāh prasād* (sanctified food).

The central feature of the key lifecycle rituals is always the *Guru Granth Sāhib*. When a child is to be named, the family takes the baby to the *gurdwira* and offers *karāh prasād*. After offering thanks and prayers through *Ardās*, the *Guru Granth Sāhib* is opened at random and a name is chosen beginning with the same letter as the first composition on the left-hand page. Thus, the process of *vāk lainā* (divine command) functions to provide the first letter of the chosen name. The underlying principle is that the child derives his or her identity from the Guru's word and begins life as a Sikh. To a boy's name the common surname Singh is added, and to a girl's name Kaur is added at the end of the chosen name. In some cases, however, particularly in North America, people employ caste names (for example, Ahluwalia, Dhaliwal, Grewal, Kalsi, Sawhney, or Sethi) as the last elements of their names, and for them Singh and Kaur become middle names. In addition, the infant is administered sweetened water that is stirred with a sword, and the first five stanzas of Guru Nānak's *Japjī* are recited.

A Sikh wedding, according to the *Ānand* (Bliss) ceremony, also takes place in the presence of the *Guru Granth Sāhib*, and the performance of the actual marriage requires the couple to circumambulate the sacred scripture four times to take four vows. Before the bridegroom and the bride make each round, they listen to a verse of the *Lāvān*, or 'wedding hymn' (*Ādi Granth* pp. 773–74), by the fourth Guru, Rām Dās, as given by a scriptural reader. They bow before the *Guru Granth Sāhib* and then stand up to make their round while professional musicians sing the same verse with the congregation. During the process of their clockwise movements around the scripture, they take the following four vows: to lead an action-oriented life based upon righteousness and never to shun the obligations of family and society; to maintain a bond of reverence and dignity between them; to keep enthusiasm for life alive in the face of adverse circumstances and to remain removed from worldly attachments; and to cultivate a 'balanced approach' (*sahaj*) in life, avoiding all extremes. The pattern of circumambulation in the *Ānand* marriage ceremony is the enactment of the primordial movement of life, in which there is no beginning and no end. Remembering the four marital vows is designed to make the life of the couple blissful.

The key initiation ceremony (*amrit sanskār*) for a Sikh must take place in the presence of the *Guru Granth Sāhib*. There is no fixed age for initiation, which may be done at any time the person is willing to accept the Khālsā discipline. Five Khālsā Sikhs, representing the collectivity of the original Cherished Five, conduct the ceremony. Each recites from memory one of the five liturgical prayers while stirring the sweetened water (*amrit*) with a double-edged sword. The novice then drinks the *amrit* five times so that his body is purified from the influence of five vices; and five times the *amrit* is sprinkled on his eyes to transform his outlook toward life. Finally, the *amrit* is poured on his head five times to sanctify his hair so that he will preserve his natural form and listen to the voice of conscience. Throughout the procedure the Sikh being initiated formally takes the oath each time by repeating the following declaration: '*Vahigurū jī kā Khālsā! Vahigurū jī kī fateh!*' (Khālsā belongs to the Wonderful Lord! Victory belongs to the Wonderful Lord!) Thus, a person becomes a Khālsā Sikh through the transforming power of the sacred word. At the conclusion of the ceremony a *vāk* is given and *karāh prasād* is distributed.

Finally, at the time of death, both in the period preceding cremation and in the postcremation rites, hymns from the *Guru Granth Sāhib* are sung. In addition, a reading of the entire scripture takes place at home or in a *gurdwārā*. Within ten days of the conclusion of the reading, a *bhog* ('completion') ceremony is held, at which final prayers are offered in memory of the deceased.

ETHICS AND HUMAN RELATIONS

The *Ādi Granth* opens with Guru Nānak's *Japjī* where the fundamental question of seeking the divine Truth is raised as follows: 'How is Truth to be attained, how the veil of falsehood torn aside?' Guru Nānak then responds: 'Nānak, thus it is written: submit to the divine order (*hukam*), walk in its ways' (*Ādi Granth* p.1). Truth obviously is not obtained by intellectual effort or cunning but only by personal commitment. To know truth one must live in it. The seeker of the divine Truth, therefore, must live an ethical life. An immoral person is neither worthy of being called a true seeker nor capable of attaining the spiritual goal of life. Any dichotomy between spiritual development and moral conduct is not approved in Sikh ethics. In this context Guru Nānak explicitly says: 'Truth is the highest virtue, but higher still is truthful living' (*Ādi Granth* p. 62). Indeed, truthful conduct (*sach achār*) is at the heart of Sikh ethics.

The central focus in the Sikh moral scheme is the cultivation of virtues such as wisdom, contentment, justice, humility, truthfulness, temperance, love, forgiveness, charity, purity, and fear of Akāl Purakh. Guru Nānak remarked, 'Sweetness and humility are the essence of all virtues' (*Ādi Granth* p. 470). These virtues not only enrich the personal lives of individuals but also promote socially responsible living. The Gurus laid great stress on the need to earn one's living through honest means. In particular, living by alms or begging is strongly rejected. Through hard work and sharing, Sikh ethics forbid withdrawal from social participation. The Sikh Gurus offered their own vision of the cultivation of egalitarian ideals in social relations. Such ideals are based on the principle of social equality, gender equality, and human brotherhood/sisterhood. Thus, it is not surprising that any kind of discrimination based on caste or gender is expressly rejected in Sikh ethics.

The key element of religious living is to render service (*sevā*) to others in the form of mutual help and voluntary work. The real importance of *sevā* lies in sharing one's resources of 'body, mind, and wealth' (*tan-man-dhan*) with others. This is an expression toward fellow beings of what one feels toward Akāl Purakh. The service must be rendered without the desire for self-glorification, and in addition, self-giving service must be done without setting oneself up as a judge of other people. The Sikh Prayer (*Ardās*) holds in high esteem the quality of 'seeing but not judging' (*anadith karanā*). Social bonds are often damaged beyond redemption when people, irrespective of their own limitations, unconscionably judge others. The Sikh Gurus emphasized the need to destroy this root of social strife and enmity through self-giving service.

Finally, Sikhism is dedicated to human rights and resistance against injustice. It strives to eliminate poverty and to offer voluntary help to the less privileged. Its commitment is to the ideal of universal brotherhood, with an altruistic concern for humanity as a whole (*sarbat da bhala*). In a celebrated passage from the *Akāl Ustat* (Praise of Immortal One), Guru Gobind Siṅgh declared that 'humankind is one and that all people belong to a single humanity' (verse 85). Here it is important to underline the Guru's role as a conciliator who tried to persuade the Mughal emperor Bahaadur Shah to walk the ways of peace. Even though Guru Gobind Siṅgh had to spend the major part of his life fighting battles that were forced upon him by Hindu hill *rājās* and Mughal authorities, a longing for peace and fellowship with both Hindus and Muslims may be seen in the following passage from the *Akāl Ustat*: 'The temple and the mosque are the same, so are the Hindu worship [*pūjā*] and Muslim prayer [*namāz*]. All people are one, it is through error that they appear different. ... Allah and Abhekh are the same, the Purana and the Qur'ān are the same. They are all alike, all the creation of the One' (verse 86). The above verses emphatically stress the irenic belief that the differences dividing people are in reality meaningless. In fact, all people are fundamentally the same because they all are the creations of the same Supreme Being. To pursue this ideal, Sikhs conclude their morning and evening prayers with the words 'Says Nānak: may thy Name and glory be ever triumphant, and in thy will, O Lord, may peace and prosperity come to one and all.'

Society: caste and gender issues

Guru Nānak and the succeeding Gurus emphatically proclaimed that the divine Name was the only sure means of liberation for all four castes: the Khatrī, originally the Ksatriya (warrior), the Brāhman (priest), the Śūdra (servant/agriculturalist), and the Vaiśya (tradesman). In the works of the Gurus, the Khatrīs were always placed above the Brahmaris in the caste hierarchy while the Śūdras were raised above the Vaiśyas. This was an interesting way of breaking the rigidity of the centuries-old caste system. All the Gurus were Khatrīs, which made them a top-ranking mercantile caste in Punjab's urban hierarchy, followed by Arorās (merchants) and Ahlūwālīās (brewers). In the rural caste hierarchy an absolute majority (almost two-thirds) of Sikhs are Jāts (peasants), followed by Rāmgarhīās (artisans), Ramdāsīās (cobblers), and Mazhabīs (sweepers). Although Brāhmans are at the apex of the Hindu caste hierarchy, Sikhs place Brāhmans distinctly lower on the caste scale. This is partly because of the strictures the Sikh Gurus laid upon Brāhman pride and partly because the reorganization of Punjabi rural society conferred dominance on the Jāt caste.

Doctrinally, caste has never been one of the defining criteria of Sikh identity. In the Sikh congregation there is no place for any kind of injustice or hurtful discrimination based upon caste identity. In the *gurdwārā* Sikhs eat together in the community kitchen, share the same sanctified food, and worship together. The *Sikh Rahit Maryādā* explicitly states, 'No account should be taken of caste; a Sikh woman should be married only to a Sikh man; and Sikhs should not be married as children.' This is the ideal, however, and in practice most Sikh marriages are arranged between members of the same endogamous caste group. Caste, therefore, still prevails within the Sikh community as a marriage convention. Nevertheless, intercaste marriages take place frequently among urban professionals in India and elsewhere.

The Sikh Gurus addressed the issues of gender within the parameters established by traditional patriarchal structures. In their view an ideal woman plays the role of a good daughter or sister and a good wife and mother within the context of family life. They condemned both women and men alike who did not observe the cultural norms of modesty and honor in their lives. It is in this context that images of the immoral woman and the unregenerate man are frequently encountered in the scriptural texts. There is no tolerance for any kind of premarital or extramarital sexual relationships, and rape in particular is regarded as a violation of women's honor in Punjabi culture. Rape amounts to the loss of family honor, which in turn becomes the loss of one's social standing in the community. The notion of family honor is thus intimately linked to the status of women.

The issue of gender has received a great deal of attention within the Sikh Panth. It is notable that the Sikh Gurus offered a vision of gender equality within the Sikh community and took practical steps to foster respect for womanhood. They were ahead of their times when they championed the cause of equal access for women in spiritual and temporal matters. Guru Nānak raised a strong voice against the position of inferiority assigned to women in society at the time: 'From women born, shaped in the womb, to woman betrothed and wed; we are bound to women by ties of affection, on women man's future depends. If one woman dies he seeks another; with a woman he orders his life. Why then should one speak evil of women, they who give birth to kings?' (*Ādi Granth* p. 473). He sought to bring home the realization that the survival of the human race depended upon women, who were unjustifiably ostracized within society. Guru Amar Dās abolished the customs among women of the veil and of *satī* (self-immolation) and permitted the remarriage of widows. He further appointed women as Sikh missionaries. Indeed, Sikh women were given equal rights with men to conduct prayers and other ceremonies in *gurdwārās*. In actual practice, however, males dominate most Sikh institutions, and Sikh women continue to live in a patriarchal society based on Punjabi cultural assumptions. In this respect they differ little from their counterparts in other religious communities in India. Although there is a large gap between the ideal and reality, there is clear doctrinal support for the equality of rights for men and women within the Sikh Panth.

MODERN EXPRESSIONS

The modern religious and cultural transformation within the Sikh tradition took place during the colonial period on the initiatives of the Siṅgh Sabhā (Society of the Siṅghs). This reform movement began in

1873 at Amritsar. The principal objective of the Siṅgh Sabhā reformers was to reaffirm the distinctiveness of Sikh identity in the face of the twin threats posed by the casual reversion to Hindu practices during Sikh rule and the explicit challenges from actively proselytizing religious movements such as Christian missionaries and the Arya Samāj. The Tat Khālsā (Pure Khālsā), the dominant wing of the Siṅgh Sabha movement, succeeded in eradicating all forms of religious diversity by the end of the nineteenth century and established norms of religious orthodoxy and orthopraxy. The reformers were largely successful in making the Khālsā ideal the orthodox form of Sikhism, and they systematized and clarified the Khālsā tradition to make Sikhism consistent and effective for propagation.

Indeed, the Tat Khālsā ideal of Sikh identity, which was forged in the colonial crucible, was both old and new. In addition to the economic and military policy of the British, there were other elements that meshed together to produce a great impact on the emerging Sikh identity. These additional elements in the larger colonial context were new patterns of administration, a new technology, a fresh approach to education, the entry of Christian missionaries, and the modernist perspective based on the scientific paradigm of the Enlightenment. All these factors produced a kind of Neo-Sikhism, characterized by a largely successful set of redefinitions in the context of the notions of modernity and religious identity imposed by the dominant ideology of the colonial power closely associated with Victorian Christianity. As such, modern Sikhism became a well-defined 'system' based on a unified tradition, and the Tat Khālsā understanding of Sikh identity became the norm of orthodoxy.

Among the 23 million Sikhs in the postmodern world, however, only approximately 15 to 20 percent are *amrit-dhāris* (initiated), those who represent the orthodox form of the Khālsā. A large majority of Sikhs, however, about 70 percent, are *kes-dhāris*, that is, those who 'retain their hair' and thus maintain a visible identity. These Sikhs follow most of the Khālsā Rahit without having gone through the initiation ceremony. The number of Sikhs who have shorn their hair, and are thus less conspicuous, is quite large in the West in general, and in particular in North America and the United Kingdom. Popularly known as *mona* (clean-shaven) Sikhs, they retain their Khālsā affiliation by using the surnames Siṅgh and Kaur. These Sikhs are also called *ichha-dhāris* because they 'desire' to keep their hair but cut it under some compulsion. They are frequently confused with *sahaj-dhāri* (gradualist) Sikhs, those who have never accepted the Khālsā discipline. Although *sahaj-dhāri* Sikhs practice *nam simaran* and follow the teachings of the *Ādi Granth*, they do not observe the Khālsā Rahit and in general do cut their hair. The number of *sahaj-dhāri* declined during the last few decades of the twentieth century, although they have not disappeared completely from the Sikh Panth. Finally, there are those who violate the Khālsā Rahit and cut their hair after initiation. These lapsed *amrit-dhāri*, who are known as *patit* or *bikh-dhāri* (apostate) Sikhs, are found largely in the diaspora. There is thus no single way of being a Sikh, and the five categories of Sikhs are not fixed permanently. Punjabi Sikhs frequently move between them according to their situation in life.

Transmission of the Tradition outside of India

There are now more than 1 million Sikhs who have settled in foreign lands as a result of successive waves of emigration over the past 100 years. It is not surprising to find the establishment of more than 400 *gurdwārās* in North America and the United Kingdom alone. The recent years have witnessed among the Sikhs of North America a revived interest in their inherited tradition and identity. This awakened consciousness has produced a flurry of activities in children's education. Sikh parents realize that worship in *gurdwaras* is conducted in Punjabi, which scarcely responds to the needs of children born in North America. At schools these children are being trained to be critical and rational, and they are therefore questioning the meaning of traditional rituals and practices. Traditionally trained *granthīs* and *gyanīs* are unable to answer their queries. Moreover, without adequate knowledge of Punjabi, the language of the *Ādi Granth*, the new generation of Sikhs is in danger of being theologically illiterate.

Moreover, a steady process of assimilation is in progress among second- and third-generation Sikhs. Western culture has added new challenges and obstructions to the Sikh tradition. This situation has created new responses from the Sikh community. Many Sikh parents have started home-based worship in both Punjabi and English in order to meet new challenges from the diaspora situation. They have introduced another innovative feature in the form of Sikh Youth Camps to pass on the Sikh traditions to the children. These camps last one or two weeks. Through them a spiritual environment is created which provides the children with continuous exposure to Sikh values and traditions.

Finally, in the 1970s a group of Caucasian Americans and Canadians converted to the Sikh faith at the inspiration of their Yoga teacher, Harbhajan Siṅgh Khālsā (Yogi Bhajan), who founded the Sikh Dharma movement. These so-called white, or *gorā*, Sikhs, male and female alike, wear white turbans, tunics, and tight trousers. They live and raise families in communal houses, spending long hours in meditation and chanting while performing various postures of Tantric *yoga*. They have thus introduced the Sikh tradition into a new cultural environment. Most Punjabi Sikhs have shown an ambivalent attitude toward these converts. On the one hand, they praise the strict Khālsā-style discipline of the white Sikhs; and on the other hand, they express doubts about the mixing of the Sikh tradition with the ideals of Tantric *yoga*.

Relations with Other Religions

The ability to accept religious pluralism is a necessary condition of religious tolerance. Religious pluralism requires that people of different faiths be able to live together harmoniously, which provides an opportunity for spiritual self-judgement and growth. It is in this context that Sikhism expresses the ideals of coexistence and mutual understanding. Sikhism emphasizes the principles of tolerance and the acceptance of the diversity of faith and practice. It is thus able to enter freely into fruitful interreligious dialogue with an open attitude. Such an attitude signifies a willingness to learn from other traditions and yet to retain the integrity of one's own tradition. It also involves the preservation of differences with dignity and mutual respect.

The Sikh Gurus were strongly opposed to the claim of any particular tradition to possess the sole religious truth. Indeed, a spirit of accommodation has always been an integral part of the Sikh attitude toward other traditions. The inclusion of the works of the fifteen medieval non-Sikh saints (*bhagat bāṇī*, 'utterances of the Bhagats'), along with the compositions of the Gurus, in the foundational text of the Sikhs provides an example of the kind of catholicity that promotes mutual respect and tolerance. For instance, the Muslim voice of the devotee Shaikh Farid is allowed to express itself on matters of doctrine and practice. This is the ideal that Sikhs frequently stress in interfaith dialogues.

The presence of the *bhagat bāṇī* in the Sikh scripture offers a four-point theory of religious pluralism. First, one must acknowledge at the outset that all religious traditions have gone through a process of self-definition in response to changing historical contexts. Thus, in any dialogue the dignity of the religious identities of the individual participants must be maintained. One must be able to honor a commitment as absolute for oneself while respecting different absolute commitments for others. For this reason the quest for a universal religion and the attempt to place one religious tradition above others must be abandoned. Second, the doctrinal standpoints of different religious traditions must be maintained with mutual respect and dignity. Third, all participants must enter into a dialogue with an open attitude, one that allows not only true understanding of other traditions but also disagreements on crucial doctrinal points. Finally, the 'other' must somehow become one's 'self' in a dialogue, so that the person's life is enriched by the spiritual experience.

The tradition in the study of religions

The first North American conference on Sikh Studies was held in 1976 at the University of California, Berkeley. At that conference it was generally felt that the Sikh tradition was indeed 'the forgotten tradition' in scholarly circles in North America. In particular, Mark Juergensmeyer argued that in the textbooks in world religions the study of Sikhism was either completely ignored or misrepresented. He examined the various reasons for this treatment. He suggested that there are two prejudices in Indian Studies that function against the study of the Sikh tradition. The first prejudice is that against the modern age. Many scholars, following the Orientalist perspective, have been more interested in the classical texts on Indian philosophy rather than a medieval devotional tradition. Since Sikh tradition is relatively modern, it has been completely ignored in Indian Studies. The other prejudice that faces Sikh Studies in Indian literature is the prejudice against regionalism. Sikhism is not only relatively modern but also almost exclusively Punjabi. In his arguments, Juergensmeyer made the case for the utility of Sikhism for the studies of religion.

In the last two decades the study of Sikh tradition has received a great deal of scholarly attention, and there are now five programs of Sikh and Punjab Studies established in North America with the active financial support of the Sikh community. In the West, Sikh Studies is a new field that is slowly gaining the academic respectability that it richly deserves. It provides interesting data to scholars of Religious Studies to address the fundamental question of how Sikhism has become meaningful to 23 million followers around the world. Its doctrines, myths, rituals, practices, and symbols are the channels of the expression of a faith in which one may grow and fulfill one's life. Throughout Sikh history the faith of its adherents has kept them steadfast in the face of adverse circumstances.

Suggested further readings

Cole (1982, 1984); Grewal (1991, 1998); McLeod (1989, 1997, 1999, 2003); Oberoi (1994); H. Singh (1983, 1992–98); N.-G. Singh (1993); N. Singh (1990); P. Singh (2000, 2003); Thursby (1992, 1993).

Chapter Review

1. Describe the Sikh world view.
2. What is the Adi Granth?
3. Explain Sikh worship.
4. Describe a Sikh wedding.
5. Explain and describe the Khalsa.

Understanding Taoism

By Russell Kirkland

REALITIES, CONSTRUCTS, AND HERMENEUTICAL CHALLENGES

The Chinese public today, like most in the outside world, generally know little about the Taoist tradition, though some are curious about whether it might have something to contribute to their lives. Meanwhile, many Westerners still imperialistically assume that the primary reason for them to study the religions of other cultures is to identify elements that can be appropriated into their own lives, or even new religious identities that can be assumed at will by "any of us." A proper understanding of Taoism requires one to recognize *all* such motivations, to ensure that they do not interfere with one's interpretive efforts, for instance by causing one to discount elements of Taoism that do not suit one's own taste or reinforce the biases of one's own age or culture.

The efflorescence of Taoist studies among scholars of the late twentieth century gave rise to a new set of interpretive perspectives, which consciously repudiated the Orientalist assumptions that had theretofore

Russell Kirkland, "Understanding Taosim," *Taoism: The Enduring Tradition*, pp. 1–19. Copyright © 2004 by Taylor & Francis Group LLC. Reprinted with permission.

been the dominant interpretive paradigm. Those new scholarly perspectives generally insisted (1) that we must recognize the *Chinese-ness* of Taoism; (2) that we must privilege the factual *data* of Taoism itself, in social, historical, and textual terms; and (3) that we must acknowledge the importance of the living forms of Taoism that survive among Chinese communities today.

As the twenty-first century opens, the educated public needs to be made very aware of aspects of Taoist history, thought, and practice that have heretofore been ignored or misinterpreted. And scholars of Taoism need to do more to show the public how such heretofore unappreciated realities expand and correct our understanding of what "Taoism" is.

For one thing, most scholars who have seriously studied Taoism, both in Asia and in the West, have finally abandoned the simplistic dichotomy of *tao-chia* and *tao-chiao*—"philosophical Taoism" and "religious Taoism." A few have begun offering new models for understanding the continuities among the ideas and practices presented in the data of Taoist texts of various periods. In the early 1990s some scholars, myself included, suggested that we try to understand Taoism in terms of a heuristic contrast between two soteriological models: "mystical" models—seen both in *Chuang-tzu* and certain later traditions—and "liturgical" models that developed in other later traditions. More recently, Livia Kohn suggested that, "within the Daoist tradition ... one can distinguish three types of organization and practice: literati, communal, and self-cultivation."

> Literati Daoists are members of the educated elite who focus on Daoist ideas as expressed by the ancient thinkers. ... They use these concepts to create meaning in their world and hope to exert some influence on the political and social situation of their time, contributing to greater universal harmony, known as the state of Great Peace *(taiping)* [*t'ai-p'ing*] ... Communal Daoists ... are found in many different positions and come from all levels of society. They are members of organized Daoist groups [who] have priestly hierarchies, formal initiations, regular rituals, and prayers to the gods. ... The third group of Daoists focus on self-cultivation. ... They, too, come from all walks of life, but rather than communal rites, their main concern is the attainment of personal health, longevity, peace of mind, and spiritual immortality.

Today, none of those interpretive models seems sufficiently nuanced to ensure a full and accurate understanding of all the diverse but interrelated forms of Taoism that evolved over the long history of China. But every time thoughtful scholars test out such models, we seem to move closer toward a more subtle, and more useful, perception of how to understand Taoism. It should be noted in this connection, however, that Taoists have never made *any* distinctions of such kinds, and it is such very facts that challenge our hermeutical imagination.

In addition, today's best specialists are still only beginning to appreciate some of the basic realities of Taoism in terms of *social and political history*, not to mention in terms of the realities of *gender*. The present book is, in part, intended to stimulate further awareness that our concept of "what Taoism is" needs to assimilate it on those terms as well.

It should also be noted that many of today's specialists in all lands still privilege the Taoist traditions that evolved during the Han to T'ang dynasties, i.e., from about 200 to 600 CE. While all such traditions are important, there remains an unfortunate tendency for scholars to say "Taoists believe X," when in fact such "X belief" may have been true only in a certain generation, in a certain region, or even in a single individual's mind. For instance, a historical study of the Taoist priesthood might adduce a single Taoist text, explicate its contents, and reify them as "Taoist tradition." Far too seldom have scholars asked the degree to which *the social realities of Taoists* truly correspond to the data that we find in such texts. To reify the contents of any such text, or group of texts, as "Taoism" can warp our perspective just as deeply as scholars of bygone days did when they reified the contents of *Lao-tzu* or *Chuang-tzu* as "Taoism."

Only at the very end of the twentieth century did scholars of Taoism even really begin to give consideration to the distinct Taoist subtraditions that emerged in China during the past millennium—an era that nearly all twentieth-century minds regarded as the heyday of "Neo-Confucianism." Even the expert contributors to the *Daoism Handbook*—a wide-ranging state-of-the-field reference work published in the year 2000—often caution that their findings, particularly regarding the Sung and later dynasties, should be read as an "interim report" rather than a definitive analysis. And the editors of a collection of expert articles on the Ch'uan-chen (Quanzhen) tradition published in 2002 note: "Few comprehensive surveys of Quanzhen Taoism exist, and most of those are unpublished dissertations." Such "modern" forms of Taoism deserve much greater attention, for a variety of reasons:

1. they survived, more or less intact, into the twentieth century, which is not true of such well-studied Six-Dynasties subtraditions as Shang-ch'ing or Ling-pao;
2. they have often featured prominent roles for women practitioners and even women leaders;
3. they maintained the ancient Taoist practices of *self-cultivation*, thereby revealing vital continuities between "classical Taoism" and the Taoism practiced from the T'ang period to today;
4. they compare favorably with other Chinese and non-Chinese traditions in terms of both religious *thought* and *models of personal practice*, which was not true of most pre-T'ang subtraditions.

Also, today's specialists often ignore a helpful heuristic distinction that modern Taoists often make between "Northern Taoism" (i.e., traditions like Ch'üan-chen) and "Southern Taoism" (i.e., Cheng-i). "Northern Taoism" displays more of the charactistics listed above than does "Southern Taoism," and as members of the educated public become more aware of "Northern Taoism," they may develop the same intense interest and respect that they showed toward other major traditions, such as Buddhism, throughout the twentieth century.

Perhaps the most important new emphasis that we should give to our presentations of Taoism today should be upon those historical and living realities of Taoism, which belie the misconceptions that dominated the twentieth century. For instance, the misconception that "religious Taoism" was the province of the "illiterate masses"—not of "the educated elite"—can be corrected simply by directing attention to the hundreds of Taoist texts preserved in the *Tao-tsang* and elsewhere, only a few of which have yet been translated into Western languages. Similarly, giving due attention to the models of *personal practice* articulated by Chinese intellectuals such as Ssu-ma Ch'eng-chen easily disproves the misconception that Taoism "degenerated into superstition" after classical times. Above all, the many versions of *Nei-tan* ("Inner Alchemy") theory and practice—a fundamental element of Taoism for the last thousand years—demonstrate the absurdity of the lingering "anti-Catholic" charge that later Taoism was "ritualistic nonsense" that ignored the spiritual needs and aspirations of individual practitioners. Increasing sophistication in ritual theory can help us understand and explain the depth and richness of all forms of Taoist ritual, past and present. Not only do we now know that the training and practice of Cheng-i liturgists were grounded in Taoist models of self-perfection that we see in such "mystical" models as Inner Alchemy. But even today's "Northern Taoism" values ritual action as an element of the Taoist life.

Further attention is due to the rich diversity of Taoist conceptions of the religious life. Virtually no one today knows, for instance, that T'ang-dynasty Taoists wrote extensively about "Tao-nature" (*tao-hsing*)—a concept of "the true reality of all things, including ourselves," which parallels the concept of "Buddha-nature" that many know from Ch'an (Zen) and other East Asian forms of Buddhism. Nor do most know that much of Ch'uan-chen thought actually parallels, and interacted historically with, that of Ch'an Buddhism, and with many elements of late imperial Confucian thought and practice. To explain that, for hundreds of years, Taoist practice was often taught in terms of "cultivating the heart/mind (*hsin*)" or of "integrating our inherent nature (*hsing*) with our destined lives (*ming*)" will correct and greatly expand the very narrow and misleading depictions of "Taoist thought" and "Taoist practice" that characterized most twentieth-century presentations.

It is also important to draw attention to the historical facts that demonstrate that Taoism was not, as has often been taught, a tradition practiced by people who stood outside the normal social order and attacked it, whether philosophically or politically. At no point in Chinese history were the majority of Taoists actually hermits, misfits, members of rebel movements, or critics of conventional values—all common stereotypes that still flourished even among some specialists of the late twentieth century. During most periods, Taoists came from all segments of society—including the educated "upper-classes"; supported—and often helped legitimize the imperial government; and were often well known and well respected by other members of China's social and cultural "elite."

Finally, the public needs to know much more about the living realities of Taoism in China today. Today's Taoists still maintain many elements of premodern Taoism, including personal self-cultivation, a monastic life for men and women alike, and a rich panoply of traditional practices. It should be noted that the liturgical traditions of Taoism survive not only in the "Southern Taoism" of Taiwan and the southeast coast, but also in temples throughout mainland China, even at those identified as Ch'üan-chen. But it should also be noted that, by the end of the twentieth century, decades of Communist rule and secularistic trends may have left Taoist practice marginalized in new ways. Among the general public, practices that had become loosely associated with Taoism—such as *t'ai-chi ch'üan (taiji juan)* and *ch'i-kung (qigong)*—remained popular, but often without the practitioners knowing their full historical background or religious implications (though, in some circles, T'ang texts such as the *T'ien-yin-tzu (Tianyinzi)* continue to inform such practices). And in temples and monasteries, Taoist clerics continued to keep a relatively low profile, and sometimes taught outsiders a quite modernized understanding of Taoist meditative and ritual traditions. As China's economy and society evolves away from the Communist restrictions of the third quarter of the twentieth century, observers should remain alert to possible redomestication of elements of Taoism among the expanding middle class in China, especially reformulations of the more intellectualized traditions of "literati Taoism."

WHAT "TAOISM" IS: FACT, TRADITION, AND SELF-IDENTIFICATION

Through the twentieth century, general discussions of Taoism usually came from, or pandered to, an audience that felt entitled to gratify itself by defining "Taoism" in terms that made "us" feel good about ourselves. For the general public in the West, Taoism was often to be defined as something "for us," specifically, a set of ideas and values that (a) complement and/or correct our own cultural/religious heritage, yet (b) do not require us to learn anything that we do not already believe, or to do anything that we would find difficult or unpleasant to do. For scholars, meanwhile, Taoism was to be defined in terms of the arguments already going on among Chinese intellectuals of the late imperial and modern age, with such adaptation as was needed to integrate them with the arguments that were already going on among non-Chinese intellectuals. To the best of my knowledge, no one has ever suggested that we ought to define Taoism, in the first instance, by asking *Taoists* to guide us in learning to understand what Taoism is.

There have been some legitimate, or at least unavoidable, reasons for past interpreters' refusal to take Taoists as their conversation partners. Those reasons involve certain stubborn realities of history, geography, politics, and language, not to mention the subtler hermeneutical problems—i.e., problems of understanding what we are told because we are different from the people telling it to us. All those problems still exist at the dawn of the twenty-first century. Consequently, this very book is still, in certain regards, a colonialistic product. That is, it is written by an outsider—someone who is not a Taoist, was not raised in a society where Taoists flourished, was not educated in a culture informed by Taoist values, and has never been taught to understand Taoism by living Taoists. Yet it is conceivable that this book may make some contribution to the decolonialization of our understanding of Taoism, by approaching some of the basic issues in a new way.

To a great extent, all that someone like me can do, at the present juncture in history, is to argue for the development of an interpretive playing-field that may be suitable for us—i.e., all modern people, in the West and in Asia alike—to learn to see "how Taoism is played" by Taoists and how it has been played by Taoists of earlier ages. When challenged to answer the question "Who is 'a Taoist'?", I shall say that the correct answer must begin by determining how *Taoists* of past and present have answered that question. In deciding what we should acknowledge to be "Taoism," therefore, we do *not* get to choose an outcome that will result in the satisfaction of any of *our own* needs or desires. Instead, we have to recognize and acknowledge what the *Taoists* have understood to be Taoism, whether or not we happen to enjoy, or find benefit to ourselves in, their self-understanding.

In twentieth-century terms, this approach is a methodological oddity, for throughout that century most explainers (even the most elite postmodernists) presumed that they—not the people whom they were explaining—were ideally or even exclusively qualified to decide the terms of their explanatory process. My own approach begins from the premise that I am not in an ideal position to explain Taoism. Yet, my own position is the only one that I have to work from, and I presume that intellectual honesty, awareness of my own historical moment, respect for those whom I am "explaining," and careful avoidance of past interpretive errors should yield a useful, if not definitive, window on the subject. Here I offer a new architectonic model, one designed to provide structural support for an understanding of Taoism that is honest and accurate—i.e., a non-colonialized understanding—while providing little support for older, more insidiously colonialistic models.

THE DATA-SET OF "TAOISM": A TAXONOMIC APPROACH

Our preliminary task is to identify a reasonable set of criteria for determining the range of data that represent "what Taoists say Taoism is," and for weighing those criteria in the balance with other criteria that might otherwise seem reasonable and appropriate. It is not my contention that we must *conclude* our interpretive efforts by understanding Taoism as the Taoists do, for at times an outsider sees given realities more clearly than someone who has a vested interest in perceiving him/herself (or in being perceived by others) as having a special and important relationship to those realities. For instance, in Taiwan today, one can easily find a given person who will, with sincerity and self-assurance, tell observers that "Taoism is basically to be defined in terms of the texts and practices that are in my possession." But in Boston or Birmingham, one can likewise find persons who will tell us that Christianity is basically to be defined in terms of how that person and his or her community understand and practice. Yet, we know that there is significant diversity in how Christians understand their own tradition, despite the fact that certain central elements are nominally "agreed upon." And we know that over the centuries even those "central elements" of Christianity have been deeply debated among members of the Christian community. To privilege as "central" to Taoism the positions of certain specific groups or individuals would be improperly to disenfranchise other Taoist groups and individuals. And to privilege the positions common in certain specific periods would be improperly to disenfranchise the Taoists of other periods. It shall be my position that we may not, at the outset, legitimately identify any particular Taoist data as normative, but must make a concerted attempt to take fully into account *all* the data pertaining to *all* the Taoists of every period, past and present.

My approach here is different from that of most scholars who were trained in the twentieth century. My criteria for deciding who we should regard as representatives of "Taoism" are fairly new. I begin with a taxonomic analysis that (1) casts its net as broadly and inclusively as the facts today seem to allow, and (2) neither endorses nor denies the inherent validity or value of any particular element of any particular phase or tradition of Taoism. We may not, I contend, legitimately privilege ancient Taoists over medieval or modern Taoists, or vice versa. We may not legitimately privilege the experiences of expressions of male Taoists over females, or vice versa. We may not legitimately privilege intellectualized expressions of Taoism over those that are "just lived"—a common bias among scholars who study *any* tradition. And we may not legitimately privilege the Taoists of one particular region over those of another, even if we know much about one region and little about another. In sum, we may not legitimately privilege any particular *form* of Taoism as intrinsically *normative* for proper identification of the category. There are certainly Taoists today who may wish us to believe that their particular form should be accepted as normative, just as there are Hindus and Christians who do so. But I shall argue that no Taoists' claim to have a normative understanding of Taoism may legitimately be accepted. Rather, I shall argue that *all* such claims must be *evaluated*, not only in terms of *each other*, but also in terms of *all* the claims of *all* of the Taoists of the past.

This definitional reasoning—and its consequences—will shock many of those who are satisfied that they already know what Taoism is, for what this reasoning reveals is often deeply at odds with what was commonly believed about Taoism by most twentieth-century minds. It will also shock those who would argue that "Taoism" is merely a construct, and that, since the validity of all constructs is contestable, it is theoretically impossible for anyone ever to present an understanding of "Taoism" that is anything but arbitrary. I will argue that that position—common among "post-modern" theorists of "continental" sensibilities—need not be taken seriously. Such issues will need to be addressed more fully in other settings. Suffice it here to say that the pronouncements of all "post-modern" theorists are themselves a product of a particular time and place, and are themselves therefore unreliable guides for anyone attempting to determine how we can determine what is true. The doctrines of that particular school of relativism—though quite popular among members of an intellectual elite in the present day—may no more be logically privileged than any other doctrines accepted by anyone of past or present. One such doctrine—accepted by many as a cardinal tenet of faith—is that we can never actually identify a "fact." But that doctrine is demonstrably false: most facts are arguable, but some pertinent arguments can easily be shown to be much better than others, and some arguments can be shown to be utterly absurd. Whatever emerges from a process of rational analysis and debate regarding the facts, their pertinence, and their significance may never quite be "objective truth," but it is certainly far from arbitrary, and will certainly help the better-informed better to inform the less-well informed about the subject under discussion.

There are indeed quite *a lot of facts* in regard to Taoism, *most* of which remain generally unknown to most people who discuss Taoism. The discovery of facts is a historical process. Today, scholars know many more facts about Taoism than did scholars of the early twentieth century. And scholars of the future will know yet more, by means of which they will be able to correct and refine whatever statements about Taoism we make today. That having been said, it is legitimate to discuss what we know about Taoism today, and to demonstrate that certain things that were said about Taoism in past ages can be shown to have been false. For instance, among the general public at the turn of the millennium, it was quite common to hear that "Taoism is basically about *wu-wei*." There can be little legitimate dispute about such a contention, because the number of actual facts that are at variance with such a statement are so overwhelmingly superabundant that no reasonable person—once made aware of those facts—would ever again seriously consider entertaining it. What scholars can do is discover more and more of the facts of Taoism, and to make more and more of them part of the twenty-first-century discourse about Taoism. Only in the last generation or two have scholars who specialize in the study of Taoism made serious progress in identifying many of those facts. Yet, a sound and reasonable understanding of Taoism must be based upon such facts, and a non-colonialistic understanding must begin with *what the Taoists of China, in every age, have said and practiced.*

Transcending invalid reifications of "tradition"

Late in the last century, the theorist Bernard Faure "examined the constitution of Chan/Zen as an epistemological object," attempting "to unsettle the object (Chan/Zen) by the use of alternative methods, while avoiding to dissolve this object into mere ideological discourse." My approach to Taoism is on the same level. But Faure also argued that "Chan is not primarily a concrete social reality, but a complex and elusive epistemological object that never existed as a given outside representations, but was always in the making, through the classificatory decisions of people who saw themselves as members of the tradition." Yet, if such shifting and disparate "classificatory decisions" can be taken as constitutive of the "epistemological object" that we call Chan/Zen, then it seems to follow that the life-actions of the centuries of men and women who made those decisions can properly be regarded as a "social reality." And while those people's decisions may not have been "concrete," there is certainly a concreteness to some of the *results* of those decisions. For instance, some very "concrete" individuals built and rebuilt the White Cloud Abbey in Beijing, from the time of the T'ang emperor Hsuan-tsung in the eighth century down to the present day. Such concrete individuals engaged in pertinent "classificatory decisions," as did those who staffed the abbey over the centuries, those who came there to engage in practices of self-cultivation, and those who articulated the code of personal conduct expected of all who engaged in such practices there. And another quite concrete *result* of those people's decisions was a massive collection of writings left behind by people of earlier ages who had likewise engaged, sometimes quite consciously, in such "classificatory decisions"—the *Tao-tsang*, a collection of writings by and about "Taoists" who had lived, and had made their own "classificatory decisions" about being "Taoist," in every age of imperial and pre-imperial China. The *Tao-tsang*, the White Cloud Abbey, and even the Lung-men subtradition, whose leadership has been housed in that abbey for centuries, can certainly be regarded as quite concrete "facts" of Taoism.

But what such facts show about Taoism is that it was not "a tradition" whose leaders ever even sought to articulate any "orthodoxy," nor one that sought to impose any particular set of ideas about "what Taoism is" upon its practitioners. Therefore, to acknowledge that there was, and is, historically and socially such a "tradition" as Taoism does not, as Faure seems to have feared, tacitly reify such "orthodox" positions, nor does it tacitly import such positions into the thought-processes of today's careful interpreters. So I contend that we should acknowledge and seek to understand "Lungmen Taoism" as a social and historical reality, while recognizing the data of history and society as tools to help us put into proper perspective any traditional claims by or about Lungmen Taoists. I shall also recognize that Lung-men Taoism has, on various levels, important continuities with other subtraditions of Taoism, though not necessarily on terms that any of its historical representatives may have recognized.

"Self-identification": the value of the Tao-tsang for identifying "the facts of Taoism"

Are there, or have there ever been, ideas or practices that "were generally agreed upon" by all, or even most, Taoists? The data with which I am familiar today leads me to say no. It is important to remember that—if we accept, for instance, the *Tao-tsang* as representative of "Taoism"—Taoists did not generally regard themselves as followers of a single religious community that shared a single set of teachings, or practices. Unlike Buddhism, Confucianism, or Christianity, Taoism did not begin from the efforts of a community to practice the teachings of a great leader. And since there were no "original teachings" of any such "original community," Taoists through history never felt obliged to hew their beliefs and practices to any putative original "standard." The diversity of Taoist beliefs and practices cannot reasonably be explained in terms of orthodoxy versus non-orthodoxy, of orthopraxy versus non-orthopraxy.

Nor would it be correct to reify traditional terminology and identify "Taoists" as those who "believed in Tao." By that token, the facts would make *Confucius* a key early Taoist, and would *not* include many of the centuries of men and women who understood themselves to be Taoist, were understood to be Taoist by their contemporaries, and were understood to be Taoist by those of later ages who self-identified as Taoists. It is true that in many Chinese temples, as in late imperial art, one often sees a depiction of

Confucius alongside a depiction of a Taoist figure such as Lord Lao. But the decisions of such artists and temple-arrangers do not seem to be explainable primarily as decisions by a self-identifying Taoist to portray Confucius as "Taoist." The message of such phenomena lies on different social and cultural levels.

The primary fact that I shall use here to determine the proper criteria for identifying "Taoist phenomena" is that there have been people for centuries who self-identified as Taoists, and were generally recognized as "Taoist" by others around them. "Taoism" must be identified, in the first instance, in terms of that historical heritage. If, therefore, someone says that clouds found in Chinese landscape paintings represent "Taoist values," we can test such statements against the pertinent social and historical data from all periods. While we may eventually revise and refine such approaches in many ways, it is quite defensible for us to take the position today that we can identify "the self-identifying Taoists" *as the people whose ideas, values, practices and institutions are expressed in the writings that have been included in the vast, amorphous collection called the Tao-tsang, its predecessors and later continuations.*

The people involved in the production of the extant *Tao-tsang* were, quite indisputably, leading participants in the Ming-dynasty community of self-identifying Taoists. And their work was also recognized as "definitionally significant" by the ambient society, for the emperor of China in the Cheng-t'ung era—like various emperors in earlier centuries—ordered *Taoist leaders* to collect all the writings of their tradition, past and present. In 1445, as at the completion of such earlier compilation processes, both "the Taoists" of that era and the imperial government agreed that the result consisted of *all* the extant written materials, from every preceding age, that should be regarded as a worthy element of the Taoist tradition. The "definitiveness" of this particular set of "classificatory decisions" lies in the fact that they were accepted by two distinct groups of people: first, the period's Taoist leaders, as so regarded by themselves and, at the very least, by the imperial government, if not also by most members of the living communities who practiced various forms of Taoism in Ming times; and, second, the government authorities, who recognized Taoism as important—in cultural and political terms alike—and wished it to endure, or at least wished to be perceived as rulers who wished it to endure.

To study the data of Taoism, one must study all that is revealed, intentionally and unintentionally, by the centuries of material preserved in the *Tao-tsang* and related collections. That material has very diverse origins, and thus reveals many distinguishable "Taoist" messages. Some of that material can now be identified, more or less clearly, as the patrimony of certain identifiable historical groups. Some of them did not survive more than a generation or two, others survived for centuries, and several survive today. There is also material in the *Tao-tsang* from some groups whose historical realities we can now show to have been deliberately *contrived* to give an *impression* of a group that had "survived for centuries," when in reality no such "survival" is demonstrable on any objective analysis of the known facts. By means of available historical data, we can today establish, to some degree, the historicity of certain "traditions," and draw into question the historicity of others.

We must also bear in mind that when we examine a given text we often cannot know how many people believed or practiced what that text suggests. We cannot even know how many people took a given text seriously as a representation of Taoism. It is conceivable that at times the collectors of anthologies such as the *Tao-tsang* may have made some of their decisions with some degree of reluctance, as when the Hebrews and Christians decided to include *Ecclesiastes* in their canons. So to accept the *Tao-tsang* as a general collection of "the texts of Taoism" does not necessarily entail any recognition that any given text within it was, in practice, truly embraced by centuries of Taoists as a valid representation of their own values, beliefs, or practices. The preponderance of historical data, and sociological data from our own times, makes clear that some of the texts in the *Tao-tsang*—such as the classical *Mo-tzu* (HY1168) and *Han-fei-tzu* (HY1169)—were seldom, if ever, regarded by Taoists as texts whose teachings "we, as Taoists, should follow." We may thus ultimately conclude that some of what is found in the *Tao-tsang* is not particularly pertinent for determining "what Taoism is," just as we may conclude that certain texts that did not survive in the *Tao-tsang* are indeed quite relevant. After all, over the centuries, wars and fires often destroyed the libraries where precious Taoist manuscripts were housed. Some such texts survived elsewhere, in collections that were not generally regarded as "Taoist," or buried away at sites such as Tun-huang. Thus, we may find good reason to acknowledge as "Taoist" materials such as the *Pen-chi ching*, the *Nei-yeh*, or the writings of various Taoist literati of T'ang and later times. Yet, to accept the *Tao-tsang* as reasonably representative of the voices of centuries of Taoists, however diverse, seems to be a quite valid way of establishing the boundaries of what Taoists considered Taoist, and of assessing the contents of their tradition.

Beyond those boundaries, our historical sources sometimes recognize as "an important Taoist" someone regarding whom it is, at best, unclear that he or she ever participated in any of the activities of his or her Taoist contemporaries, or that he or she ever imagined that anyone would ever identify her or him as a Taoist. One such example was the T'ang-dynasty thaumaturge Yeh Fa-shan (631–720). Yet, Taoist tradition did in time certainly embrace Yeh as an ideal exemplar of some of its most cherished values, as seen by the texts in the *Tao-tsang* which so represent him. Then again, there are those such as Lin Chao-en (1517–1598) who have sometimes been called "syncretists," because their lives and thought clearly included elements of Buddhism and Confucianism as well as Taoism. There are doubtless many comparable cases of men and women who may perhaps be worth including in our discussion of "Taoism," even though we may not always be able to show that the individual self-identified as "a Taoist."

My contention here is *not* that "Taoism" is, or ever was, a monolithic social or historical entity: the evidence makes clear that Taoism never had the coherence that we see in "the Christian Church" over the centuries, much less that organization's social, political, or economic power. Nor is it my contention that "Taoism" is now fully known, and must be explained in a single, specific way. Rather, my contention is that Taoism is *well enough* known for us to sort out *certain* explanations that are clearly *correct*; others that are *not entirely certain* but are supported by *most* readings of the pertinent data; and a variety of explanations that we can now clearly demonstrate to be *unsupported* by the pertinent data.

For instance, through the twentieth century it was common to read that Taoism after *Lao-tzu* and *Chuang-tzu* had no intellectual content and is best understood in terms of "popular religion." Scholarship of the last quarter of that century began to show that such beliefs are clearly incorrect. Likewise, through the twentieth century it was common to read that Taoism was "escapist," that Taoists had no real regard for the realities of social life, no interest in government, and no moral teachings. Such contentions, of course, were almost always made by people who had never made any attempt to read, much less carefully study, the material preserved in the *Tao-tsang* and related collections. Likewise, through the twentieth century it was common to read that Taoism was historically "marginal" to the Chinese "mainstream," for that mainstream was essentially "Confucian." But that belief was grounded in the contentions of Confucians, and reflects the biases of modern interpreters.

It is now possible to offer sound, if not quite fully definitive, explanations of what Taoism was to various practitioners from age to age, provided that we set aside the preconceptions that plagued past generations, and look objectively at the data of Taoism, as defined primarily in terms of the materials found in the *Tao-tsang* and related materials. And we may emend and expand what we learn from those materials by means of fieldwork in Chinese societies, analysis of pertinent works of art and material culture, and examination of pertinent documents that were preserved at places such as Tun-huang, in the Buddhist canon, in "eclectic" collections such as the *Lü-shih ch'un-chiu* and *Kuan-tzu*, in inscription texts, in local histories, in "standard histories" and other imperial collections, such as the *Tai-p'ingkuang-chi*, and even in literary works, such as *ch'uan-ch'i* tales, novels, and plays.

The historical Taoist "community"

The first socio-cultural group whose participants consciously identified themselves as "Taoist"—and began conceiving the first comprehensive collection of Taoist texts—appeared in what some would call "early medieval China," during the fifth century CE. That group consisted specifically of people whose sense of Taoist identity was stimulated by the fact that Buddhism had gained acceptance and political favor throughout the land, which was, at that time, politically divided, with one imperial regime in the north and another in the south. There were many then, in the north and south alike, who had no wish to identify themselves with Buddhism. Data pertaining to the lives, and decisions, of "the common people" in that period is scant: most of our textual data clearly originated among the aristocracy. And what that data reveals is that members of the aristocracy who respected and cherished *indigenous* religious traditions— what they regarded as "our" religious heritage—began trying to *organize* those traditions—institutionally, textually, and even conceptually—so that "our religion" could better compete with Buddhism.

Those efforts, which were moderately successful, constituted the *creation* of what *the Taoists* called "Taoism"—*Tao-chiao*. "Taoism" was thus not—as has often been wrongly claimed—a development among those in China who rejected Confucianism. The facts of history generally show that Taoists actually had *no problem at all* with Confucians or their values. In fact, Taoists and Confucians were generally partners and allies, up to the time of the Mongol conquest. Even beyond that point, they continued to influence each other's ideas and practices, and in late imperial times many Confucians and Taoists were quite happy to acknowledge the value of both as elements of "the Three Teachings."

The only Confucians who ever really claimed to be resisting an antagonistic Taoist tradition were members of a very narrow community consisting of followers of the twelfth-century ideologue Chu Hsi (1130–1200). Chu claimed to inherit a "transmission of the Way" (*tao-t'ung*) that originated with Confucius and Mencius then jumped over a millennium to the eleventh-century teacher Ch'eng I, then of course to Chu himself. The ideologues of the "Ch'eng/Chu school" essentially gained political control of the mechanisms for expression of ideas in late imperial China, and, from their hostility toward all other religious, intellectual, and cultural systems—including Confucians outside their own school—modern minds throughout the world gained the false impression that Taoism should be understood in relationship to Confucianism. The facts clearly show that Taoists never understood *themselves* on any such terms.

If there was anything that Taoists of imperial times really feared, it was not Confucianism, or even Buddhism. Rather, Taoists of several periods feared—often with good reason—that the rulers of their day could be misled into imagining that the activities of Taoists were somehow continuous with disreputable "cults." Thus conceived, "cults" (whatever their actual social or cultural dynamics) had little appeal to rulers or to aristocrats—a segment of society that increasingly included Taoists as well as Confucians. In fact, when the Taoists of the fifth century first tried to put together a collection of their sacred writings—a collection that could compete with that of the Buddhists both in scope and in diversity—they conceived that collection as consisting primarily, indeed perhaps exclusively, of those writings that interested *aristocrats* of that day. As first designed, the corpus of the *Tao-chiao* gave *no place* to such ancient works as the *Lao-tzu* and *Chuang-tzu*: those writings were *not*, at that time, writings that Taoists considered foundational for their tradition or important for defining their identity.

More tellingly, these Taoists' first corpus—their first great effort to tell the ruler and the people of China "this is who we are, and this is what we value"—specifically *excluded* writings by, and about, the "Heavenly Masters" of the late Han period—an organization that had long struggled to differentiate itself from the disreputable "cults" with which it was sometimes apparently confused. That exclusion is ironic, for some of the medieval aristocrats' traditions were in some ways tied back to the earlier "Heavenly Masters" movement, and some "Heavenly Masters" traditions were maintained, albeit in new forms, throughout medieval China, across all social levels. But the problem for the creators of the aristocratic *Tao-chiao* was that, by the time Buddhism had begun posing a threat to those of Taoist sensibilities, the "Heavenly Masters" movement—which had not originally emerged from the "upper classes"—had become marginalized, not in terms of the Chinese social order, but within "Taoism" itself: new "revelations" among fourth-century aristocrats—the Shang-ch'ing and Ling-pao revelations, in particular—now gave "respectability" to aristocrats who were trying to construct *a comprehensive non-Buddhist religious tradition* of their own. Among those "aristocratic Taoists" of the fifth century, the traditions and practices of the earlier "Heavenly Masters" appear to have been, at best, a profound embarrassment, certainly *not* something to be featured in any public exposition of "what we, as Taoists, do and value." Only a century later was the original three-section Taoist "canon" expanded with four "supplements," including one for "Heavenly Masters" materials, as well as other texts that interested the aristocratic target audience, such as the *Lao-tzu* and *Chuang-tzu*.

Taoism *qua* Taoism thus developed within a specific historical setting, within a specific social setting, for specific and easily explainable reasons. Once such realities are understood, it is quite easy to see the silliness of many of the inherited misconceptions in modern minds about "what Taoism is." For instance, most modern minds inevitably link "the origins of Taoism" with the "person" who was long believed to have produced the *Lao-tzu*. We shall see that there is no sense in which such beliefs have any historical validity, though the ideas and images in the *Lao-tzu* were certainly appropriated by many later Taoists, and the figure of "Lao-tzu"—a creation of early Han historians, as I shall show—was appropriated for its legitimatory value by emperors of many periods, and by some Taoists as well.

We shall also see that modern minds are quite mistaken when they imagine that "early Taoism" consisted of a "school of thought"—to be understood in terms of a set of ideas found (or imagined to be found) in the *Lao-tzu* and the *Chuang-tzu*—an unrelated text of quite dissimilar provenance. I shall lay out what we can now say about those texts on the basis of actual fact, and about the historical context from which they sprang. It will quickly become apparent that back in "classical times"—before "the first Ch'in emperor" unified "the middle kingdoms" and all neighboring states in 221 BCE—there was actually no "school of Taoism" on any intellectual terms, and certainly *no group of people* who considered themselves "Taoists" or wished to be understood as "Taoists" by others. That is not to say that there were no people in that age whose understanding of life, and whose way of living life, can now be seen to have been, in certain important ways, *continuous* with those of the Taoists of imperial China. But scholars have still only begun to sort through some of those continuities. And until they give full respect to the many varieties of "Taoism" that came and went over the course of later centuries, they will remain unable to say much about the continuities and discontinuities among the various phases and segments of the tradition.

CHAPTER REVIEW

1. What would you say if you were asked the question, "What is a Taoist?"
2. What is an objective truth, according to Taoism?

3. Who was Lao-Tzu?
4. Describe the historical Taoist community.
5. Differentiate between Taoism and Confucianism.

Conascianism

By Ray Billington

As we saw earlier, in philosophical and religious terms there have been three major influences in China. One is Taoism, in both its *tao-chia* and *tao-chiao* expressions; the second is Buddhism, which, while not native to China, was to establish so firm a hold there in its Mahayana mode that the Chinese could be forgiven for looking on it as native to themselves; the third, and the most typically Chinese of all, is Confucianism. This philosophy—and we shall see that, of all the schools discussed in this book, it has least claim to be termed a religion—has made such an indelible mark on Chinese personal and socio-political life that Confucianism and China are almost as ineradicably linked as Hinduism and India.

The great name in this school is of course Confucius himself, but there have been a host of Confucian scholars and philosophers over the centuries. We shall look at two of these who, by the pure originality of their thinking, have made distinctive contributions relevant to the theme of this book: Mencius, living two centuries later than Confucius, and his direct ideological descendant (he could be described as the

Ray Billington, "Chinese Philosophy III: Confucianism," *Understanding Eastern Philosophy*, pp. 118–133. Copyright © 1997 by Taylor & Francis Group LLC. Reprinted with permission.

Huxley to Confucius' Darwin); and, in the twelfth century CE, Chu Hsi, the outstanding mentor of Neo-Confucianism, which was effectively a synthesis of Taoism, Buddhism and Confucianism. Other teachers will be mentioned in passing, in relation to particular debates in which the major protagonists were engaged.

Confucius

This name, with which even children in the West are familiar, is the Latinised form of **K'ung Tzu** (sometimes transcribed as K'ung Fu-tzu), or Master K'ung. He lived from 551 to 479 BCE, during the so-called Spring and Autumn Period (722–481) of the Chou Dynasty (1111–249). Tradition had it that during its founding era this dynasty had been ruled by men who were highly principled, in particular the kings Wen and Wu. By K'ung's time, however, Chou had fallen prey to internal conflicts and attacks from beyond, and his own state of Lu (now Shantung) was in fact ruled by usurpers. This may help to explain why it was that he experienced frustration in his chosen calling as a civil servant, and why at the age of fifty he resigned to become a peripatetic teacher, a role that many other learned Chinese, including Mencius, also assumed. He gathered a large number of students around him, amounting eventually to some three thousand.

According to tradition, Master K'ung spent his final years writing a number of books, including the *Shi Ching* (Book of Songs), the *Shu Ching* (Book of Writings), and the *Ch'un Ch'iu* (Spring and Autumn Annals). All we can say for sure is that these books are among the Confucian classics and reflect K'ung's teaching. His philosophy is expressed most directly, however, in the work that, along with the *Tao Te Ching*, is at the peak of Chinese philosophical writing, the **Analects**. It is generally held that K'ung did not write this work, but that it was compiled by his disciples after his death. Here is the essence of Confucianism, and it is significant that Chan Wing-Tsit, in his comprehensive compilation *A Source Book in Chinese Philosophy*, uses only this work to illustrate K'ung's teaching. It was, along with Mencius and two other Confucian classics, the *Ta Hsueh* and the *Chung Yung*, one of the so-called 'Four Books' (*ssu-chu*), which were used as the basis of Chinese civil service examinations from 1313 CE until as recently as 1905.

Almost any extract from the *Analects* will illustrate why it is that the name of Confucius has become synonymous with sound common sense (reflected in the phrase, 'Confucius, he say …'). In Book II, 15–17, we read:

> The Master said, He who learns but does not think is lost. He who thinks but does not learn is in great danger … Shall I teach you what knowledge is? When you know a thing, to recognise that you know it; and when you do not know a thing, to recognise that you do not know it. That is knowledge.

(Perhaps even more basic is his laconic statement in IX,17 that he had 'never seen anyone whose desire to build up his moral power was as strong as sexual desire'.)

Master K'ung's prime consideration, and the central theme of the *Analects*, was how people might live harmoniously together. He was therefore concerned with ethics rather than metaphysics, although Mencius and other successors were to develop this strand in their teaching. From K'ung's point of view, it was a difficult enough task to cope with other people here and now without introducing speculation (for he viewed it as no more than that) about a future life, or a divine being who might influence events in this world from some invisible world beyond. He frequently referred to 'the Way of Heaven' (***t'ien***) and even referred to the emperor as 'Son of Heaven' (*t'ien-tzu*), but the word is normally used with an ethical connotation, signifying the highest pinnacle of human behaviour. Any ruler, as we shall see, was held by K'ung to be uniquely placed both to practise the virtues himself and to set an example for others. K'ung was questioned about *t'ien* apropos of 'God in heaven' but was at best agnostic and generally sceptical on the matter. It seemed to him absurd to believe that the 'will of heaven' could be modified as a direct consequence of prayers sent 'up' by people on Earth: so the sensible procedure was to forget about praying and tackle the problems of living as they stared one in the face. In this, to be sure, all people have the examples of their ancestors to inspire them; but K'ung refused to speculate about any influence that the spirits of the dead might have on the human situation. *Analects* XI,11 states:

> Tzu-lu asked how one should serve ghosts and spirits.
> The Master said, How can there be any proper service of spirits until living men have been properly served?
> Tzu-lu then ventured upon a question about the dead (whether they are conscious).
> The Master said, Until a man knows about the living, how can he know about the dead?

This perspective is reminiscent of the New Testament words: 'He who does not love his brother whom he has seen, cannot love God whom he has not seen' (I John 4:21); but K'ung's philosophy is totally humanistic in its suggestion that relationships with others should be based on secular, rather than spiritual, considerations. To make the love of God one's ultimate aim in human encounters, rather than to have regard for others for their own sakes, would have seemed to him an unrealistic diversion from the clearly defined, self-disciplined way that he was offering to his followers.

The way of Confucius is based on two definable and unambiguous human qualities, which have given Confucianism its distinctive stamp. They may be described as the *yin* and the *yang* of relationships, in the sense that each, while apparently poles apart (like justice and mercy), needs to be tempered by the other. They are ***jen***, or loving kindness, and ***li***, or propriety.

The Chinese pictogram for *jen* gives a clear indication of its meaning. It shows the sign for a human being, together with the sign for 'two'. Thus *jen* embraces all the qualities that enable one human being to express ideal behaviour towards another. It is the equivalent of the Greek word *agape*, for which, as for *jen*, the word 'love' is too general and too vague a translation. It is based on sympathy for others, an empathy with them, and a desire for them to achieve their best good. It is mirrored in Kant's description of goodwill, which to him was the ideal basis of all human intercourse. It meant that no other person was to be treated as a means to an end (that is, one's own selfish end) but rather should be treated as at all times an end in him or herself. 'Respect for persons' would be a not inapposite translation of this quality, fostered by a sense of mutuality (***shu***) and loyalty (***chung***) in any relationship. Master K'ung himself, when asked if there was a single saying that one could act on all day and every day, gave the simple and straightforward guideline [...]: 'Never do to others what you would not like them to do to you' (XV,23). This expression of the Golden Rule in negative form is probably easier to follow than its converse, especially if it is the case that human beings are more united in what they dislike than in what they like. On the other hand, he also said (VI,28): 'To apply one's own wishes and desires as a yardstick by which to judge one's behaviour toward others is the true way of *jen*.'

The roots of *jen*, he affirmed, were piety *(hsiao)* and obedience *(ti)*. These were the qualities that characterised the ideal man, or ***chun-tzu***, literally 'duke's son', one whose nobility of title is reflected in his behaviour. The piety called for is the veneration of parents by children, and the obedience that of the younger brother to the older, whether within a family or in the community generally; thus respect for the old became a central feature of the Chinese cultural tradition. This does not always mean yielding to them whatever the issue, but treating them in the way to which, by their years, they have become entitled. Confucius (IV,18) was typically practical:

> In serving his father and mother a man may gently remonstrate with them. But if he sees that he has failed to change their opinion, he should resume an attitude of deference and not thwart them. He may feel discouraged, but not resentful.

Mencius, Confucius' natural heir, later (*Mencius* IV,19) linked respect for parents with self-respect:

> Which is the greatest service? The service of parents is the greatest. Which is the greatest of charges? The charge of oneself is the greatest. I have heard of keeping oneself, and thus being able to serve one's parents. But I have not heard of failing to keep oneself, and yet being able to serve one's parents.

The expression of *jen* in relationships is an ideal that Confucius shared with, or in which he was to be joined by, representatives and leaders of most of the major world religions. The second of the two pivots of Confucian ethics is, however, more idiosyncratically K'ung Tzu's emphasis. *Li* is normally translated as 'propriety'; it was originally (that is, in pre-Confucian times) related to the correct conduct of rites and ceremonies, that everything should be done, in St. Paul's words, 'decently and in order'. It was extended to embrace the customs and traditions of the community, with the implication that these should be faithfully preserved. Master K'ung went a step further and applied it to inter-human relationships, giving a structure to the ideal of *jen*. Just as mercy without justice is likely to encourage crime, so *jen* without *li*, he suggested, could easily degenerate into a simplistic expression of mawkish sentimentality. K'ung Tzu could no more have joined the Beatles in singing 'All you need is love' (the idea is in fact hilarious) than he could have deliberately deceived a neighbour over a commercial transaction. The combination of *li* and *jen* makes it possible to win an argument without losing a friend; to accept one's superiority over another without making him or her feel belittled (and inferiority without feeling humiliated); or—quint-essentially Chinese—allowing a defeated opponent to 'save face'. The emphasis of *li* is that some arguments must be won, some people are superior to others, and some opponents have to be defeated.

Master K'ung indicates the significance of *li* with great clarity in the *Analects* (VIII,2, Wilhelm translation):

> Deference ['courtesy', in Waley's translation] that lacks propriety (form, *li*) becomes servility ['tiresome'], caution without propriety becomes timidity, courage without propriety becomes rebelliousness, honesty without propriety beomes rudeness [or 'inflexibility becomes harshness' in Waley].

The distinction here is subtle, and an insensitive person may well be incapable of appreciating it. In order to learn what *li* means in practice, any person will need to acquire **chih**, or wisdom, the ability to discriminate between the nicely differing modes of behaviour that are in tune with the forces of *yin* and *yang*. To express propriety in one's dealing with others, therefore, means that nothing is done in excess, whether in words or in actions. In the harmony of *yin* and *yang*, one is never too strident, never too muted; happy doing ordinary things well rather than constantly attempting the extraordinary or the impossible; living well, but living well within oneself. 'Nothing in excess' could be a Confucian catchword, reminiscent of the ideal of the mean as taught by Aristotle, with whom Master K'ung is sometimes compared.

A key element in the practice of *li* is the fulfilling of one's duty, for which the Chinese word is *i* This quality can be translated as righteousness, honesty, uprightness; people who observe *i* observe the requirements demanded of them by their roles and stations in life, and the care shown in making this observance must inevitably give direction to any expression of *jen* toward others. This may sound a bland statement, but in fact it is highly pertinent. Master K'ung considered that loving kindness can manifest itself only in ever-widening circles, with the inevitable consequence that the *jen* that is expressed abates in its intensity as the circle widens: this, for K'ung, was a natural state of affairs, an unalterable condition of humanity. An individual's first duty is filial piety, **xiao**, followed by duty to his clan; and although, as we shall see, K'ung laid great significance on the subject's duty to the state, he viewed this as secondary to the primary duties. He would probably have agreed with E.M. Forster, who remarked that, given a choice between betraying a friend or betraying his country, 'I hope I should have the courage to betray my country.'

This concept of circles of relationships is in direct conflict with a philosophy that was to be expressed a century later by the founder of the Mohist School, Mo Tzu, or Mo Ti (Master Mo, c. 468–376 BCE). He taught that loving kindness (*jen*) should be shown to others without distinction or favouritism: the needs of distant strangers or local enemies should rank as highly in any person's consciousness as those of his family or clan. Mo was in fact expressing an early form of utilitarianism as was to be taught in the nineteenth century by John Stuart Mill, whose argument was that any moral decision should have as its end the increase in human happiness. With that K'ung would have agreed; where they would have parted company was in Mill's assertion that, when decisions are required about how best to achieve this end in any given circumstance, 'everyone [is] to count as one, nobody to count as more than one'.

To Confucius, and even more to his successor, Mencius, this aim would have seemed both unnatural and against the ground rules of propriety. Each of them had more than his share of common sense, based on calm observation of people. From this they concluded that most people find it difficult enough expressing goodwill to those around them without multiplying the problem by introducing the whole of the human race into the equation. On the other hand, they were also aware that some people find it is easier to express love for people they are never likely to meet than for those with whom they share the frustrations of daily living.

K'ung therefore had no truck either with the ideal of loving one's enemies, which was to receive superb expression in the New Testament, or with the utilitarian ideal of having neither favourites nor 'also-rans' in one's relationships. If love were to be shown as much to one's enemies as to one's friends, what advantage lay in being a friend? And what wife could cheerfully accept that, while her husband loved her no less than all the other women in the world, he loved her no more than them? What was needed, according to Confucius, was the quality of conscientiousness to others (**zhong**); this means that, while one may make a diligent effort to practise *jen*, one is not called upon to repay evil with good.

Master K'ung taught that there are five relationships (**wu-lun**), which together form the basis of human interaction (*wu-ch'ang*, or 'five constants'). The constants are *jen, li, i, chih* (wisdom or insight) and *hsin* (trust); by observing *wu-lun* meticulously (that is, by living according to the implications of the relationships) people may achieve order in their personal lives and, by extension, the community as a whole may coexist harmoniously. In each of the *wu-lun*, the first named should have the dominant, *yang* role, and the second the submissive *yin*. The five are:

father and son;
husband and wife;
older brother and younger brother;

(older) friend and (younger) friend;
ruler and subject.

Thus a man can expect to show both *yin* and *yang* qualities in his relationships. A father, for example, will be *yang* in relation to his wife or his children, and *yin* in relation to the ruler (or older friend). A son will be *yin* in relation to his father and *yang* in relation to any younger brother or friend. K'ung does not discuss the problems that may arise in a family if number two son (to use a Chinese phrase) has more innately dominant qualities than his older brother; nor—and this is a considerably larger sticking-point—does he allow women anything but *a yin* position *vis-a-vis* any male. The *Analects* hint that he was married, with a son and a daughter, but there are no domestic details. We may conclude that, like two other pioneer visionaries of the ideal society, Plato and St. Paul, there is a lacuna at this point in his thinking, so that effectively he has nothing to teach us on the subject. K'ung himself seems to have been aware of this omission, suggested by his comment in the *Analects* (XVII,25):

> Women and people of low birth are very hard to deal with. If you are friendly with them, they get out of hand, and if you keep your distance, they resent it.

Some interpreters soften the saying by making it apply to 'maids and valets'.

Master K'ung's main public concern was with the selection of rulers, and the style in which they should govern. His view was that a 'trickle-down effect' operated between ruler and subjects, whereby if he showed virtue in his dealings, they would follow his example. To one ruler he said (XII,19):

> If you desire what is good, the people will be good. The character of a ruler is like wind and that of the people is like grass. In whatever direction the wind blows, the grass always bends.

He accepted in general that rulers reached their position 'with the mandate of heaven', but he argued that this situation was not irreversible. If ever, by despotism or greed, they betrayed the trust thus conferred upon them, it was right that they should be overthrown and replaced. Where this occurred, the qualities to look for were integrity and strength of character, fostered by a love of education. These qualities would enable them to overcome the pettiness that leads to the mistreatment of subjects, causing them in their turn to become rebellious. Mencius was later to give unambiguous expression to this admonition:

> If a ruler regards his ministers as his hands and feet, then his ministers will regard him as their heart and mind. If a ruler regards his ministers as dogs and horses, his ministers will regard him as any other man. If a ruler regards his ministers as dirt and grass, his ministers will regard him as a bandit and an enemy.
>
> (IV ,B,3)

A particular concern of Kung Tzu's was what he termed 'the rectification of names', meaning that there should be a correspondence between a person's title and his behaviour. 'Let the ruler *be* a ruler,' he said (XII,11), 'the minister *be* a minister, the father *be* a father, and the son *be* a son.' A ruler who is too lazy to tackle the problems in his region, a minister who is too greedy to serve others, a father who ignores his paternal obligations and a son who is indifferent to his filial responsibilities: all are, in their different ways, catalysts of disorder and dissension. Get the names right, suggested K'ung, and there arises the possibility of justice and order in the land; ignore the names, and the door is open to contention, disharmony and strife. Every name contains qualities that correspond to the essence of whatever or whoever is referred to by that name. If ruler, minister, father or son follows the *Tao* of his role by living up to the ideal that the name indicates, there will be harmony between the name and the expression of it in practice. 'A noble person [*chun-tzu*] will not tolerate disorder in his words. That is what matters', he said (*Analects* XIII,3).

The School of Names was later to become an autonomous school, but without Master K'ung's wise, non-obsessional and, above all, comprehensively human perspective it came to represent a somewhat narrow, even pedantic, form of what Western philosophy might describe as linguistic analysis.

We may summarise Confucius' views on government in the following statements:

1. The purpose of government is to provide for the welfare and happiness of all its people.
2. The right to govern is not sustained by heavenly decree, but by the ability to make its people happy and secure, with equal justice before the law.
3. In the selection of leaders, no role should be played by wealth or breeding, but by integrity and virtue, arising from a love of education.
4. Excessive taxation, barbarous punishments and aggression towards people within the state and beyond should be outlawed.
5. The best government is that which governs least, dedicating itself to the development of the character and culture of the people.

This last statement is a reflection of Taoist thought, especially about *wu-wei*. [...] Confucius's commendation of the legendary ruler, Shun, who seems to have been content to let things be and not to intervene in his subjects' affairs (XV,4):

> To have taken no [unnatural] action [*wu-wei*] and yet have the empire well governed, Shun was the man.

Confucius constantly emphasised education as the key to happy and successful living, 'to go on learning so that you do not notice yourself growing old', as he stated in the *Analects,* and this emphasis puts him among the foremost of the world's humanists. He was one of the first people in history, and certainly the first in China, to take up teaching as a full-time occupation, and to suggest that the educational process was life-long. He thus stands among the protagonists of *educere*, rather than *educare*, as the essence of education: to go on growing, humbly aware that, however learned one is, there is infinitely more to know, rather than viewing education simply as the gateway to a qualification that offers economic opportunities to its owner. L.C. Wu closes his study of Confucius (*op. cit*, p. 31) with these words:

> Confucius' ethic is a rational approach to human happiness and good society without any supernatural grounding. Confucius taught the Chinese that happiness and virtue are correlatives which are complementary to each other ... This spirit of happiness can be readily found among the Chinese regardless of their educational level, social or financial status. This is Confucius' contribution. It is the noblest of human achievements.

This may explain why it is that, after some years of neglect, Master K'ung has returned as a compulsory subject of study in Chinese schools. Even Mao Tse-tung acknowledged that he ranked worthy to be studied alongside Marx, Engels and Lenin. How far he would have been happy in their company is, however, a matter of some speculation. Independently of their political views, one suspects that, like any other claimants to possession of the 'truth', their self-assuredness, a corruption of self-assurance, would have made it difficult for him to relate to them at any more than a surface level. To be a *chun-tzu* (gentleman), he knew, a key virtue was the humility to accept that one may be wrong on any issue, however firmly that belief be held.

MENCIUS (MENG-TZU)

Second only to K'ung Tzu in the Confucian hierarchy is Mencius (*c.* 372–289 BCE). In many respects both his life and his teachings were remarkably similar to those of his mentor. He was born in the same province, followed in his earlier years the same profession, experienced similar frustrations because of the political and moral chaos brought about primarily through selfish and ineffectual government, eventually became a roaming teacher and counsellor, offering advice to rulers, and disputing with those whom he believed to be the authors of 'perversive doctrines'; and, like Confucius, he felt at the end of his life a sense of disappointment and failure.

The philosophy of Mencius is often described as 'idealistic Confucianism', an expression based partly on his optimistic view of human nature, partly on his greater emphasis on the spiritual dimension in following the Confucian virtues. If Confucius was China's Aristotle, Mencius was more akin to its Plato, of whom he was a contemporary, and with whom he is often compared. He was also a contemporary of Chuang Tzu, but there is no record of their ever having met each other—an encounter that would surely have been beneficial not only to both of them but also to all whose lives have been enriched by their teaching.

Like the *Analects*, the book *Mencius* was probably edited by disciples, although under closer supervision by their mentor than was the earlier book. It is structured more carefully than the *Analects*, and from it we can infer that Mencius was a sharp debater, uncompromising in his views, and not so ready as Confucius to admit that he might be wrong on any matter. He seems to have spent considerable time in arguing his case with rival philosophers, who were more numerous in his time than two centuries earlier.

Mencius accepted Confucius's emphasis on the twin virtues of *jen* and *li*: how they embrace *chung* and *shu*, express themselves in *xiao (hsiao)* and *chun-tzu*, and are directed by a sense of righteousness, or *i*. So far as guidelines for successful living are concerned, therefore, Mencius offered no radical departures from the Confucianist canon. Where he differed was on a matter that has been the subject of continual debate over the millennia, to which he offered an unambiguous standpoint: human nature, and his view, for which he remains one of the key historical protagonists, that it is inherently good.

Confucius had held the belief that human nature cannot be characterised as inherently either 'good' or 'bad' (the reason for putting those words in quotations will emerge later). In a sense, he took an existentialist view, arguing that each person's nature (what Sartre called 'essence') developed as a direct consequence of the path they followed through life: the choices they made, the priorities they established, the extent to which they observed the five relationships, and so on. Above all, he held that the most certain route to goodness lay along the path of education. The broadening of the mind that this would ensure would enable a person more comprehensively to show loving kindness, observe the proprieties and express righteousness in his or her dealings. In other words, goodness was a product of the *educere* process [...], and, while many were prevented from following this way because of factors beyond their control, nobody was inherently incapable of achieving it. Confucius could, therefore, well have been the first to declare, 'Existence precedes essence.'

Mencius disagreed with this neutral position. His view was that people were born with their natures intact, and that the natural human instinct is towards goodness. 'Which of you,' he asked his audience during one debate on the subject, 'seeing a child playing on the edge of a well and stumbling, would not instinctively spring to its aid, lest it fall to its death?' To Mencius, this—what we should today call reflex—reaction proved that people are predisposed to be altruistic. He observed the generations of people throughout history who had willingly accepted personal inconvenience, sacrifice, suffering and even death for the sake of others: was this to be described as unnatural behaviour? This seemed to him to be necessarily the case if the opposite position were taken.

There is a close similarity here between Mencius's view and that of Plato and, two millennia later, Jean-Jacques Rousseau, although without the Platonic concept of reincarnation after a period in heaven, the world of forms, or ideals, which was an integral feature of their philosophy. Mencius did not discuss *why* people were altruistic from birth; he simply affirmed that this was the case, based on empirical evidence.

Confucianism | 143

His critics wanted to know why, in that case, many people in a host of situations—as observation would continually confirm—behaved selfishly, showing indifference towards others' needs, and even going to the extent of causing them deliberate harm. Mencius's reply was that evil was the result of unnatural behaviour. Because of circumstances, people's natural goodness could be distorted or suppressed; what was needed, therefore, was a community that allowed free rein to their natural constituents: loving kindness, righteousness, respect for others, piety. In a famous passage, he compared human nature to the way water behaves:

> Man's nature is naturally good just as water naturally flows downward. There is no man without this good nature; neither is there water that does not flow downward. Now, you can splash water and cause it to splash upward over your forehead; and by damming it and leading it, you can force it uphill. Is this the nature of water? It is the forced circumstance that makes it so. Man can be made to do evil, for his nature can be treated in the same way.
>
> (VI,1,6)

Mencius lived, of course, 2,000 years before Newton's discovery of gravity, otherwise he would at the very least have needed to find a different analogy. More important philosophically is the question, which relates to Plato's and Rousseau's theories also, of how, if all people are born with perfect natures, imperfections arise at all. Logically it seems the case that, if they are naturally altruistic individually, they will be so collectively; the only escape-route from this logic would be to assert that the natural life is one of isolation, so that all social intercourse is unnatural: which would leave a question mark over the need for altruism in any case.

The fact is that Mencius's whole position is tautological, since by the word 'good' he means whatever is fully in tune with human nature, and by human nature he means whatever may be described as 'good'. This is a circular argument: if, on the one hand, whatever is inborn is defined as human nature, and, on the other, human nature is characterised as 'good', then Mercius's conclusion that 'bad' behaviour must be characterised as 'unnatural', may follow, but only by a monumental process of question-begging. It is as if a person were to argue that Christians live good lives and, on being told of a practising Christian who treats others shabbily, replies, 'In that case I would not describe him as a Christian at all.' (We leave unexplored the vexed questions of how far 'goodness' and 'badness' are absolute terms, and whether the words have any definable meaning at all. Mencius lived not only before Newton, but before the age of postmodernist relativism cf. p.100.)

Independently of these considerations, Mencius made the following statements, which encapsulate the logical consequences of accepting his basic proposition:

1. The ability possessed by men without their having to acquire it is innate ability, and the knowledge possessed by them without deliberation is innate knowledge ... These feelings are universal in the world.

   (VII,A,15)

2. He who exerts his mind to the uttermost knows his nature. He who knows his nature knows Heaven. To preserve one's mind and to nourish one's nature is the way to serve Heaven.

   (VII,A,1)

3. When there is repeated disturbance, the restorative influence of the night will not be sufficient to preserve [the proper goodness of the mind] ... People see that he acts like an animal, and think that he never had the original endowment [for goodness].

   (VI,A,8)

4. Pity the man who abandons the path and does not follow it, and has lost his heart and does not know how to recover it.

   (VI,A,11)

5. Confucius said, 'Hold it fast and you preserve it. Let it go and you lose it.' He was talking about the human mind ... *The way of learning is none other than finding the lost mind.*

   (VI,A,11,8)

Those italicised words perfectly express the humanist approach to education, and they are reflected in Pope's famous couplet in his *Essay on Man*:

Men must be taught as if you taught them not, And things unknown proposed as things forgot.

One practical expression of Mencius' idealism was his proposal for the 'well-field system' in agriculture. Each square (*li*) of land (about one-third of a mile squared) is divided into nine equal squares in the shape of a noughts-and-crosses chart. Eight farmers each own one of the outside squares, leaving the central square to be farmed by all of them on a rota basis. Each keeps the proceeds from his own patch, but the proceeds from the central square provide the taxes for all eight of them. (This square can of course be expanded or contracted according to the rate of taxation.) Mencius proposed this as a middle way between totally individualised and completely communalised farming; he believed that it would leave the way open for people both to cooperate with one another and to have the personal satisfaction of reaping the fruits of their own labour.

It is interesting to speculate whether this system would work in practice. Would each farmer work as hard on the central square as he did on his own patch? It would need only one backslider to upset both the system as a whole, and the feelings of the other seven at the same time. One wonders how many of them would find themselves feeling unwell on the eighth day when it was their turn in the middle. Who would be held to blame if the tax authorities felt underpaid? The resolution of this conundrum depends on whether one is an idealist or a cynic: it would certainly be a test of Mencius' theory.

One Confucianist who would have scorned the well-field system on the grounds that it would lead to controversy brought about by self-interest was **Hsun Tzu** (*c.* 298–238 BCE), generally revered as the 'third sage' in the Confucian hierarchy. While in essential aspects he agreed with Confucian teaching, he disagreed with Mencius about human nature. In fact, if Mencius was the Rousseau of Confucianism, Hsun Tzu was its Hobbes. Two of his disciples became leading figures in the Legalistic School, and he has (wrongly, according to many modern sinologists), been characterised as the midway figure between it and Confucianism. The *Hsun-Tzu* consists of thirty-two chapters, which are effectively a series of essays on a range of subjects. They indicate that, if on some issues he was more legalistic than Confucius, in others, such as his view of *T'ien* (Heaven), he was more Taoist. His writings are not included among the Chinese classics, but his critical and analytical approach to philosophy makes him a particularly attractive subject of study in modern China.

Chapter 23 of the *Hsun-Tzu*, probably the best-known essay in the book, is entitled, 'The Nature of Man is Evil'. Its first two paragraphs give the gist of his beliefs on the subject, and because of their simplicity of expression they need no further elucidation:

> The nature of man is evil; whatever is good in him is the result of acquired training. Men are born with the love of gain; if this natural tendency is followed they are contentious and greedy, utterly lacking in courtesy and consideration for others. They are filled from birth with envy and hatred of others; if these passions are given rein they are violent and villainous, wholly devoid of integrity and good faith. At birth man is endowed with the desires of the ear and the eye, the love of sound and colour; if he acts as they dictate he is licentious and disorderly, and has no desire for *li* or justice or moderation.
>
> Clearly, then, to accord with man's original nature and act as instinct dictates must lead to contention, rapacity, and disorder, and cause humanity to revert to a state of violence. For this reason it is essential that men be transformed by teachers and laws, and guided by *li* and justice; only then will they be courteous and cooperative, only then is good order possible. In the light of these facts it is clear that man's original nature is evil, and that he becomes good only through acquired training.

Hsun Tzu's theory is in some respects a reflection of Aristotle's contention, expressed a century earlier, that the law exists to spur people on in the pursuit of 'the good'.

One other emphasis in Mencius' teaching distinguishes him from Confucius and links him somewhat more closely with the Taoist and *Yin–Yang* schools. This is his philosophical mysticism, in accordance with which he speaks not only of cultivating order in the community, but also of achieving order within oneself by cultivating *ch'i*: vital breath, or energy. We have seen [...] how important is the concept of *ch'i* in Taoism, both as a focal point of meditation and as a means of achieving physical harmony, both within oneself and in relation to the universe as a whole. *T'ai-ch'i* is the term used for the supreme ultimate, and *T'ai-Ch'i Ch'uan*, [...] is a form of physical exercise designed to create a sense of personal harmony with it.

Mencius wrote (II,A,2 and VII,A,1,1):

> When I cultivate this great *ch'i* within me, all things are then complete within me ... [therefore] he who completely knows his nature, knows Heaven.

By 'Heaven', he was referring to the cosmic order, which for him was a moral one:

> his view was that moral principles both reflect and devolve from the metaphysical principles of the universe (there is a nuance of Kantianism in this perception). All people are at the same time citizens of society and of Heaven. With this emphasis he went further in the direction of mysticism than had Confucius. The Master had certainly introduced the concept of Heaven into his teaching, but more as an indication of the source of the values he taught than as a goal for people to attain. Mencius stressed that, in the process of cultivating the great *ch'i*, we need not only human principles such as duty and righteousness, which Confucius had unambiguously outlined, but also both an understanding of, and sense of harmony with, the *Tao*.

Mencius thus combines two of the disciplines of Hinduism: Jnana Yoga, or spiritual understanding, and Karma Yoga, the discipline of action and work. This balance gives his teaching the completeness found in the harmony of *yin* and *yang*, which may well be seen as the aim of all religious philosophies and their practitioners [...].

Neo-Confucianism

During the centuries immediately following Mencius' death, the mystical element in his teaching was given little prominence among students of Confucianism, who preferred to concentrate on the school's practical emphases. Advocates of other philosophical schools and perspectives were viewed, on the whole, as rivals rather than exponents of alternative facets of the truth they were all seeking. There were in fact numerous disputations, not all of them harmonious, between adherents of the different philosophies.

Between the third and eighth centuries CE, however, a process of synthesis took place that brought about a modification of the Confucianism taught by the Master. The main schools that were involved in this process were the two which, alongside Confucianism, still constitute the main streams in Chinese philosophy/religion: Taoism and Buddhism. Through the influence of these two schools, Confucian thought underwent a transformation, with the result that it began to acknowledge more directly the role of the mystical when interpreting both the universe in general and human life in particular. It was during this period that the *I Ching* gained its significance as a guide to a spiritual interpretation of the world; and the concept of the *Tao* as the primordial principle of the universe was seen to connect with the practical guidelines of Confucius, so that (for instance) the five relationships taught by the Master could be described as 'the *Tao* of relationships'. This synthesising process is known as Neo-Confucianism and has great significance for any modern discussion of the subject. It was during this period that the so-called Four Books, which were, [...] used in Chinese Civil Service examinations, assumed their authority.

The most important contribution of Neo-Confucianism, however, was its extension of Mencius' view of the metaphysical rationale for traditional ethics. The person most closely associated with this teaching, and generally regarded as the greatest of the Neo-Confucians, was the twelfth-century philosopher **Chu Hsi** (1130–1200), a prolific writer, and lecturer at the Confucian College of Bai Lu Dong (White Deer Grotto) near Shanghai. In his earlier years he was a student of Buddhism but turned from this philosophy because of its teaching of *anatta*; Chu Hsi held that there is a basic self, and his philosophy is built around this belief.

The two fundamental components of his teaching are *li* and *ch'i*. We have met both these words already, but his interpretation of them, particularly his combination of them, is distinctive. In traditional Confucian teaching, *li* means propriety; but Chu Hsi used it in its second (although not secondary) sense of the absolute, the cosmic order: in fact, as he interprets the word, it becomes highly reminiscent of the *Tao*. *Li* is the principle, the formal aspect of a thing (the thing-in-itself); *ch'i*, as used by Chu Hsi, is its material representation in any specific instance. *Ch'i* cannot exist without *li*, and *li* cannot be known without *ch'i*. Things are thus the instruments by which *li* finds expression; everything has its *li*, which alone establishes that thing's nature. Furthermore, the *li* of a thing pre-exists the actual coming into being of that thing (as opposed to Confucius' more existentialist perspective): the essence of anyone or anything precedes their actual coming into existence. One is reminded of Plato's theory of forms in this teaching, although the emphasis in Chu Hsi is on what Christians would term 'realised eschatology', described by Dietrich Bonhoeffer as 'the beyond in the midst'. For Plato, the forms remain in Heaven, either dimly remembered by the philosophers who have escaped from the shadows of the cave, or encountered in moments of revelation by those who 'can suddenly perceive a nature of wondrous beauty' (*Symposium*, 211).

For Chu Hsi, the form of a thing (or person), and its actual expression in a particular instance, are potentially one, and he summarised this idea with the words, 'Everything has an ultimate *ch'i*, which is the ultimate *li*' (*Recorded Sayings*, chapter 94). In the same passage, however, he added words that link his teaching more closely with *tao-chia* and, although not quite so directly, with the Hindu idea of *brahman* and the ground of being:

> That which unites and embraces the *li* of heaven, earth, and all things is the Supreme Ultimate [*T'ai-Ch'i*].

In the *Complete Works of the Master Chu*, chapter 49, he adds:

> The Supreme Ultimate is what is highest of all, beyond which nothing can be. It is the most high, most mystical, and most abstruse, surpassing everything.

Thus *T'ai-Ch'i* is, as Chu expresses it (p.244), 'the *li* of all *li*, the *li* of the universe as a whole'. Every individual therefore has not only his or her own *li* within his or her *ch'i*, but also partakes of the ultimate *li*. Chu Hsi states:

> This one Supreme Ultimate is received by each individual in its entirety and undivided. It is like the moon shining in the heavens, of which, though it is reflected in rivers and lakes and thus is everywhere visible, we would not therefore say that it is divided.
>
> (*Recorded Sayings*, chapter 94)

If we accept the findings, such as they are, of Chapter 2, this must be judged to be a highly religious statement. Chu Hsi adds to this perspective a cosmological consideration. He taught that the universe's existence is a consequence of the continually alternating phases of *ch'i*, which he held to oscillate between rest and motion. It is at rest in *yin* and in movement in *yang*, and from the oscillation arise *wu-hsing*, the five elements of earth, fire, metal, wood and water [...], which, by their infinite combinations, give rise to the material world. There are some reflections here of the alternating appearance and disappearance of the universe (evolution and involution) taught in the Hindu school of Sankya Yoga [..].

Laurence Wu comments on this teaching with these words (*op. cit.* p.245):

> All creation was an evolutionary process from simple to complex life, through a continuous succession of birth, decay, death, and re-creation. In view of the role played by *li* and *ch'i* in the production of things, Joseph Needham's translation of *li* as 'principle of organisation' and *ch'i* as 'matter—energy' in *Science and Civilisation in China* are quite apt.

Whether religious or otherwise, these ideas have played a formative part in creating one feature of the Chinese mind.

[...]

Chapter Review

1. Explain *jen*.
2. Explain *li*.
3. According to Master Kung, what is the purpose of government?
4. Who was Mencius and how did he differ from Master Kung?
5. What were the five relationships?
6. Describe Neo-Confucianism.
7. What is the *ch'i*?

What is Shinto?

By Inoue Nobutaka

SHINTO AS A RELIGIOUS SYSTEM

The term 'Shinto' is notoriously vague and difficult to define. A brief look at the term's history confuses more than it enlightens. Its first occurrence is in the *Nihon shoki* (720), which writes of Emperor Yomei (r. 585–7) that he 'had faith in the Buddhist Dharma and revered Shinto.' Here, as in most early usages of the word, it seems to serve as a synonym for Japan's native deities, in Japanese called kami, in contrast to the new 'foreign kami' that entered Japan with the introduction of Buddhism in the sixth century. Only during the medieval and early modern periods was the term applied to specific theological and ritual systems. In modern scholarship, the term is often used with reference to kami worship and related theologies, rituals and practices. In these contexts, 'Shinto' takes on the meaning of 'Japan's traditional religion', as opposed to foreign religions such as Christianity, Buddhism, Islam and so forth.

Inoue Nobutaka, "Introduction: What is Shinto?" *Shinto: A Short History*, ed. Inoue Nobutaka, Itō Satoshi, Endō Jun, and Mori Mizue, pp. 1–11. Copyright © 2003 by Taylor & Francis Group LLC. Reprinted with permission.

A central element in a practical definition of Shinto will have to be systems of kami worship and shrine ritual that date back to classical times. Few will doubt that the kami and their cults form the core of what we call Shinto. However, when we try to pin down more specifically what teachings, rituals, or beliefs have constituted Shinto through the centuries, we soon run into difficulty. Some scholars have attempted to categorise Shinto into 'shrine Shinto', 'sect Shinto', and 'folk Shinto', and others have added 'imperial Shinto' (referring to imperial rituals focusing on kami), 'state Shinto' and 'Shinto-derived new religions'. However, many questions remain both as to the legitimacy of these categorisations, and as to their relationship to each other. In particular, it is well-nigh impossible to separate 'shrine Shinto' from 'folk Shinto'. In extreme cases, some have even resorted to labelling all religious folk traditions in Japan 'Shinto'.

In the field of Religious Studies, Shinto is usually described as an 'indigenous religion'. By this term is meant a religion that emerged naturally within the historical development of an indigenous culture, in contrast to 'founded religions', which are based on the teachings of historical founders. These latter are often described as 'world religions', because they spread across national boundaries to assume a global role. In contrast, Shinto as an 'indigenous religion' is inextricably linked with a single nation, Japan.

Shinto also displays many features of what we may call 'folk religion'. This term is here used as a generic term for popular beliefs and practices that are not directly controlled by a shrine, temple or church, or led by a religious professional such as a priest, a monk or a minister. As such beliefs and practices in Japan, we may mention the worship of various deity tablets (*ofuda*), the tabooing of certain dates or directions, belief in different kinds of spirits (such as spirits of the dead, or 'revengeful spirits', *onryō*), worship of natural objects such as trees and mountains, and worship of the kami of fields and mountains (*ta no kami* and *yama no kami*). Most of what is commonly called religious folklore, local customs, or superstition belongs in this category.

Not only Shinto, but also Buddhism and the new religions of Japan are closely connected with folk religion. Even Christianity, both in Japan and elsewhere, contains many folk influences. In the case of Shinto, however, such elements are so prominent that it is impossible to draw a line between folk religion and some fictional 'pure Shinto'. This is a direct result of Shinto's history, which is rooted in a long tradition of kami worship that developed in close relation with the rhythms of everyday life, both cultural and economic.

There is another reason why it is difficult to follow Shinto through history as a distinct religious tradition: the fact that Shinto has been profoundly influenced by other religious traditions. The influence of the religions of China has been prominent since ancient times, and among them, the religion that left the most profound impact was Chinese Buddhism. Even if we were to use the term 'Early Shinto' to refer to some archaic prototype of Shinto, we would find that such a distant ancestor of Shinto would already have been transformed in important ways by Chinese forms of Buddhism. In addition, other continental traditions such as Confucianism, Taoism, and theories about Yin and Yang and the Five Phases of matter (wood, fire, earth, metal and water) left their imprint in ideas about, and practices around, the kami from an early date. These facts further complicate our question, which appears so simple at first sight: what is Shinto? One is reminded of the onion of Peer Gynt: will there really be a 'core' to be found after we have peeled off layer after layer of foreign accretions?

These are the sort of fundamental problems one is faced with when trying to define Shinto. Looking for Shinto's 'core' or 'true essence' will not take us very far in resolving the issue. In this volume, we have chosen a different approach. Here, we will introduce the concept of a 'religious system' as a new angle on Shinto and its historical development.

The concept of a 'religious system' is here proposed as a tool to explore the historical development of religion in its intimate relation with the structural characteristics and changes of society as a whole. Traditionally, religious history has occupied itself with the histories of individual religions, schools or sects. We have histories of Christianity, Islam, Buddhism and Shinto, histories of the Methodist church and of Pure Land Buddhism, and histories of Tenrikyō and Sōka Gakkai. While this is a valuable approach to the history of religion, it tends to ignore the fact that the concept of religion itself can vary widely from period to period, or from religious group to religious group. It is obvious, for example, that the Catholic Church in Korea and its counterpart in Japan differ in many respects, in spite of the fact that both are grounded in the same religion. Similarly, Buddhism in classical Japan was fundamentally distinct in character from modern Japanese Buddhism. Conversely, we find that different religious groups display similar characteristics when developing in a common social and cultural environment. The new religious movements of modern Japan, which are collectively known as the 'new religions', are a good example of this: behind the multitude of sect names we find many similarities in actual teaching and practice. If we were to compare, for example, the modern Risshō Kōseikai and Myōchikai (both Buddhist-derived new religions), we would find that they are much more similar to one another than, say, the Buddhism of the Nara period (710–94) and the Edo period (1600–1867).

If we think of a religion in terms of written doctrine, individual religions or sects display a great deal of continuity over the centuries, but when we consider the roles these same religions or sects have played in actual society in different historical periods or in different cultural areas, we notice radical differences. If we regard individual religions as part of a wider religious 'ecosystem', it becomes clear that traditional histories of religion need to be reconsidered in various ways. It is to tackle these issues that the concept of a 'religious system' is useful. This concept allows us to treat clusters of religious groups that display typological similarities as one religious system. When studying such clusters as a religious system we relate their development to changes within society as a whole. This makes it possible to consider, say, the Sōtō Zen sect and the Jōdo Pure Land sect of the Edo period as two members of the same religious system: early modern Japanese Buddhism. Conversely, the Shingon school in the Heian period (794–1192) can be studied as belonging to a different religious system from its Edo period counterpart.

To study religion from this angle is to exchange the metaphor of religion as an organism for that of religion as an ecosystem. The boundaries of different religious systems are regarded as fluid, both with regard to individual religious movements, and with regard to different historical periods.

When we isolate a particular religious system and try to make out its characteristics, it is necessary to approach it from three angles: the system's *constituents*, its *network*, and its *substance*. The *constituents* of a religious system are the people who carry and maintain it. In most cases, we can distinguish between two groups: the 'makers' and the 'users' of the religion. The first include the founders of religious groups and their successors: monks, shrine priests, ministers, missionaries, and so forth. These are the people who work actively to sustain a particular religious tradition. This category also includes those who carry out the administrative tasks of religious institutions. The 'users' of a religious system are the believers, followers and church-goers who participate in religious activities. It is important to note that not all 'users' are necessarily 'believers'; those who do not necessarily have 'faith' but are active in the periphery of religious groups must also be included in this category. This is because they are important to religious groups as possible future believers, and as targets for missionary education or conversion. The category of 'users', then, can be defined as those who already are, and those who may become, believers of a religion.

This takes us to the term *network*. We use this term to refer to the various elements that are related to the organisational upkeep of the religious system: the channels the religious system uses to ensure its future existence. Here, we can distinguish between 'hard' and 'soft' aspects: the sacred sites, shrine buildings, temples, churches and headquarters of religious groups constitute the first, while the latter includes institutional hierarchies, pilgrimage routes, etc.

The third and last key aspect of religious systems is termed *substance*. This refers to the message that a religion tries to convey to its users through its teachings, practices and rituals. A religion's teachings include both the doctrines laid down in its scriptures, and the contents of the sermons of its preachers—two aspects of teaching that are not always identical or even consistent. Practices and rituals range widely from secret, esoteric rites to public ceremonies.

Religious groups which display a clear similarity in structure or type can fruitfully be studied as components of a single religious system. A new religious system emerges when the three elements of *constituents*, *network* and *substance* come together in some new way. Changes in religious systems occur when one of these three elements is transformed to such a degree that it affects the other two.

If religious systems are formed and transformed in close interaction with the society in which they partake, it follows that Shinto cannot be considered as a single religious system that existed from the ancient to the modern period. Nonetheless, it is also true that the religious system that emerged with the systematisation of kami worship in ancient Japan is connected with modern shrine Shinto through a long string of gradual transformations. The method we will take in this volume is to follow this long history of transformations. As our point of departure, we will choose kami worship as the characteristic that distinguishes Shinto from other religious traditions and gives it continuity through the ages. It will become clear, however, that the concrete beliefs and practices of kami worship changed considerably from period to period, and took on a great variety of disparate forms.

The classical system of kami worship clearly possessed all the elements of a fully fledged religious system. Its origin is difficult to date, but it was completed as a system after the establishment of a central imperial state governed by an adapted version of Chinese law (J. *ritsuryō*). Shrines from all over the country were included in a system of 'official shrines' (*kansha*). This network of official shrines formed the *network* of kami worship as a religious system. Also, the *constituents* of kami rituals were clearly identified, and their message (the system's *substance*) was transmitted to society through ritual prayers (*norito*) and imperial decrees (*senmyō*). It is not possible to identify a religious system that might be described as 'Shinto' before the systematisation of kami worship by the new imperial state during the classical period, because the constituents, network, and substance of kami cults during this early period were too ill-defined.

Together with the decline of the rule of *ritsuryō* law, the classical system of kami worship gradually lost its character as a distinct religious system. The system's network was lost, and as kami cults amalgamated with Buddhism, its substance was radically transformed. During the medieval period, warrior groups became important carriers of kami cults, leading to a partial shift of the religion's constituents. The spread of private estates (*shōen*) and the popular practice of 'inviting' spirits of the deity Hachiman to such estates encouraged the formation of a new network which partly replaced the classical 'network' of official shrines.

Simultaneously, the amalgamation of kami cults and Buddhism that had begun already in early classical times penetrated into all nooks and crannies of kami worship in the course of the medieval period, and in the process not only transformed the classical system of kami worship but also encouraged the founding of new religious systems, such as that of Shugendo. This amalgamation generated changes in the substance of kami cults, because it placed kami cults under the strong influence of Buddhist doctrine. On the other hand, the process of amalgamation also encouraged the development of theological kami thought in opposition to Buddhism. During medieval times, Shinto as a religious system was all but absorbed by the much more powerful system of Buddhism, but nevertheless survived. Developments in the early modern and modern periods proved that medieval Shinto, though largely subsumed in Buddhism, still remained sufficiently autonomous as a religious system to move once more into a direction of its own.

Elements of the classical system of kami worship survived through the middle ages into the early modern period. This period saw the emergence of a new form of Shinto thought in the form of National Learning (*koku-gaku*) and Restoration (*fukko*) Shinto. This form of Shinto can be regarded as a new religious system in its own right, and also proved essential in the later formation of sect Shinto in modern times. On the level of substance, we see that the multitude of medieval kami theories of the medieval period were rearranged into a new, close-knit discourse through the labours of successive thinkers of the National Learning movement. This was an important step in the formation of a new religious system. With regard to the network of Shinto, the early modern period saw the formation of a range of religious 'confraternities' (*kō*), whose existence was an important factor in the development of the Shinto sects of the modern period.

The Buddhist and Confucian forms of Shinto that were prominent during the medieval and early modern periods were incomplete as a religious system, because they did not provide for a network of their own, or only a fragmentary one. On the other hand, they prepared the ground both for the modern system of kami worship and for the formation of sect Shinto and Shinto-derived new religions. Therefore, it is not impossible to regard them at least as a religious system *in nascendo*.

Shugendo, finally, developed in the power field between kami cults and Esoteric Buddhism, and gradually matured into a religious system of its own. Shugendo will not be discussed in detail in this volume, but it was a factor of great importance in the historical development of Shinto.

THE EAST-ASIAN SPHERE OF RELIGIOUS CULTURE AND SHINTO

Traditionally, there has been a tendency to stress the 'uniquely Japanese' character of Shinto, and little effort has been made to compare kami worship in Japan with the indigenous religions and folk beliefs of other East-Asian countries. It is only recently that researchers have focused on the similarities between kami cults and Taoism, and on the profound influence of Chinese folk religion and Chinese theories of Yin and Yang and the Five Phases of matter on Japanese kami cults.[1]

Worship of spirits, spirit possession, divination, oracles and polytheism are all features that Japanese kami cults share with East-Asian folk religion. Also, the amalgamation of kami cults with Buddhism in Japan has parallels in the amalgamation of Taoism and Buddhism in China, and of Confucianism and Buddhism in Korea.

The influence of Chinese religion in East Asia is so prominent that the whole region may well be regarded as a single 'Chinese religio-cultural sphere'. Until recently, scholars who have wished to identify the characteristics of Japanese religion did so by comparing Japanese religious traditions with the monotheistic religions of the West. As a result of such comparisons, syncretism, polytheism and animism have frequently been highlighted as typical of Japanese religion as a whole. However, even a superficial glance at the religions of Japan's closest neighbours reveals that these are all features shared by the large majority of religions in the Chinese religio-cultural sphere.

Shinto worships an untold multitude of different kami deities. While this represents an important difference with monotheistic religions such as Judaism, Christianity and Islam, it is a feature that Shinto shares with many other religions across the world, and that constitutes the norm in East Asia. Buddhism incorporated many Hindu deities in India, and once again expanded its pantheon in China with a host of Taoist deities. These countless regional deities play an especially important role on the level of popular religion.

Moreover, popular beliefs and practices revere not only deities but also a multitude of other kinds of spirits and supernatural creatures. Japanese religion recognises many deities and, to some extent, attributes different functions to different deities. The dividing line between deities and human beings is vague, and extraordinary humans are frequently worshipped as 'living kami' *(ikigami)* or as 'emanations of a Buddha' *(keshin)*. These features of Japanese religion, too, are widely shared by other religious traditions within the Chinese cultural sphere.

It goes without saying that polytheistic and animistic forms of religion can be found across the globe, and constitute one of the basic types of religion. In East Asia, these features are especially common. Moreover, East-Asian versions of polytheistic and animistic religions can perhaps be further defined as a special sub-species of this form of religion. Here, the role of Mahayana Buddhism and ancient Chinese deity worship, ancestor worship, and beliefs in demons must be emphasised.

The universal religion of East Asia has been Mahāyāna Buddhism, a religion of an exceptionally accommodative character. In the Chinese cultural sphere, Mahāyāna Buddhism absorbed multifarious forms of ancestor worship and deity worship, and through its flexible attitude and its tendency to transform differences and oppositions into expressions of a single religious truth, it contributed to the multifaceted and yet closely interconnected character of East-Asian religion as a whole.

An important issue in all religious traditions is the question of how contact with deities, or with God, can be established and maintained. Christianity and Islam describe how God 'appears' to human beings to convey messages to them (a phenomenon termed theophany); in East Asia, we find a corresponding phenomenon in the various forms of shamanism that are common throughout this region. Shamans can be defined as those who deploy some well-developed technique of interacting with deities or spirits. In contrast to those who encounter a theophany in Christianity or Islam, shamans actively establish contact with deities or spirits and, on occasion, control and use them for their own aims.

Shamanism is often mentioned as a constituent of Shinto. Oracles have formed part of kami cults since the ancient period, and spirit possession is a common element of folk religion to this day. It is perhaps questionable whether all of these phenomena should be termed shamanism, but there is no doubt that they have functioned as important means of communication between kami and their worshippers throughout history. The question remains how exactly kami possession in Shinto relates to shamanic practices current in modern Korea, Taiwan or Mongolia; the least we can say is that all these practices are religious techniques to fathom the will of deities or spirits. Practices of this nature can be found throughout East Asia, and Japan is no exception. In Japan, shamanic features are especially apparent in the activities of different types of spirit ritualists, which are known variously as *ogamiya, reinōsha, kitōshi*, or, in specific regions of Japan, *yuta* (Okinawa), *kamisan, itako,* and *gomiso* (Northern Honshu). The former of these are occupied mainly with healing practices, and the latter specialise first and foremost in contacting the dead and conveying messages from them, and in making predictions for the future.

Another common method to fathom the will of the gods is divination *(uranai)*. Techniques to interpret utterances, natural events, or the movements of special contrivances as the will of supernatural beings have been common in most religions since ancient times. In modern Shinto, the drawing of *omikuji* lots springs to mind; older are the reading of cracks in burnt tortoise shells (a technique of Chinese origin), and 'hot-water ordeals' *(kugatachi)*, in which a priest sprinkles hot water over the worshippers in the kami's presence. A large variety of annual divinatory rites and ceremonies to predict the prosperity of the coming year are practised at different localities throughout Japan. There are also forms of divination which include an element of spirit possession, such as *yudate*, a ritual closely related to *kugatachi* in which a *miko* priestess sprinkles hot water over herself and the worshippers to become possessed by the kami. Most forms of divination in Japan have been heavily influenced by Chinese folk religion, by Chinese theories of Yin and Yang and the Five Phases of matter, and by the Book of Changes *(Yijing)*. In fact, the very idea that good and bad fortune alternate, and the notion that we can read the 'will of Heaven', have their roots in China.

Even more important in the history of kami cults was their interblending with Buddhism. Throughout most of the historical period, kami have been worshipped together with buddhas or bodhisattvas, as a primarily Buddhist set. This not only assimilated the characters of different kami with those of buddhas and bodhisattvas, but also resulted in a situation in which the same individuals or communities followed different religious traditions parallel to each other. Both of these phenomena are commonly termed syncretism.

Syncretism develops naturally in a society where different non-exclusionistic, open-ended religions exist side by side. In Japan, Shinto amalgamated not only with Buddhism but also with Confucianism. Also, most modern new religions are rooted in more than one established religious tradition. In China, Confucianism, Taoism and Buddhism have produced a variety of combinatory cults and theologies, and Korea saw the partial amalgamation of Confucianism with Taoism. In Korea one can even find cults that combine Christian with shamanic elements. It is no exaggeration to argue that syncretism is characteristic of East-Asian religion as a whole.

In addition to this traditional syncretism, we can observe a new trend of forming new religious systems by selecting and combining the 'best points' of more than one religion. This tendency is distinguished from traditional syncretism as 'neo-syncretism'. Neo-syncretism is particularly prominent in modern Shinto-derived new religions, but can also be encountered in some of the new religions of modern Taiwan, Korea and other East-Asian countries.

Another prominent aspect of East-Asian religion is ancestor worship. In Japan, memorial services for ancestors are largely the domain of Buddhist sects, and ancestor worship is often regarded as an element of popular Buddhism; nevertheless, ancestors also play an important role in popular kami practices. In East Asia, ancestor worship has often been tied in with Confucianism, and has played a prominent role in people's religious life. Ancestral genealogies have usually followed the paternal line and are, in China and Korea, linked with specific places of origin. In some modern Japanese Buddhist-derived sects (notably

Reiyukai and sects split off from it), there is a tendency to include maternal ancestors as well. In general, it can be said that the concept of ancestors in Japan is more inclusive than in China or Korea, and the practice of paying reverence to ancestors has consistently occupied a larger proportion of religious activity than in other parts of East Asia. The fact remains, however, that the notion of a shared ancestry has played an important role in the formation of group identities in most societies throughout East Asia.

Ancestor worship mostly takes the form of ritual practice by kin groups or clans, and continues to perform the function of promoting group solidarity, often in secularised ways. Originally, such rituals were strongly religious in character. The ancestors were connected to living individuals or groups not only genealogically, but also as active ancestral spirits that protect their descendants in the present. In Japan, ancestor spirits were not necessarily related to their proteges in a strictly genealogical sense, and could therefore play an important role in community (rather than kin group) rituals. Moreover, ancestor worship has been central to modern ideologies that identify the whole of the state of Japan as an extended family, with the emperor at its head.

As will be clear already from this brief inventory of shared East-Asian features, research into Shinto as a member of the family of East-Asian religions is a promising and necessary avenue to a better understanding of this religious tradition, which has all too often been described as 'uniquely Japanese'.

Note

1. Examples are Fukunaga Mitsuji, *Dōkyō to Nihon bunka* (Jinbun Shoin 1982), and Yoshino Hiroko, *In'yō gogyosetsu kara mita Nihon no matsuri* (Kōbundō 1978).

Chapter Review

1. How could Shinto be called an indigenous religion?
2. Explain how kami are viewed.
3. Explain constituency, substance and network with regard to Shinto.
4. How is Shinto uniquely Japanese?
5. Explain syncretism with regard to Shinto and Buddhism.

160 | Religions of the World

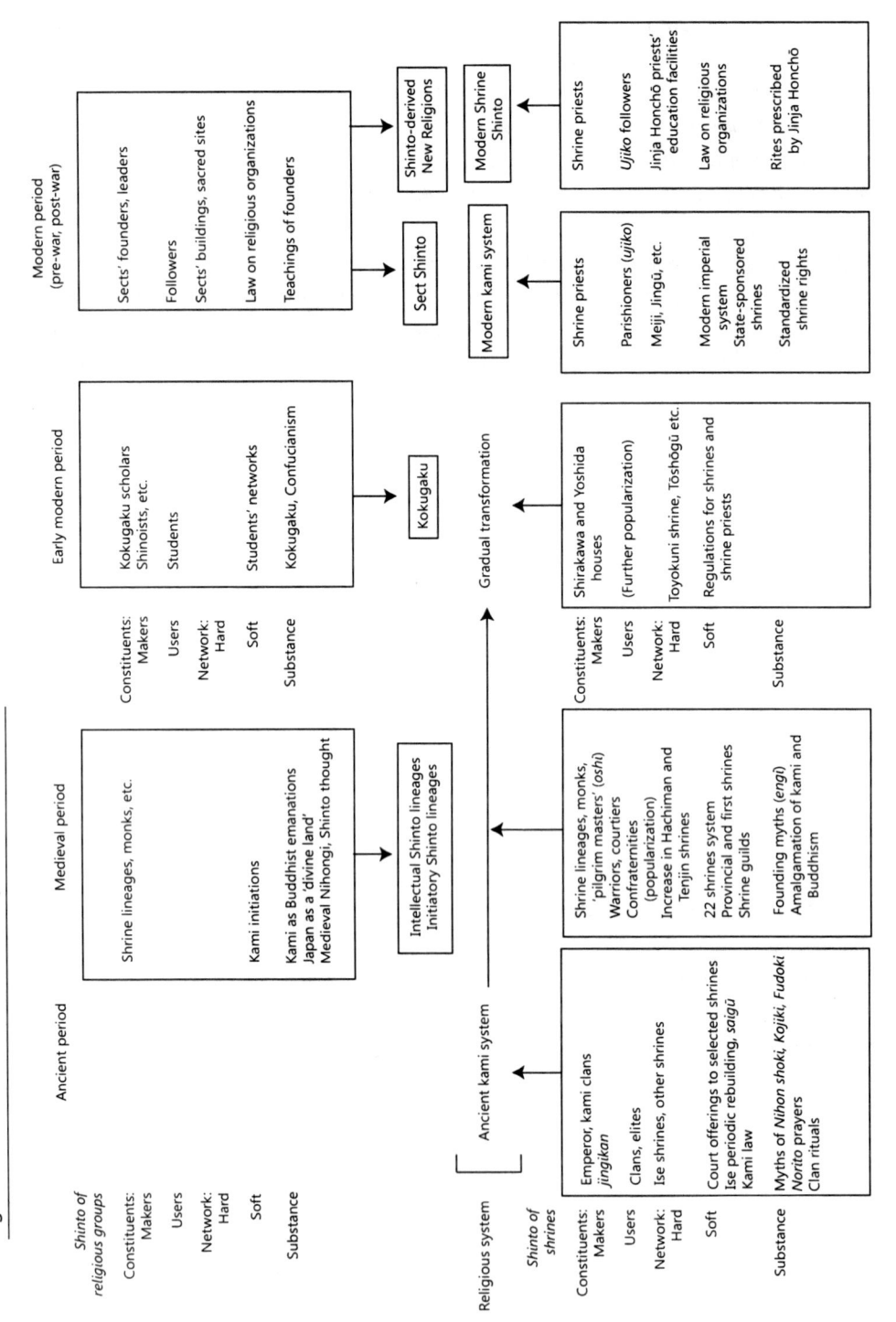

Figure 1: An Overview of Shinto history

	Ancient period	Medieval period	Early modern period	Modern period (pre-war, post-war)
Shinto of religious groups				
Constituents: Makers		Shrine lineages, monks, etc.	Kokugaku scholars Shinoists, etc.	Sects' founders, leaders
Users			Students	Followers
Network: Hard		Kami initiations	Students' networks	Sects' buildings, sacred sites Law on religious organizations
Soft				
Substance		Kami as Buddhist emanations Japan as a 'divine land' Medieval Nihongi, Shinto thought	Kokugaku, Confucianism	Teachings of founders

→ Intellectual Shinto lineages / Initiatory Shinto lineages → Kokugaku → Sect Shinto / Shinto-derived New Religions

→ Modern Shrine Shinto

Religious system	Ancient kami system	→ Gradual transformation →		Modern kami system
Shinto of shrines				
Constituents: Makers	Emperor, kami clans *jingikan*	Shrine lineages, monks, 'pilgrim masters' (*oshi*) Warriors, courtiers	Shirakawa and Yoshida houses	Shrine priests
Users	Clans, elites	Confraternities (popularization)	(Further popularization)	Parishioners (*ujiko*)
Network: Hard	Ise shrines, other shrines	Increase in Hachiman and Tenjin shrines 22 shrines system Provincial and first shrines Shrine guilds	Toyokuni shrine, Tōshōgū etc.	Meiji, Jingū, etc. Modern imperial system State-sponsored shrines
Soft	Court offerings to selected shrines Ise periodic rebuilding, *saigū* Kami law		Regulations for shrines and shrine priests	Standardized shrine rights
Substance	Myths of *Nihon shoki, Kojiki, Fudoki Norito* prayers Clan rituals	Founding myths (*engi*) Amalgamation of kami and Buddhism		

Modern Shrine Shinto:
- Shrine priests
- Ujiko followers
- Jinja Honchō priests' education facilities
- Law on religious organizations
- Rites prescribed by Jinja Honchō

Zoroastrianism

By Eugene F. Gorski

To set the background for our study of Zoroastrianism [...] we focus first on the stepping stones to these traditions, that is, the ancient Aryans[1] and their pre-Axial religion.

THE ARYANS: AN ANCIENT PEOPLE

We begin with Central Asia in the millennium before the Axial Age by examining the cultural and religious practices of an ancient, loose-knit network of tribes that inhabited, from about 4500 BCE, the steppes of southern Russia, east of the Volga River and north of the Caspian Sea. Today this area is roughly the Ukraine to west Kazakhstan. Five thousand years ago, this territory was for the most part barren desert that had little rainfall and that suffered severe cold winters and unkind summers. A great deal is not known about these people of the Central Asian steppes in the pre-Axial period. But there is a consensus

Eugene F. Gorski, "Zoroastrianism," *Theology of Religions: A Sourcebook for Interreligious Study*, pp. 45–62. Copyright © 2008 by Paulist Press. Reprinted with permission.

among scholars that they shared a common culture and identified themselves as the Aryans. Their name meant something like "noble" or "honorable" and, therefore, was not an ethnic or racial term but rather an assertion of their tribal pride. Because they spoke a language that would form the basis of several Asiatic and European tongues, they are also identified as Indo-Europeans. In the middle of the third millennium BCE, some of the tribes began a gradual migration to northern Europe, the northern Mediterranean region, as far west as Ireland, and southward to Iran and India. Careful analysis of the languages as diverse as Icelandic, German, Gaelic, Latin and Greek, Russian, Persian, Sanskrit, Sinhalese, and English has determined that these languages derive from what was once a single language. Over a period of time, the descendents of these Central Asians dispersed through Eurasia, and this single language developed into the dozens of tongues and dialects that are referred to as the Indo-European family of languages.

Of the several groups that migrated from the Central Asian region, we are most interested in those who traveled southward into regions now occupied by the countries of Iran and India. To distinguish this group from the other members of the Indo-European peoples, we refer to them as *Indo-Iranians*. These people remained together on the Caucasian steppes until about four thousand years ago, when they slowly drifted apart and migrated in two separate directions. The Iranian branch entered into and remained in Iran, while some of them ventured further into Mesopotamia, the area of present-day Iraq. The Indo branch immigrated into Afghanistan and then into the Indus Valley, gradually expanding across northern India. As the Indo-Iranians separated, their languages evolved from one another, but because they were similar enough, communication was still possible. The Iranian tribes spoke a dialect we call *Avestan* because now it only exists in a collection of sacred scriptures known as the *Avesta*. The group that migrated to India spoke a form of the language we now know as Sanskrit.

When each group arrived at its final destination, they called their new territory "the land of the nobles." For the sake of clarity, we use the term *Indo-Aryans* to refer to the group that settled in India and the word *Iranians* to identify the group that ended up in Iran. In what follows we focus on these two groups before they split, when they were united in Central Asia and beginning their southward movement. For this period we simply call them the Indo-Aryans.

Indo-Iranian Life and Religion

What we know about the Indo-Iranians comes mainly from two sources: the *Rig Veda*, the oldest extant Indo-European text, and the *Avesta*, a somewhat later text from Iran; both were originally kept in oral tradition. Because these documents were composed before the split, they communicate not a small part about the life of the Indo-Iranians. These people lived peacefully together and shared the same culture and religious traditions until about 1500 BCE.[2] They were arranged into tribes with no formal governing structures. As nomadic and semi-nomadic shepherds and cattle herders, they wandered about in relatively small areas, seeking pastureland for their animals. Because they had no real enemies, and no desire to conquer new territories, they were a peaceful people with a static, sedentary existence. Since they had not yet learned to tame horses, the earliest Indo-Iranians did not travel far, and they knew nothing about the kind of warfare that the horse made possible for other ancient societies. It seems they existed for centuries with hardly any significant cultural changes.

As much as it can be reconstructed from our limited resources, the simple and serene religion of the Indo-Iranians was based on a commonsensical view for people living in a harsh environment of Central Asia. Like other pre-Axial peoples, they had their gods, their beliefs about the nature of the world, and their rituals that enabled them to understand and influence those gods and that world.

The gods were of several kinds, related to the various aspects of everyday life. Especially important to the common people were the gods who controlled parts of the natural world, like the Sky and the Earth, the Sun and the Moon. In addition to these gods of nature, the deities associated with ritual practices were particularly important, namely the Fire, the Water, and a vision-inducing substance called *haoma* in the Avestan dialect and *soma* in Sanskrit. These divinities had special significance for the priests.

A third category of divine beings was the *ahuras* in Avestan, or *asuras* in Sanskrit, words that simply mean "lord." The greatest of the *ahuras* was Mazda, the Lord of Wisdom. Later, in the Zoroastrian religious reform, we will see how Lord Mazda is given a very prominent role, becoming the most important god of all Iranians. And finally, there were many lesser divinities called "the shiny ones": *deva* in Sanskrit and *daeva* in Avestan. The shiny ones represented such qualities as courage and justice.

In addition to this complex world of spirit and gods, the Indo-Iranians believed in a more abstract and impersonal principle of order. Those who spoke Sanskrit called it *rta*, and the Avestan speakers referred to it as *asha*. Both words signify a type of natural law that preserved cosmic order, maintaining the sun on its path and the seasons following in proper sequence. *Rta* and *asha* had a moral as well as a cosmological dimension, and in this sense meant an absolute principle for appropriate human behavior and for divine behavior, since the deities themselves were also obliged to conform to *rta* and *asha*.

Conformity to the moral law promoted harmony and well-being for the individual and for society. But the principle of order was opposed by another power that accounted for disharmony and chaos; by the Iranians it was called *druj*. Since these two principles were diametrically opposed to one another, the Indo-Iranians thought it necessary to help maintain and strengthen *asha*, the element of order. They were convinced they could do this by means of ritual. Proper observance of the religious rites thus enhanced the force of *asha* and promoted harmony in the world. This is one instance of the pre-Axial practice of cosmic maintenance, founded on the responsibility that people experienced for collaborating with the processes on which their lives depended.

Indo-Iranian Creation Story

We observe how these ritual practices promoted social and cosmological harmony. To understand pre-Axial rituals in any culture, it is important to have a grasp of its belief about the origins of the world as treated in its cosmologies or creation stories. Those who perform religious rites often understand themselves as reenacting the divine work of creation and thereby renewing creation. To illustrate this, we consider the world's creation taken from the Avestan texts and then show its relationship to ritual practices.

The Indo-Iranians' creation story in the Avestan version states that the Earth was created in seven stages. First, the sky was depicted as a gigantic inverted bowl made of beautiful stone. Second, water was created, covering the bottom of the sky shell. Third, solid earth was brought into being, floating on the water. In the fourth, fifth, and sixth stages, life was added in the form of one plant, one animal, a bull, and one man with the name of Yima or Yama. In the seventh stage, fire was added. In a last act of creation, the gods performed the first ritual sacrifice. By crushing and dismembering the plant, the bull, and the man, they created new life. The world now was populated and began the course of *asha* by means of death and reproduction.

Indo-Iranian Rituals

In a setting of rituals of various sorts, the Indo-Iranians reenacted the primordial sacrifice to preserve the cosmic and moral order and to ensure that new life properly replaced the old. The rituals performed were of many types, from the simple to the complex.

Those that were the simplest were offerings of libations to the gods of Water and Fire. In the arid and cold regions of Central Asia, the importance of these two elements is evident. Water was given a libation of milk and plant leaves to symbolize the animal and vegetable domains. These libations gave back to the divine powers the necessary elements that they needed to continue productivity and harmony. The Water goddess was fortified by these gifts. Fire had great importance for warmth in the cold of winter and for the cooking of food stuffs. Offerings to Fire, like libations to Water, were from the two realms: incense and wood from plants and animal fat from cooked meat. Melting fat made the flames blaze up, strengthening the fire.

The most sacred of the fire rituals often involved blood offerings, usually of goats, sheep, or cattle. This was done to replenish the energies the gods used to maintain world order and to obtain from them other practical goods. It was believed that the sacrifices placed an obligation on the deities worshiped to respond with benefits of purely material and mundane value, such as wealth, health, abundant harvests, and security. It should be noted that since they felt very close to their cattle and desired to respect the sacred life that united all creatures,[3] the ritualistic slaughter of a beast was executed in a humane manner, and its spirit consecrated to the sacred archetypical domestic animal. Consecrated and cooked meat offered to the gods was then eaten by the participants of the sacrifice. Because of their respect for animal life, the Indo-Iranians ate only consecrated meat of their domesticated animals. Even before killing a wild animal for food, hunters said prayers to assure the safe return of the animal's spirit to the Soul of the Bull. The Aryans would never lose this deep respect for the *spirit* that they shared with others, and this would become an important principle of their Axial Age. And as they came to realize that it was necessary that other creatures give up their lives in sacrifice so that others may live and the cosmos continue in existence, self-sacrifice became highly valued. No progress, material or spiritual, could be made without self-sacrifice. This too would become one of the principles of the Axial Age.

The priest conducted rituals that also involved a beverage known by *soma* in Sanskrit or *haoma* in Avestan. This substance, regarded as a deity, was found in a special species of plant whose identity is unknown today. Soma's properties induced in those who imbibed it to feel ecstatic, liberated from their ordinary world and transported to the realm of the gods. By drinking soma, the Indo-Iranians experienced what they believed to be the apex of existence: a temporary ecstasy that gave a sense of immortality, freedom from suffering and fear, communion with the gods and the spirits, and intense pleasure. Soma, then, was the means of expanding the mind to ponder the deepest possibilities of human existence; it gave a glimpse to the Indo-Iranians of a life free of suffering and fear. In the centuries to come, those who inherited their traditions would endeavor to seek similar experiences by means of meditation and ascetic practices rather than by physical substances.

Conclusion

We have now come to that time in history that marks the eve of the Axial Age, even though further developments in Indo-Iranian religions will occur before it dawns. But we are now able to make some statements about Indo-Iranian religion and culture that will facilitate our understanding of the Axial transformation that will come about in Iran and later in India. We have seen that the main purpose of religion for these peoples at this time was to collaborate with the gods and goddesses, or with an abstract impersonal principle, in the processes and functions of life. They were convinced that they experienced a close affinity with various aspects of the natural and divine worlds, and that it was necessary for them to do their part in keeping both the natural and social worlds in good working order, and it was clear that they had a close relationship with other aspects of the natural and divine worlds.

As supported by religious practices that promoted cosmic maintenance and keeping the world working in an orderly fashion, their culture was fairly conservative and not especially interested in change. Critical thinking and innovation in such societies tended to be viewed with suspicion and frequently looked upon even as sacrilegious since it represented departure from the primordial acts of the gods.

Indo-Iranians on the Threshold of the Axial Age

In spite of the conservative forces operative in the Indo-Iranian culture, the way of life of these people did eventually undergo dramatic changes. We discuss these changes now and their consequences for religious life on the threshold of the Axial Age.

Aggression Begins

As the Indo-Iranians drifted south from the Central Asian steppes, they came in contact with one of the great civilizations of the ancient world, that of the highly advanced people of Mesopotamia. Around 1500 BCE, they began to trade with them, and from them they learned about the making of bronze weaponry and how to domesticate the horse and how to construct and use war chariots. As they mastered the skill of taming the wild horses of the steppes and harnessing them to their chariots, they experienced the exhilaration of mobility and long-distance travel. And thus the tranquil and serene life of the Aryans came to an end. Their access to the chariot and the implements of war completely disrupted their once-stable culture. A new method of livelihood now surfaced to supplement the passive tending of sheep and cows; this was stealing sheep and cows. Many of the later Indo-Iranians became cattle rustlers who conducted fierce attacks on neighboring settlements, engaging in raiding and stealing cattle and crops.

Violence escalated on the steppes and a heroic age began. "Might was right, chieftains sought gain and glory; and bards celebrated aggression, reckless courage, and military prowess."[4] The Sanskrit-speaking Aryans, who had become cattle rustlers, no longer cherished the values of their old religion concerning reciprocity, self-sacrifice, and kindness to animals. Their new fundamental purpose was to gain wealth and glory. For a long time, cattle and sheep had been the measure of prosperity among the Indo-Iranians. In addition to providing meat and milk, the animals were the source of leather and bones for tools, dung for fire, and also urine for the consecration of sacred implements used in rituals.

The violence of raiding not only changed the economy of the Indo-Iranians, it also upset their moral concerns and respect for the law. The pillaging cattle rustlers showed little concern for the weak and defenseless; whole villages might be destroyed in an afternoon just to enhance another clan's livestock holdings. As a result of this new way of life, there emerged a third class of individuals alongside the priests and the producers: the warlords and professional warriors. This new class soon became known for their love of rough living, hard drinking, and gambling. "There was an excitement and a thrill to living on the edge and outside the constraints of conventional society."[5] New gods who were more acceptable to the rising warrior caste began to appear and even dominate the forms of religion. Their hero was the god, Indra, the slayer of dragons, who rode in a chariot upon the clouds of heaven. As they fought, killed, and stole, they experienced themselves as one with Indra and the aggressive *devas* who had founded the world order by force of arms. Actually, by the time the *Rig Veda* got to India, Indra was already the dominant divine being. More than one-quarter of the one thousand hymns of praise are addressed to him alone.

Not all of the Indo-Iranians took on the cattle-rustling and village-pillaging style of life. And in fact a new type of nomenclature entered the vocabulary to identify and distinguish the two types of people. In ancient Iran, those who were the wicked ones, devoted to the way of disorder, were called *drujvants;* those who followed the old way of order, the path of stability, were call *ashavans*. The *ashavans* were shocked by the violent aggression of their kin. And because they believed that events on Earth always reflected cosmic events in the heavens of the gods, they concluded that the terrifying raids must have a divine prototype. Their fellow Aryans who hustled cattle and fought according to the model of Indra must be his earthly counterparts.

Zoroastrianism

Zoroastrianism was once the dominant religion of much of Greater Iran. Until about 2002 (CE), most of the published estimates for the world total of Zoroastrians were 100,000 to 125,000. Recent publications of many major encyclopedias and world almanacs indicate a population of 2 to 3.5 million.[6] Small Zoroastrian communities are found in India, Pakistan, and Iran, as well as major urban areas in the United States, Canada, the United Kingdom, Australia, and a worldwide diaspora. There are two main groups of persons who are adherents of this tradition: those of Indian Zoroastrian background, who are know as *Parsis* (or *Parsees*), and those of Iranian background. They are numerically small, but their influence in the present-day world is more than proportionate to their number. And from a historical point of view, the religion founded by Zoroaster is of inestimable significance.

Zoroaster is a later Greek translation of *Zarathustra*. Little is known about him. The leading scholar in this area, Mary Boyce, dates him around 1200 BCE. Most recent scholars place him somewhere before the beginning of the Axial Age. He lived in the eastern area of present-day Iran and came from a modest family living in semi-nomadic conditions, at a time when the cattle rustlers and outlaws were in the prime and *druj*, the principle of disorder, appeared to be dominating *asha*, the principle of order and harmony. Except from much later traditions and legendary sources, all the information we have about Zoroaster is from a text called the *Gathas*, or the verses, which are a part of the oldest *Avesta*, the basic scripture of Zoroaster's religion. It is believed that these verses were composed by Zoroaster himself as he was moved by forces of inspiration. They are written in an archaic dialect very close to the Sanskrit of the *Rig Veda;* they are not sermons and didactic statements but rather spontaneous prayers addressed to the deity.

Zoroaster: Priest and Prophet

The *Gathas* indicate that Zoroaster was a priest, an authorized specialist. He believed that Mazda was the greatest of the *ahuras*: he was the single divine transcendent source of everything that was good, Lord of Wisdom and Justice, different in kind from any other divinity.[7] In Mazda's retinue there were seven luminous beings—the "Holy Immortals"—who were also divine, each manifesting one of Mazda's benign attributes. It is probable that Zoroaster came to this position by reflection on the creation story, which claimed that in the beginning there had been one plant, one animal, and one human being. It was logical to assume that originally there had been one god.[8]

According to tradition, at the age of thirty he had a compelling mystical experience in which he was led into the presence of Ahura Mazda and six other resplendent beings known collectively as the *hepatad*, the "seven." There he was graced with a special disclosure that persuaded him that he had a new life goal, a new vocation: this was to oppose the popular polytheism of his time and to effect a religious reform, to call his people to practice a true and final religion based on faith in Mazda.

Zoroaster's response to his new life goal was both conservative and revolutionary. As a priest and prophet faithful to the tradition, he urged his fellow Iranians to return to a respect for the principle of good order and harmony. As an innovator, however, he added a new perspective to the traditional worldview that made it an extremely engaging vision of the world. His innovative theology of reform had two principle dimensions, both directed to simplification. First, with passion he urged worship of Ahura Mazda as the superior deity, greater even than Varuna, the other *ahuras,* and the seven luminous beings. He claimed that the other *ahuras* and divinities were simply emanations or partial manifestations of Mazda, who was the only uncreated God and the agent of the seven stages creation theme.

Monotheistic Tendency

His second innovation was to simplify the pantheon by attributing specific moral characteristics to the other deities. All the beings that constituted the ensemble of spirits, *daevas* and *ahuras* were now plainly associated either with good or with evil. Because the *daevas* like Indra were worshiped by cattle rustlers, whom Zoroaster called the "Followers of the Lie," he reserved the word *daeva* exclusively for the wicked gods and the word *ahura* for the gods who were good and just. In accord with this theological simplification, he also declared the existence of an independent evil deity among the *daevas*, an entirely evil supernatural being called *Angra Mainyu,* or later by the name of *Ahriman.* The source of everything evil was Angra Mainyu, the wicked deity believed to be equal in power and opposed to Lord Mazda. Angra Mainyu had inspired the cruelty of Indra and the cattle raiders, who allied themselves with him and decided to fight alongside him in his battle against the good. Zoroaster therefore conceived of two superior beings, one completely good and other completely evil, hooked in mortal battle since the beginning of time, each one fighting for victory of his principles and powers.

Zoroaster's faith, then, was in several deities, but nevertheless, there was a monotheistic tendency in his religious convictions. For Lord Mazda was believed to be the Supreme God, the first deity to exist, the creative source of the Holy Immortals, who were of "one mind, one voice, one act" with him and fought with him in war against the forces of evil (identified in later time with Satan).[9]

Fundamental Moral Option

In line with his experience of the good and the evil transcendent deities, he taught that each human being must make a choice between one or the other. Persons are not able to avoid the responsibility of associating themselves with good or with evil, and they are obliged to live accordingly. As the *daevas* had made a choice, individual human beings are also faced with a similar decision. Everything resolved to a simple, uncomplicated choice, a fundamental option. Are you on the side of the good or of evil? It should be noted here that this is one of the points at which Zoroaster anticipates the transformation of the Axial Age. Repeatedly, as our study of the religions of the Axial Age continues, we encounter this call to make a decision, fundamentally to align one's life with the good or the evil as it is experienced and conceived of by the Axial sages. It is a situation in which demands are made on persons as individuals to accept responsibility for the moral quality of their words and actions.

In cooperation with Lord Mazda, men and women were to oppose the violence that had destroyed the peaceful world of the steppes and to resist all forces of evil. A new era had dawned; everybody, gods and humans alike, were obliged to make a fundamental choice between good and evil. Good persons must no longer invite Indra into the sacred precinct and offer sacrificial worship. Instead their calling was to defeat the *daevas* and their wicked henchmen, the cattle raiders. Only with the power of Mazda could peace, justice, and security be secured in the steppes. While he continued in his life to receive the revelations of Mazda, this initial visionary experience was a principle turning point in his life; it transformed him from a priest to a prophet.

The command given to Zoroaster was to mobilize his people in a holy war against the terror and violence of their environment and the evil in the human soul. While human beings are vulnerable to the suggestions of the evil forces, they are also endowed with freedom to determine their own actions, and therefore they are able to choose between right and wrong. It was Mazda's will and their religious duty to transcend their human weaknesses, believe in him, and freely choose what is good and virtuous. The eternal fate and salvation of each person would be determined by the choices he or she made between good and evil.

In the religion established by Zoroaster (which was originally called *Zarathustrianism*), life was now seen as a battlefield in which all persons had a role. This basic message and theology of Zoroaster were reinforced by the various rituals of Zoroastrianism. Men and women who had committed themselves to Mazda were to purify their environment from dirt and pollution. In their efforts to separate good from evil, they would liberate the world for Lord Mazda. They were to pray five times daily and counter the influence of evil by meditating on the menace of evil and falsehood. In their reflections they would see that the world was in a period of raging cosmic conflict, racing toward an apocalyptic conflict. Prayer was to be performed standing in the presence of fire. If the devotee was outside in natural setting, the fire might be the sun. The sun had now become closely connected with Ahura Mazda. Like their Indo-Aryan relatives, the Iranians followed the custom of keeping the sacred fire continuously lit. These fire rituals were actually a part of the Zoroastrian practice of purification. The elements that made up the world need to be made clean and uncontaminated. The Zoroastrians also celebrate seven major festivals, associated mainly with the rhythms of agricultural life.

Zoroaster believed that individual persons would be judged on the fourth day after their death. Those who were judged good were to be led to the heavens across a wide bridge. There in the heavens they would enjoy the company of Mazda and the other *ashavans*. Those who were judged evil were obliged to cross an extremely narrow bridge. Without fail, they tumbled as they crossed and landed in the abyss of hell, where they suffered painfully for their sins in the place ruled over by the Evil One.

Apocalyptic Conclusion

A final cosmic destiny was also envisioned by Zoroaster; the assignment to heaven or to hell was only temporary. He believed the history of all humankind was directed in a specific direction toward a unique end. In a final battle it was anticipated that Ahura Mazda would bring the present world order to an end and save all of creation by a complete triumphant victory over evil and establish a reign of right and truth. There would be a general resurrection, and in a final judgment the eternal fate of each person would be determined by the choices he or she had made between good and evil; the wicked would be wiped from the face of the world and, along with the evil god, Angra Mainyu, sent to hell. The universe would be restored to its original pristine condition. Those human beings who had been observant of the divine will and were saved would be rewarded with everlasting life in heaven in union with Mazda; they would be like gods, free from sickness, old age, and mortality.

Zoroaster was unlike his contemporaries around the world in that he saw time moving forward in a linear fashion, from a beginning to a final apocalyptic conclusion. The end of the world would come in the universal battle between good and evil to a final climax. Then the forces of good would prevail and the devil would be completely crushed and banished from all existence. The Evil One and his associates, as well as hell and all its dwellers, would be exterminated, and paradise would be established on Earth.

It is possible that Zoroaster connected this vision of the final end with a bodily resurrection of the dead; those who had initially gone to heaven would return to Earth to continue life, joined again with their material parts. It seems too that Zoroaster anticipated the coming of a savior or apocalyptic judge who would play a role in the final drama. The Avestan texts allude to this future redeemer as a *saoshyant*. The *saoshyant* would be born of a virgin who had conceived by bathing in a lake in which Zoroaster's semen had been miraculously preserved.

Zoroaster's Innovative Concepts

These ideas—a grand cosmic struggle between good and evil, time progressing toward a final apocalyptic climax, the appearance of a redeemer-judge, the resurrection of the dead, and the need of humans to choose sides—all comprise Zoroaster's innovative concepts. "We can't say for certain that all these ideas originated with him; perhaps he was in conversation with like-minded persons or with ancient traditions. But we can say that it was through Zoroaster's influence and prophetic message that these ideas were widely decimated among the Iranians."[10] Mark W. Muesse points out the features that made Zoroaster's vision so compelling to many of his contemporaries:

First, Zoroaster's vision implied a decisive role for human beings. To Zoroaster, people were not the pawns of the gods. The gods did not intervene and fool with the lives of hapless human beings. Persons had a choice to make, and that choice was essential. It determined the individual's future and shaped the cosmic drama itself. The gods were at war, and human beings had to act to ensure the side of right prevailed. In this way Zoroaster greatly elevated the importance of human moral responsibility.[11]

On the whole, the call to this kind of personal choice and obligation is an innovation in the history of religions because it is connected with fresh ideas about what it means to be human. For Zoroaster, the moral and religious decision of the individual now determines the status and quality of his or her personal destiny. The future existence of a person, especially in the world to come, depends on one's behavior here and now in history. So to the simple choice concerning the decision for the good or for evil, Zoroaster added another reality. The individual's ultimate destiny was dependent on the choice he or she made. He was of the conviction that a person's final end as a human being was contingent on whether he or she opted for the wholly good Mazda or the wholly evil Ahriman. This idea is something new for the times and common across the axial centers in history the notion of the moral choice and its consequences for the future constituted a remarkable concept. The first atypical element about it is its implication that the individual person in fact has a destiny beyond this historical life. Before the dawning of the Axial Age such a belief was not widely accepted. It is true that some may have had the belief that prominent individuals like the king were favored with a life after death. But even these notions were rarely well defined and clearly developed. With the coming of the Axial Age, however, the thought that individuals might have a destiny in a world to come came to be more commonly accepted.

But even more unusual was Zoroaster's claim that one's prospects for a life hereafter were contingent on the quality of one's moral choices. Even in those civilizations that held to a conception of an afterlife, very rarely was one's destiny dependent on one's moral behavior. An individual's existence after death might be predicated on the effectiveness of ritual practice, whether or not one had pleased the gods with sacrifices of enough quality, or perhaps on the doing of exceptional deeds, such as heroic bravery in battle. But seldom do we find the claim before the Axial Age that the individual's destiny is contingent on moral decision and behavior. This is in fact one of the important themes of the Axial transformation.

Mark W. Muesse also underlines the important way Zoroaster's vision gave meaning to human suffering and promised ultimate reward for it.

> Those suffering from an unkind fate from thieves and cattle rustlers, from illness and deprivation could see their plight in much larger context. Their anguish and misery was part of a grand drama involving the entire world and was not just bad luck or random happenstance. For their suffering the righteous would be given ample reparations. Immortal life in paradise—free of any and all evil—would suffice to make earthly suffering seem insignificant by comparison. And they would be satisfied by the sense the evil ones, too, would receive their just deserts.[12]

Foreshadowing the Axial Age

Zoroaster's teaching was based on a cosmic combat between good and evil, a traumatized vision that was vengeful and filled with imagery of burning, terror, and extermination. It inspired a militant spirituality. In this sense it participated in the piety of pre-Axial religion. In making a cosmic agon between good and evil central to his message, Zoroaster belongs to the old spiritual world. However, because his vision was passionately ethical, he did look forward to the Axial Age. For he tried to bring some morality to the ethos of war: heroes were to make efforts to counter aggression and not to terrorize their fellow creatures; the holy warrior was dedicated to peace; those who opted to fight for Lord Mazda were characterized by the virtues of patience, discipline, courage; they were to defend all good creatures from the assaults of the wicked. When Zoroastrians defended the weak, cared for their cattle, and purified their natural environment, they became bonded with Mazda and joined the struggle of the Immortals against the Hostile Spirit. Consequently, because of his strong emphasis on ethics, Zoroaster foreshadowed the Axial sages who came centuries later and made efforts to counter the cruelty and aggression of their time by promoting spirituality based on nonviolence.

Opposition, Growth, and Impact

In spite of its being rooted in ancient Aryan tradition, Zoroaster's vision was received with strong hostility. The people of his time found it too difficult, and some were shocked by his belief that all persons, not just the elite, could reach salvation. The established religious authorities opposed his teaching because it threatened to undermine their own traditional doctrine. After years of preaching to his own tribe, Zoroaster gained only *one* convert! Eventually he departed from his village and found a patron in the chief of another tribe, who established the Zoroastrian faith in his territory. One tradition states that Zoroaster was killed by rival priests who were furious because of his rejection of the old religion. By the end of the second millennium BCE, the Avestan Aryans had migrated and settled in eastern Persia, where Zoroastrianism became the national religion.

It should be noted that parallels exist between Zoroastrianism and some of the doctrines of the Middle Eastern religions. In Judaism and Christianity, parallels may be found with Zoroaster's doctrine of transcendence and salvation: the end of the world, the resurrection, heaven and hell, immortality, the last judgment, and God's operation through the Spirit. In the beliefs of Islamic Arabs, parallels can be observed with the vision of the approaching last judgment foretold by Zoroaster, and then by Jews and Christians. One may wonder whether the parallels among the traditions are coincidental or whether there has been some actual historical influence from one tradition to the others. This has been, and still remains, a controversial issue. Some scholars working in this area propose that formative Judaism, Christianity, and Islam were shaped directly or indirectly by the more ancient Zoroastrian beliefs. "This influence," states Mark Muesse,

> is difficult to document and prove conclusively because the case is based largely on circumstantial evidence. There are no passages in the Bible or the Qur'an that quote from the Gathas or even paraphrase it ... Early Jewish and Christian theologians probably never read any of the Zoroastrian scriptures because most of Zoroaster's religion remained in oral tradition for centuries.[13]

We may hold that if there was infiltration of Zoroastrian ideas, perhaps it occurred in a less formal way as Jews came into contact with Zoroastrian adherents and engaged in conversation and trade with them and observed their practices. In any case, there are no valid grounds to detract from the conviction of Jews, Christians, and Muslims that their religions are unique and of divine origin.

With the rise of Islam, the twelve hundred years of Zoroastrian imperial history came to an end in the seventh century CE. Within one hundred years of the Arab conquest, many Zoroastrians departed from Persia. In the tenth century, a band of Zoroastrians sought religious freedom in India, where they are known as *Parsis*, people of Pars (Persia). There the original teaching endures to the present. And Zoroaster is often revered more than a prophet, almost as a manifestation of the divine. For all Zoroastrians, he is the great role model, the strong defender of the true faith, the uncompromising enemy of evil, and the supporter of all that is good. In modern times it is estimated, as we have seen, that there are 2 to 3.5 million Zoroastrians in the world.

Notes

1. Here the term *Aryans* is to be distinguished from the same term as used by Adolph Hitler. He twisted the theories of the German archeologist and ethnohistorian Gustaf Kossinna (1858–1931) to put forward the Aryans as a master race of Indo-Europeans, who were supposed to be of Nordic appearance and directly ancestral to the Germans.

2. Mary Boyce, *Zoroastrians: Their Religious Beliefs and Practices* (London, Boston and Henley: Routledge & Kegan Paul, 1979), 2; Peter Clark, *Zoroastrianism: An Introduction to an Ancient Faith* (Brighton, Portland, UK: Sussex Academic Press, 1998), 18.
3. Mircea Eliade, *The Myth of the Eternal Return, or Cosmos and History*, trans. Willard R. Trask (London: Routledge & Kegan Paul, 1955), 1–34.
4. Karen Armstrong, *The Great Transformation: The Beginning of Our Religious Traditions* (New York/Toronto: Knopf, 2006), 7.
5. Mark W. Muesse, *Religions of the Axial Age: An Approach to the World's Religions* (Chantilly, VA: Teaching Company, 2007), part 1, 39.
6. *Major Religions of the World Ranked by Number of Adherents.* Available at: http://www.adherents.com/Relgions_By_Adherents.html.
7. Clark, *Zoroastrianism*, 4–6.
8. Boyce, *Zoroastrianism*, 20–23
9. Yasna 19:16–18. Quotations from the Zoroastrian scriptures are taken from Mary Boyce, ed. and trans., *Textual Sources for the Study of Zoroastrianism* (Totowa, NJ: Barnes & Noble Books, 1984); cited in Armstrong, *Great Transformation*, 8. The term *Yasna* refers to the Zoroastrian daily liturgy of preparation of *haoma* and offerings to Fire and Water; the term, as used here, also refers to the title of the text recited in the ceremony.
10. Muesse, *Religions of the Axial Age*, part 1, 55.
11. Ibid.
12. Ibid., 55–56.
13. Ibid., 57.

Chapter Review

1. How much do we know about Zarathustra?
2. Describe Zarathustra's view of divinity.
3. How did Zarathustra arrive at a monotheism.
4. Explain Zoroastrian judgement.
5. Describe Zoroastrian apocalypticism.
6. What is the origin of the Aryan people?
7. Describe the most sacred of the fire rituals.

Judaism

By Marc H. Ellis

Where We Have Come From/Where We Have Arrived

I was born in 1952 and, like all Jews of my generation, the shadow of the Holocaust permeated everything. Or almost everything. In those early years of my life, the Holocaust was as yet unnamed; the mass murder of Jews was too close at hand. The enormity took time to absorb and become articulated. The very name *Holocaust* lay years ahead, the experience awaiting that horrific name. I was surrounded by Hebrew schoolteachers from Europe, but their experience was kept from us, spoken, if at all, only in whispers. Something terrible had happened to Jews and I knew this without the direct speech and visuals we have become accustomed to today. The film reels we did see in movie theaters, as trailers to the main event, were about the victorious Allies in World War II. The suffering of the war seemed even, in these news reels, to be immense. The victims, however, remained unnamed, shorn of their particularity. Jews there were—we all knew this—but the enormity was, quite correctly, kept from us.

Marc H. Ellis, "Judaism," *The Hope of Liberation in World Religions*, ed. Miguel A. De La Torre, pp. 65–89. Copyright © 2008 by Baylor University Press. Reprinted with permission.

America was already engaged in a new war, the cold war, and Europe, undergoing its own reconstruction, needed Germany, at least West Germany, to pull its weight in defense of freedom and democracy. Dwelling on the old war—over just a decade or so—was too dangerous. The air raid drills we took part in at school were needed because of the Soviet Union, not the dreaded but defeated Nazis. The Nazis were old hat and besides, we were in America, a country that looked toward the future; we represented the ever-present dawn of freedom. In our minds Americans were victors, not victims. As Jews we are part of this new dawn; we did not want to be known or to see ourselves as victims.

All of this changed and rapidly, the late 1950s and early 1960s turning on the pivot of the 1967 Arab-Israeli war, six days in June when the Holocaust was named and its twin Israel became the center of Jewish existence. Israel, of course, was already there, founded in 1948, just three years after the end of World War II. Like the Holocaust, Israel had not yet been named as central to Jewish existence; I, like most American Jews, knew Israel as a small pioneering state that we should support and of which we should be proud. The naming of the Holocaust was a political response to and for the suffering of the Jews of Europe, the ones who were forced to or had chosen to settle in Palestine during and after the war. The 1967 war came upon us like a wave, gathering momentum as it came closer to our shore. The reports of the modernizing media were more vivid and direct; the threat to the Jews of Israel through what we knew at the time to be hostile Arab countries became palpable. When the war began there was almost a sigh of relief, and the heightened tension now had a release point. Yet many also were filled with despair, the sense that Israel might lose the war, that there would then be another slaughter of Jews. Another Holocaust?

The threat of another slaughter and the incredible lightning victory of Israel—the breathtaking capture of Jerusalem—ignited a heightened Jewish sensibility that is difficult to describe. I had always been proud to be a Jew; now there was a public pride that moved beyond the individual, a pride that was recognized by others as well. A public sense of the importance of being a Jew was inscribed in America and Europe especially, a *novum* in Jewish history, almost as if the Holocaust and Israel had brought Jews and the world to a new level of understanding and respect for Jews and Judaism. There, basking in victory—as if all Jews had taken part in the war—we could now articulate and name our suffering as having experienced a Holocaust. In our newfound power it was safe to speak of the terror, the terror of terrors, without being victims now and without our expression leading to a new round of victimization.

Israel, then, could also be named as the response to the horror of the Holocaust; the twinning of memory and nation became a twinning in thought and discourse. Jews were on the offense as a compensation for the years, the millennia, of being underneath, beholden, discriminated against, and murdered. Now in the light of day we could celebrate our Jewishness in the boldest manner, speaking of our suffering and empowerment without restraint. It was like a wave breaking through the dam of history; now we as Jews could enact our world-shaking drama outside the synagogue, on stage and screen, television news and drama, the daily newspapers commemorating our suffering and celebrating our new power. These were heady days to be a Jew. Yet even then there were rumblings, warnings that the glory of victory would somehow unravel, an unraveling unlike earlier times when the acceptance of Jews in society would suffer a reversal; it was acceptance followed by nightmare.

The warning first came within the naming of the Holocaust. Though named within Israel's victory, the discourse around the Holocaust was naturally somber. The visuals of the death camps were followed by dramatizations and narratives. Elie Wiesel's *Night*, his autobiography of the time spent in Auschwitz, became a constant companion to many Jews and in classrooms around the nation. First in the universities, then in the high schools, and sometimes even in junior high or elementary schools, the Holocaust began to be consumed by Jews and non-Jews alike. Questions about God and humanity were present throughout a new and ominous landscape of depictions of the Holocaust, produced by a generation of Jewish writers searching for words to evoke the horrors of an experience so outrageous and outlandish.

I experienced this in its initial phase with one of these Holocaust commentators, Richard Rubenstein, whose 1966 book *After Auschwitz* helped frame the ensuing years of Holocaust discussion. Like Wiesel's *Night*, but in theological rather than experiential language, *After Auschwitz* confronts the ancient beliefs about the God of history, doubts the efficacy of the covenant, and is suspicious about the goodness of humanity. After all, in the middle of the twentieth century, in thoroughly modern and Christian Europe, the ancient animus against the Jews took on its most radical and deadly form.

Whereas Christianity placed the Jews in a damning but ironically protecting eschatological reserve, the Nazis propounded the eschatology of annihilation. Christianity believed that the Jews were being punished for their sins of turning away from Jesus and God; one day even the Jews would see the light and at that moment the last days of creation would begin. Jesus would return as the Christ; the messianic reign would commence.

The Nazis believed none of that. There was no reason for Jews to exist; their very existence threatened the possibility that the Nazis could continue to reign on earth. The Nazi mission toward Jews was clear, and their plan of annihilating the Jews gained currency. Its implementation was indeed described in theological terms as the good that surpassed all the difficulties of the mission. The Nazis would be remembered first and foremost for accomplishing the mission of making the world free of Jews.

Where was God in the death camps? Where was humanity? What could we say of both God and humanity after Auschwitz? To some extent Wiesel and Rubenstein agreed on the answers to these questions: neither God nor humanity could be trusted with the Jews. Only Jews could take Jewish history to its depths and rebuild it. It was the obligation of all Jews, whatever their political or religious affiliations, to mourn the dead and rebuild Jewish life. At the center of that rebuilding was Israel, the state, which would lead to the rebuilding of the people Israel. They were together now, state and people, where they had been separate for too long, and tragically so.

Could the Holocaust have happened if the state of Israel had existed? Historically the answer was theoretical but Jews could never afford the test of theory again. Israel the state was absolutely necessary so that no one would attempt such an assault on Jews ever again. This time any attempt would be limited by the knowledge that Jews had their own state and their own army. If, after this warning, an attempt was made, it would be beaten back. If the state of Israel was defeated it would go down fighting. Never again would Jews be weak and helpless; never again would Jews go down without a fight.

Rubenstein in particular sounded this note; it resonated with Jews around the world. Yet there was another note within the burgeoning commentaries on Jewish life after the Holocaust. As particular victims, Jews had the responsibility of self-protection and self-empowerment. Beyond self-interest, however, was a universal applicability of the need for protection and empowerment; never again should anything approaching genocide happen to any community or people. This was the reason for the subtext of reflections on the Holocaust. In light of Jewish suffering, the world should be on permanent guard against other political, military, and religious configurations that might lead to genocide.

Over the years the emphasis on Jewish particularity in suffering and empowerment took hold. The secondary, more universal emphasis remained, though in a weakened way. Jewish empowerment in Israel assumed a role of its own and soon, by the 1980s for sure, a defensive posture toward Israel, and thus toward the Holocaust, took center stage.

The reason for this was simple and continues today. The lightning victory of Israel in the 1967 war yielded territory: the eastern part of Jerusalem, immediately and unilaterally annexed by Israel days after the war's end; the Golan heights bordering Syria; the West Bank; Gaza. All of these territories were heavily populated with Palestinians and soon that population was complemented by Jews and an array of settlements that, in the ensuing decades, have grown in number and population. Today Jews number around four hundred thousand in these territories; the settlements have thickened in number and territory and, of course, the supporting infrastructure of military, economy, and transportation has developed in extensive ways.

The occupation of these territories is now legendary in its breadth and the controversy it has engendered. Since 1967 there have been numerous uprisings among the Palestinians and perhaps predictable responses by an occupying army and settlement population. Thousands of Palestinians and Israelis have died in these clashes; more and more Palestinian land has been confiscated and turned into Jewish-only areas. The land that was supposed to be divided into two states, Israel in its pre-1967 borders and Palestine in eastern Jerusalem, the West Bank, and Gaza, has been a war zone between Israel and Palestine and a constant geopolitical irritant on the international scene.

In short, the theological commentary on the Holocaust and its aftermath was born and has lived within a military struggle that continues to this day. The question of God and empowerment can be asked on the theoretical level; the lessons of the Holocaust fill volumes that are published more frequently today than decades ago. Still, the theoretical discussion has been tried through fire on both sides of the divide, in the Holocaust obviously, but also in the lost lives and dreams of Jews and Palestinians. The latest Palestinian uprisings that began in 2000 that featured, on the one hand, Israel's use of helicopter gunships in the occupied territories and, on the other, Palestinian suicide bombers within the pre-1967 borders of

Israel, bring the theoretical to a practical reality. The question now, at least for Jews, is what to do now after the Holocaust and after Israel.

The phrase *after the Holocaust* is now clearly understood. The Holocaust as a formative event in Jewish and world history has changed our understanding in a variety of areas. It remains, and appropriately so, a permanent warning of what human beings will do to other human beings when they are defined outside of the protection of the state and the dominant religious and cultural sensibility. No people should ever be too strong or too weak, and thus they would avoid the temptation of aggression or submission. Intervention on behalf of the weaker party is mandatory before the situation escalates into genocide or Holocaust.

But what happens when the formerly weak, harassed, and murdered people gain power, expand that power, occupy another nation, settle on its land, and seek to destroy its capacity to organize and define itself as a political entity? Then what if all of this is done in the name of the victims of the Holocaust, in the name of self-defense, fulfilling what everyone agrees upon—never again?

Adding to the complexity, the new and expanding state is inhabited—through settlement—by a people who has suffered dispersion for millennia, has a battered but continuous, intact, and recognized religiosity, culture, and ethnicity. This people claims a biblical right to "return" to the land of their fathers. Having recently experienced horrendous, almost unimaginable suffering, this people is returning from the West, mostly Europe, to an area of the world trying to free itself of the malignancy of Western colonialism, the proponents of which are dispersing the indigenous people of the land and claiming land, cultural, and religious rights over them. This complexity is exacerbated by the internal structure of this "returning" people as they also carry an internationalism, an anticolonial sensibility, as well as a rigorously developed, highly original ethical compass that, while honed through a travail of suffering, actually was part of the birth of their religious and political journey—the prophetic.

The people who returned to the land were, in their origins, slaves; their very birth called forth a God of liberation who led them to leave the empire of Egypt behind and bid them to construct a community of justice and equality. This community was indeed in the land but carried a special series of warnings about the recreation of the structures of empire within their community and among those that preceded them in the land. The warnings represent another level of analysis that accompanies the lessons of the Holocaust. Diminished and placed in question, the biblical canon of ancient Israel continues to provide strength to contemporary Jews and haunts them as well. Could the return to a place of security and hope within the ancient birthplace of the people Israel be thwarted by policies of injustice toward others in the land, the Palestinians, so that even a significant minority of the Jewish people must protest this homecoming as a fundamental violation of the entire Jewish ethical tradition?

The Challenge of Liberation *After*

Initially, my study with Rubenstein was completely oriented around the Holocaust and the questions he raised through and around the event. The possibility that the God of history was no longer believable or, out of ethical concerns, should be rejected, concerned me. Rubenstein's understanding that the Jewish covenant was irretrievably broken was somehow even more distressing. The continuity of Jewish life seemed in jeopardy. In the main, I read Wiesel through Rubenstein's eyes and, though fierce and bitter rivals, I resonated with Wiesel's style of lament. It yielded a feeling of attachment to a God and tradition that was efficacious in the past and somehow was still available or could be one day. While Rubenstein was direct and analytical, pursuing the logic of his understandings with a precise and unyielding rationality, Wiesel appealed to a world of hurt and pain for a solace that, while not immediately forthcoming, might one day be available—as it was in the past.

Their respective analyses of Israel followed the rhetorical patterns they established in their post-Holocaust understanding of God and the people. Rubenstein was hard and fast; Israel was a place of protection and power. While Wiesel did not disagree, his sense again was softer. Israel was a response to the Holocaust, a dream in light of the nightmare of the Holocaust, its power generated through the ages of Jewish history rather than sheer military might. At some point, perhaps soon, that might would be transformed into the messianic dream of peace, justice, and earth. Rubenstein demurred and railed against the mystical and the hope that history might turn a corner and become the peaceable Kingdom it had never been. Arming Israel was an obligation and necessary forever. If the Holocaust means anything, it is the rejection of this dream and the hope of rescue from the drama of history. For Rubenstein, Jews have one of two choices: either be on the victorious side of the cycle of violence and atrocity or be defeated by it.

The Palestinians played a peculiar place in both Rubenstein's and Wiesel's writings, a place defined mostly by their absence which, paradoxically, spoke volumes. For Rubenstein, the creation of Israel and the dispersion of hundreds of thousands of Palestinians out of their homes and locality could be considered by them an injustice. They could even protest and organize against their displacement. He understood and accepted this grievance. History and the Jewish need, however, overrode this injustice. After the Holocaust, moral concerns had to be peripheral to our needs. Our power was our need; its use required neither justification nor compromise. Moral questions only weakened our resolve. After the Holocaust, to be weak was to court defeat and another Holocaust.

Wiesel took another tack. For the most part in Wiesel's work, Palestinians, as with Rubenstein, exist as a silent other. When mentioned, they are uncomprehending of ancient and recent Jewish history; if aware, they would accept Israel with open arms. Their lack of consciousness allows them to see Israel as a settler and conquering state, whereas Wiesel sees Jews as only in search of sanctuary and peace. The fighting between Israelis and Palestinians does not emerge from the Jewish search for power and Palestinian resistance to displacement and occupation, but rather is a fundamental misunderstanding that can be solved when Palestinians stop rejecting a state project that benefits all of humanity including the Palestinians. Despite the Holocaust and in contradiction to Rubenstein, Jews do not see the world as fundamentally divided between those who have and do not have power. Israel thus may stand as a moral force and Jews are innocent in their suffering and their empowerment. Israel represents a breaking of the cycle that Rubenstein sees as pivotal to world history. Why would Palestinians resist this?

So it went, the analytical and lyrical, in the 1960s and 1970s, with a distinctly filtered message from the Arab and Palestinian world that confronted Rubenstein and Wiesel. Most Jews were content there, not knowing exactly what to think about Israel and the Palestinians, but also knowing that a fractured support for Israel might spell its doom. Within Rubenstein's and Wiesel's compelling frameworks, the ethical had difficulty gaining traction. Power and dream, wrapped in the banner of Jewish survival and identity, left little room for considered thinking and ethical reflection on the prophetic tradition and how it might apply to Jewish life after the Holocaust. Rubenstein's and Wiesel's narratives, accepted at a deep, emotional, almost primal level by the Jewish people, had little room for the prophetic critique of Jewish power. In short, their narratives, the mainstream Jewish narrative, could not envision life after Israel. After Israel meant another Holocaust.

Does this sentiment still hold true? Beyond sentiment, is it true that an engagement with Israeli power should be avoided by non-Jew and Jew alike? The twenty-first century is well under way. Is the situation of Jews in America and Israel analogous to our plight in the years around Nazi rule? Does a critique of Israeli transgressions against the Palestinians in the twenty-first century threaten a retrogression so that the Nazis of old will once again flourish?

With the Israeli invasion of Lebanon, the continuing occupation of the West Bank and Gaza and settling of Palestinian land, and the suppression of the Palestinian uprising in the 1980s, I, with other Jews, began to think through the Holocaust again and the lessons it bequeathed to Jews and the world. The emergency years after the Holocaust had passed; Jews in America and Israel were now empowered and secure. Indeed the entire Jewish world was flourishing in a substantial and unparalleled way.

Despite the fact that our security was established, Holocaust commentary continued to expand, time and again molding the terrible terrain of Jewish suffering and Israel as a response to that suffering. Jewish innocence was trumpeted over and over again and anyone who opposed Israeli policies, even while supporting the state itself, could only be on the wrong side of the Jewish narrative. In fact, those who dissented from Israeli policies were increasingly labeled as anti-Semitic; if Jewish, the dissenters were called self-haters.

Clearly this applied to Palestinians who dissented from the way they were being treated. Their grievance could not simply be political, the way any group or people would resent and resist occupation. Resistance was raised to an eschatological dimension. So too Christians and Jews who increasingly found Palestinian complaints to be justified, in need of a hearing and even action on their behalf. Again, the drama was lifted beyond the political; the prophetic, even when moderate, was deemed as threatening another Holocaust. The narrative of the Holocaust would change if in fact Jews, in their empowerment, could actually be called to account. The fear was that anything beyond the Holocaust threatened the purity of Jewish innocence and our own claim to the exercise of power without accountability.

It was becoming clear, however, that accountability was the issue. Accountability was needed everywhere; the claim that somehow the Jewish situation was different, always different, sought to distance Jews from this universal standard. The argument had to be joined yet the difficulty was ever present, since the Jewish situation had been and was, if not totally so, certainly somewhat different. As it turns out, that difference limited and directed criticism in a particular way; the peculiar situation of the Jews in history needed to be recognized and the trenchant critique of the very prophetic, which the Jews gave to the world, needed to be applied.

As with the Holocaust, a new language was needed to fit the particularity of Jewish history and the unique situation of contemporary Jews, poised as they were between Holocaust and Israel. In some ways Jews were living within an ancient history as it was being played out in the contemporary drama of Holocaust and Israel. That ancient history bequeathed the Exodus and the prophets, the very narrative of liberation that was gripping the Christian theological world at this time. The Exodus and the prophetic had applied to Christian theology, say in Latin America and among African Americans in the United States—the poor and disenfranchised. Did they still apply to Jews and the state of Israel *after*?

Within the decades since the 1967 war, I began noticing another transformation in the Jewish community. The political and cultural in America was becoming more and more conservative, taking on the label neoconservative. This transformation was startling, a drift in the Jewish world from a more liberal sensibility that I had grown up with; it would have a tremendous impact on American political life in the domestic and foreign policy realms. Was this neoconservatism also a product of the new centrality of the Holocaust and Israel to Jewish identity?

Neoconservatism makes sense within the Jewish journey from weakness to power but still, again with the inherited ethical tradition, the limits of such a drift could be qualified. The equation seemed to go like this: American power guarantees Israel's security; Jews are empowered in the United States; Jewish power here keeps the foreign policy of the United States focused on Israel as a strategic asset; the Jewish establishment has to reeducate mainstream Jews to this neoconservatism; so as to show some continuity with the Jewish ethical tradition, neoconservatism has to demonstrate how liberalism has abandoned this tradition, becoming radicalized even to the point of criticizing too harshly the economic, political, and military system that protects Jews in America and protects Israel—especially in a world that was increasingly hostile to Jewish interests, again, especially with regard to Israel.

There *was* in fact increasing criticism of Israel across the board, and not only in the Arab world and Third World. Increasingly global institutions like the United Nations and the World Council of Churches, as well as human rights organizations, were paying more and more attention to the plight of the Palestinians. The spell of the 1967 war was dissipating, yet the Israeli occupation and settlement of Palestinian territory continued apace. Secure within its own borders, Israel's reasons for occupation and its pretense that the occupation was only continuing because of Palestinian intransigence, could no longer be upheld. In the global arena, Israel felt a sense of isolation. In the end, on many issues, Israel was supported only by the United States. In return, America could count on Israel's vocal and often military support in areas of the world where it was difficult for the United States to deliver arms or training, sometimes because of divided public opinion or congressional mandates.

Thus mutual support turned into a symbiotic relationship until it was difficult for other countries to know where Israel started and America ended. Jewish neoconservatives began to ask whether Jewish criticism of American foreign policy—indeed criticism of America from any corner of the world—could be a form of self-hate and anti-Semitism. The label for this trend in the world was the new anti-Semitism, an anti-Semitism that moved individual and even collective prejudice against Jews to institutions that were critical of Jewish empowerment and the use of power by the United States.

In truth, the Jewish establishment was turning a major corner in Jewish history on a variety of fronts, not the least being the adoption of the model that Christianity had developed since it moved from a small persecuted and marginal group to inherit the keys of the earthly Kingdom—the empire Constantine ruled. In the fourth century and beyond, Constantinian Christianity pioneered the alliance of religion and the state, trading its criticism of power and its way of life that contravened the acceptable norms of its time, to become the normative faith and lifestyle of the empire. For the support of the state, Christianity was given a monopoly on religion and favors that allowed it to expand its reach. It was given carte blanche as long as it returned the favor to the state; thus the church had the freedom to monopolize religion, and the blessing of the church would be conferred upon matters properly within the purview of the state. In exchange, the Church would be silent on matters of the state.

Judaism was now doing the same thing; a Constantinian Judaism was forming that, on the one hand, demanded the freedom of Jewish identity and pursuit of Jewish interests and, on the other, promised an intellectual and economic support of the American government as it pursued conservative domestic and foreign policy goals. Still, the liberal veneer continued to be present; how else to convince the Jewish community to follow a conservative lead? The job of the Constantinian Jewish establishment was to convince the Jewish community that liberalism had lost its way; its radicalization left Jews in America and Israel especially exposed to political currents that were anti-Semitic. Involved here was the job of convincing Jewish intellectuals and ordinary Jews that their very well-being was being undermined by radicalized liberal agenda that sought to universalize Jewish particularity out of existence.

The other job was to convince these same Jews that those Jews who dissented from Constantinian Judaism were not really Jews at all. Or they were Jews, like others previously, who had not seen the Holocaust coming and were disarming the Jewish community in the present so that another threat like the Nazis could overrun the people Israel. Constantinian Jews, having learned the lessons of the Holocaust, were strong Jews. Jewish dissenters had missed those lessons, therefore repeating the same mistakes Jews had made before. They were leading the people astray and had to be disciplined, exposed, ridiculed.

Two transformations were taking place: first, an awakening to the fact that Israel and the Jewish community in America were no longer innocent and that a new post-Holocaust language of dissent was needed; second, that the Jewish community and Israel were moving toward a Constantinian Judaism, a way of being Jewish that made dissent among Jews and non-Jews even more difficult. The division in the Jewish community would widen even more in the coming years, emerging as a kind of civil war among Jews. Still by the mid-1980s, the various sides were already forming and the language of each was coming into its own.

It is within this context that a Jewish theology of liberation was born, the first article on that theme being published in 1984, and the first book on the subject, *Toward a Jewish Theology of Liberation*, was published in 1987. By 1989 a second edition of the book was published with a postscript titled "The Palestinian Uprising and the Future of the Jewish People." In less than a decade the main themes of that theology were already set; their relevance increased over the years so that a third and expanded edition was published in 2004.

A Jewish theology of liberation emerged within the context of the post-Holocaust world and the continuing conflict of Israel and the Palestinians. But another context was the world of liberation theology itself, primarily a Christian and Third World theology with North America contributing African American, Latino/a, and feminist variations. In general the world of liberation theology was the theology of the poor, marginalized, and neglected sectors and peoples of the world—and thus most of the world—in search of respect, recognition, material sustenance, and justice. The have-nots were now speaking to the haves about exclusion, enslavement, and murder in history and the present. Christian liberation theologies argued for a confession from the exploiters and justice for the exploited, all placed in the Christian paradigm of liberation. However, since Christianity had often been an engine of oppression—for many of the peoples in need of liberation Christianity had been an agent of colonial and imperial oppressive language that articulated Christianity as liberating was desperately needed.

Such a language was found in the Exodus and the prophets of the Hebrew Bible; Jesus was liberated from the captivity of colonial Christianity by placing him in the line of the prophets. Thus liberation theologians explored the foreground of Jesus as a prophet rather than his lineage as proof of his messianic line. Of course as Christians the belief in Jesus as Messiah was affirmed. Still the distinction was crucial. The messianic Jesus, understood in a static and otherworldly way, was paved by Constantinian Christianity, the progenitor of Christendom. Liberation theology wanted to move beyond both forms of Christianity to a prophetic Christianity that served the poor and marginalized rather than the state and power.

A Jewish theology of liberation also appealed to the Hebrew Bible, this as its primary focus, but the confrontation was different. A Jewish theology of liberation confronted a history of violence and massacre against Jews that culminated in the mass murder of six million Jews during the middle of the twentieth century, in the middle of Christian Europe. On the one hand, Jews were and are suspicious of a revived Christianity in any form, Christians being the primary oppressors of Jews in history; on the other hand, Jews now live safely in America, which is primarily populated with Christians, but still as a distinct minority. On the other, within that situation of living among Christians whose attitudes toward Jews have changed substantially and for the good, the lives of Jews have undergone a massive transformation. Once pariahs, now Jews are prized and full citizens of America and Europe. At the same time, and for the first time in two thousand years, Jews have their own state and army.

So, liberated after the Holocaust and living peacefully and flourishing among their former enemies—but also using empowerment to secure their situation—Jews are faced with almost an opposite situation than most who practice liberation theology. Coming from a history of oppression and just recently emerging from the death camps—and now finally empowered—Jews are now oppressing others in Palestine, using their newfound power in America to solidify their status as important elites to be cultivated, and participating fully in the upper echelons of American society. In short, the liberation of Jews is shadowed by past suffering and the use of empowerment, as perhaps any group uses empowerment, to solidify elite status and keep others, including those in need of liberation, from disturbing or displacing Jews from that position.

The question, then, for Jews is not empowerment; what impoverished and marginalized community would turn its back on this opportunity? The challenge is liberation within empowerment. Has our arrival as Jews in America and Israel liberated us or is there a new enslavement to power itself? Having survived Constantinian Christianity, does it bode well for Jews to develop and embrace a Constantinian Judaism? Though the symbolic configuration of Constantinian Christianity and Constantinian Judaism may differ, is the practice of each faith in that similar form different? What does it mean to survive a religion and a state that uses that religion to justify exclusion and murder and then to adopt it, albeit with a different name and symbol structure? Being without power after the Holocaust may be risking physical suicide. Is the use of power against others a form of moral suicide?

But then, the history of marginalization and death cannot be swept aside easily. Nor can the world be trusted so quickly. Sometimes exaggerated and often used as polemical rhetoric, anti-Semitism is a reality. Are Jews caught between realpolitik and ethics? Is there a need to choose one over the other? Can both be chosen, navigating the world of power and ethics? Or does the choice of one preclude the other? The offer of solidarity to oppressed groups is taking a risk. Would they in power continue to honor Jews and, if need be, protect them?

Theologies of liberation from the Christian side trust in the power of God to, alongside their efforts, liberate them. In essence they believe in the liberating power of the Exodus God. The experience of the Holocaust makes this belief extremely difficult for Jews. Whether or not Christians on the margins should believe in this God is certainly a question. After all, though Jesus may be with the poor and oppressed of the Third World, it seems that their worldly situation continues to deteriorate.

It seems that their very belief in a liberating God further cautions Jews against these movements of liberation and even the suggestion that such a God might return to Jewish consciousness. It may be that this fear is rooted in the critique that the prophets would bring against Jews in their empowerment—a constant refrain of the prophets in the Hebrew Bible. The God of liberation is suspect on a variety of fronts; God's absence during the Holocaust and God's critique of unjust power are two strikes against him in contemporary Jewish life. If Jews did follow God on the question of justice, would God protect Jews if we experienced another round of persecution, even at the hands of liberated Christians?

For Jews, the challenge of liberation *after* is complicated—by our history, our God, our power, and Christianity. Still, a Jewish theology of liberation cannot be silent. Its argument for justice for the Palestinians alongside Israel, its plea to recognize and work with the marginal of the world, the critique of Constantinian Christianity, even the suggestion of another look at God, struck the Jewish community like a tidal wave. On the one side were Constantinian Jews, those who opposed a Jewish theology of liberation as if it was a heresy with murderous possibilities, and on the other side were progressive Jews who embodied parts of the liberation message in their own lives.

In the end, however, and as the situation worsened, even progressive Jews could not bridge the divide to a Jewish theology of liberation. That was left to another group of Jews, Jews of Conscience, that emerged in the wake of a second Palestinian uprising that began in 2000. A few years later, the Wall inside and around the West Bank began to be built. For some this Wall was one of security and separation; for Jews of Conscience it is an apartheid or ghetto wall. Jewish history had come full circle.

Jews of Conscience: Toward a Jewish Theology of Liberation for the Twenty-first Century

With all the twists and turns of Jewish history, the question remains for every generation. What does it mean to be faithful as a Jew in our time? Jews are empowered; a Constantinian Judaism is at hand. Progressive Jews have argued within the context of Holocaust and empowerment for a more ethical Judaism in our time. Over the last decades they have opposed the expansion of Israel into Palestinian territories and have confronted the increasingly conservative politics of the mainstream Jewish community. Most recently they have endorsed the Geneva Accords that seek a compromise between Israeli expansionism and Palestinian rights to self-determination and nationhood and opposed the American invasion and occupation of Iraq. In the wake of September 11, progressive Jews have spoken forcefully against terrorism while at the same time asking difficult questions about conditions that create terrorism.

Still their critiques come from the perspective of power as they seek to negotiate the terrain of mainstream Judaism. Because of this their analyses have often been less than forthright. Too often they have been patronizing, invoking the suffering of Jews in the Holocaust as a necessity for Palestinians to understand and, to some extent, use to orient their lives and politics. Too, their new age sensibility and appeal to a politics of healing blunts the prophetic critique of injustice.

Over the years, especially with regard to criticism of Israel, progressive Jews have often blocked the critique that they later, under force of circumstance, adopted. In doing so, progressive Jews have actually held back the process of thought and action that may have made a difference in confronting Israeli power. Their timidity and fear has therefore been part of the displacement of the Palestinians. In 2000 this judgment became clear as the violence of Israeli policies in the West Bank in particular was met by violence on the Palestinian side. Many progressive Jews who opposed the violence of the Israeli military were also scandalized by Palestinian armed resistance. Suicide bombings galvanized a significant portion of Jewish progressives to conclude that Palestinians did not want to live in peace side-by-side with Israel. Thus they left the progressive Jewish community and joined forces with those who believed that only might and strict separation of Jews and Palestinians could work in the future. The memory of the Holocaust weighed in here; Jews had to be first concerned with our own safety and security and only after that could considerations of justice be permitted.

This break within the progressive Jewish community raises the question of liberation for the future. Have Jews, even with concerns for justice, gone deeply enough into the history of the formation of the Jewish state in 1948? Were Jews innocent in the formation of Israel and do Palestinians need to affirm Jewish claims to the land because of the Holocaust or because of the Bible? The expansion of Israel and the building of the Wall within the West Bank seem permanent, the Wall itself becoming the final borders of the expanded state. Are negotiations to take place within that context or do Jews need to argue for a force, whether moral, political, economic, or military, to push Israel back to the pre-1967 borders of Israel?

Critique from the Jewish ethical tradition has been ongoing for decades; it has been powerless to stop Israeli expansion. It has also been powerless to stop the neoconservative drift of Constantinian Judaism. What is the reason for this failure? Is the Jewish ethical tradition itself flawed or does it need to be abandoned in favor of some other moral impulse? Is the Constantinian Judaism of today the *real* Judaism while dissenters are new imposters? Or is the reverse true?

These questions themselves are deep and engaging, their answers elusive. Jews of Conscience at least try to approach them with vigor and honesty. At this point in Jewish history, everything is on the line. If in fact a new form of Judaism is developing, a Constantinian Judaism, will it be embraced by future generations of Jews? For those Jews who cannot embrace Constantinian Judaism, will their children identify themselves as Jews? The prophetic is the great gift to the world of the people Israel. If we cease to carry it, does the prophetic lose its foundation and therefore disappear? Or does the prophetic survive in other movements, including Christian theologies of liberation? Will Christian liberation theology preserve the prophetic and thus make it available to future generations of Jews?

Over time, as the legacy of the Holocaust and the Jewish prophetic tradition recede, can Judaism actually project itself to the world? Israel, Judaism, and Jews have always articulated Jewish identity within the concept of difference. Though this identity is still asserted even by the Constantinian Jewish establishment, time is ticking away and the historical markers of difference, especially in ethical critique and practice, are becoming more and more difficult to distinguish. Does the world have the right to take these claims at face value and demand this of Jews in reality? Or would this be considered anti-Jewish? Are Jews of Conscience reasserting this difference *after* the Holocaust and *after* Israel?

Indeed, Jews of Conscience do ask difficult questions about the Holocaust and Israel. Regarding the lessons of the Holocaust, they reaffirm the dual sensibility first surfaced by the original Holocaust theologians: never again to the Jewish people and never again to any people. Yet they mean not just the Holocaust, because concern for suffering should not be limited to the ultimate horrors. Indeed the memory of the Holocaust has too often constrained Jewish action on behalf of others. Nor is the comparison of the suffering of others to the Holocaust the litmus test for Jewish participation in the struggle against violence and atrocity. Rather, the Holocaust behooves Jews and others to fight all injustice, wherever it is.

There are no free passes when it comes to these issues—even the heirs to the Holocaust event, perhaps especially these, must be on guard against practices that are unjust. Injustice in the name of the Holocaust, used as a banner of unaccountability while claiming innocence, denigrates the victims in whose names the community acts. Though comparisons of other events of suffering to the Holocaust diminish the enormity of the event, the use of the Holocaust to pursue unjust policies trivializes it. As Irving Greenberg wrote, "The victims ask us above all not to allow the creation of another matrix of values that might sustain another attempt at genocide" (Fleishner, 1977:29). For Jews of Conscience, they also ask that we do not use the memory of the victims to cause further suffering.

The Holocaust thus stands as formative but in an almost reverse relationship to the Holocaust commentaries that have become normative for the Jewish community. Thus Emil Fackenheim's 614th commandment, issued by him after the 1967 war, that the "authentic Jew of today is forbidden to hand Hitler yet another posthumous victory"—a commandment that counsels Jewish empowerment so as to survive and flourish after Hitler's demise—is countered by the 615th commandment: "Thou shalt not demean, denigrate or dislocate the Palestinian people" (Fackenheim, 1970:84).

A more positive way of placing both commandments in a constructive forward momentum is to command that both Jews and Palestinians embark on a relationship of trust, seeking justice and forgiveness so that after this difficult history both peoples can find their own individual destiny as well as their shared destiny. After all, as enemies, the victor and victim are locked in a mortal struggle that denies both the rhythms and pleasures of ordinary life. Is there another way? Could the sharing of Jerusalem—the broken middle of Israel and Palestine—propel both on a journey of revolutionary forgiveness? (Ellis, 2004a:271–85).

Jews of Conscience ask how this can happen when the *fait accompli* is the annexation of Jerusalem, the building of the Wall within the West Bank, the projected unilateral declaration of borders that make a real Palestinian state impossible. Yet this question begs others, including a deeper understanding of and reflection about the very creation of the state of Israel. Here, even in these emergency years after the Holocaust, there is a reckoning. A Jewish state may indeed have been necessary; could it justify the displacement of seven to eight thousand Palestinians from their villages, towns, and cities?

Recently, Meron Benvenisti, the Israeli political commentator, historian, and former deputy mayor of Jerusalem, described the displacement of the Palestinians in 1948 and after as an act of ethnic cleansing. That Jews have done such things does not distinguish us from many other peoples and nation-states—the "founding" of America is another of many examples; still it removes the sense of innocence that we sometimes wear as a badge of honor. Whatever one can say about the Jewish state, it was not created without horror, violence, and bloodshed. Jewish empowerment was not innocent.

Today, long after those emergency years have come to an end, a possibility emerges to reconcile the violence, to confess it and begin again. Instead Israel has expanded steadily for decades, pushing more and more Palestinians aside, demolishing their homes, expropriating their land and, at the same time, placing Jewish settlements and settlers where Palestinians once were. Can this be explained or justified by the Holocaust? Or is this simply another example in history of those with more power taking the land of those with less power? Again, it is no worse than others but certainly not above critique; it is definitely not an example of innocence.

Raising these questions does not hinder the juggernaut of Israeli power. Nor does it seem to affect the American Constantinian establishment, but just the opposite. The policies of expropriation and expansion continue unabated, as does the defense of these policies. The labeling of Jewish and non-Jewish protestors as self-hating Jews and anti-Semites continues as well. The progressive Jewish establishment continues to seek dialogue with those who support and deflect criticism from these policies, often compromising their critique to seek converts from the powerful. Since this has not worked and also because it often softens the criticism to the point where culpability is more or less removed, should Jews of Conscience separate themselves from both groups? In essence, should Jews of Conscience abandon dialogue with mainstream and progressive Jews as a waste of time and effort, fearing cooptation as a price to win the coveted label of a good Jew?

The argument for justice within empowerment is difficult, especially in light of Jewish history. Still, even within this conundrum, the question of what it can mean to be Jewish while practicing injustice remains. The difficulty deepens: where are the resources to choose justice as a critique of our newfound power? Even if Jews of Conscience challenge the primary emphasis of Holocaust theology—never again to the Jewish people—and raise its corollary—never again to any people—to an equal status, the specifically theological questions stemming from the Holocaust cannot be ignored.

Christian liberation theology often asserts, perhaps too easily, that God is among the poor, for the poor, and working for their liberation. This emphasis on the Exodus paradigm is difficult if not impossible to assert in the face of recent Jewish history. Just the opposite, some Jews see the Exodus paradigm with reference to the emergence of the state of Israel; they see the Holocaust as a time of slavery, Israel as a time that responds to the cries of the people and liberates them. Holocaust theologians do not move overtly in this direction. To them, Israel is a human, not divine, response to Jewish weakness in the Holocaust. For the most part, Jews of Conscience also speak in human terms. The tradition speaks about ethics; Jews of Conscience embody this tradition. Still, their movement is against the grain of the community.

A typical and normal response to the Holocaust is self-empowerment without concern for the other. Going against the grain in any community is difficult. With the stakes so high, specific resources seem to be needed to imitate and then sustain what amounts to a counterintuitive sensibility. This, with power arrayed against them, demands a similar array of resources for Jews of Conscience to have the courage for a sustained struggle against the powers that be.

THE PROPHETIC WITH/OUT GOD

In a strange twist of fate, the people who gave God to the world are now without God. Or, perhaps more accurately stated, the people who gave God to the world have lost the ability to articulate God's presence. That loss is understandable: if God chose the people of Israel as God's people and promised to be with us, if God is indeed a God of history, where was God in the Holocaust? If God is the Lord of all history, where has God been in the suffering of all, then and now, in the Holocaust, but also in the genocides in the Americas after 1492, in the twentieth century after the Holocaust in Cambodia, Rwanda, and now Darfur? Perhaps the loss of the ability to articulate a God of concern and justice should not be consigned to the Jews. Does this ongoing and unremitting history of suffering also chasten the bold claims of Christian theologies of liberation to name God an efficacious and liberating God?

Surely the naming of God is less important than action on behalf of justice. This is one of the lessons of the Holocaust. The very lack of action on behalf of Jews, coupled with the piety of the surrounding Christian culture, also implicate religion and its naming of God. One conclusion, drawn from the Jewish tradition and Christian theologies of liberation, is that the naming of a God that does nothing to motivate believers to sacrifice on behalf of justice represents idolatry. Thus today, those Christians who allow the Holocaust, perhaps even laid the groundwork for it through their demonizing of Jews, were worshiping a false God. But then, Jews who cannot speak of God may ask a corollary question: Is the God of history so prominent in the Hebrew Bible a failed God in light of the Holocaust, and perhaps also a false God? Christians, worshiping a false God of discrimination and anti-Semitism, laid the groundwork for the Holocaust. Were Jews who held fast to the true God who would rescue them from their enemies also worshiping a false God, an idol that consisted of wishful thinking and a misplaced hope?

Of course the biblical witness and the tradition that emerges from the Bible is complex with regard to God. Contemporary liberation thought is also complex. In the later work of Gustavo Gutiérrez, for example, especially his work on the biblical Job and the sixteenth-century church dissident Bartolomé de las Casas, he pursues difficult questions about God. While Gutiérrez, who witnesses the ongoing suffering of his own Latin America people, does not deny the God of the Bible, the earlier certainty of his own liberation theology regarding who God is and what God is doing is compromised. At least Gutiérrez concedes that the liberation that God promises is difficult to discern, is beyond our lifetimes and knowledge. We should hesitate to name that liberation, or God for that matter, in definitive terms, as if our own naming is *the* naming.

In the end, Gutiérrez is humbled by suffering and by God. He is left, like Job, with his own voice and the voice of God—a disharmonious harmony, an inconsistent blending of assertion, denial, questioning, and power. Job engages in dialogue with God, with himself and friends, with the suffering that is and is not only among others, and with the earth and the universe that Job understands and that which is beyond his understanding. Even Gutiérrez's humility before the naming of God is of a different order than that of Jews of Conscience who hardly enter even a nuanced theological conversation. Still it seems that for Jews of Conscience a covenantal reality remains. This is true in Holocaust theology as well, though again the differences are crucial: in both, the Jewish partner remains steadfast even if God is no longer present or named. For Holocaust theology, the Jewish partner continues on, dedicated primarily to the survival of the Jewish people, thus focusing almost exclusively on empowerment. Jews of Conscience continue on as well; their focus is the ethical and moral survival of the Jewish witness. Here the prophetic is upheld and highlighted, becoming the center of Jewish commitment. This is contrary to Holocaust theology where the prophetic is downplayed and, in extreme cases, banished. If it remains alive at all it is concentrated on other issues that do not impact Jewish life or, rather the only issues that can be addressed in a prophetic style that reinforce Jewish power or deflect criticism away from it.

But the catch is here. The Jewish prophetic, illustrated in the Bible and found within the framework of the covenant, is not primarily about the other nations, for prophets are called to specifically and almost exclusively address Israel. The prophetic is internal, reminding Israel of its slavery, its deliverance, and its mission to create a new kind of society unlike the Egyptian society they had been slaves within. The prophets arise within the land that Israel has been brought into because they are not living the promise they gave to God. That promise is contained within the covenant and so the violation of the covenant is in some ways a violation of God. Jews of Conscience carry on the covenant insofar as they hold the people Israel to the justice Israel is called to in the Hebrew Bible. They do this without knowing, acknowledging, naming, or believing in that God. The drama of Israel's covenant is the mission of Israel, not of the outside world. That mission is the creation of community in a world of empire; empires, even and especially when Israel aspires to empire, are condemned. They represent a return to the empire that enslaved Israel and, as importantly, to the gods of Egypt, false gods, no-gods, the same gods that Israel is tempted to worship.

Is it better to name a God that is no-god? Or is Israel called first to be atheist toward the no-gods of Egypt? In the biblical drama, the strength to turn away from the false gods of Egypt is found in the discovery of Yahweh, the true God, the God of Israel, the God of history, the God of Israel's liberation.

Could Jews of Conscience have internalized God to such an extent, that though they are unable to name or affirm God after the Holocaust, the memory of God's presence remains and the covenant, again unnamed, remains? That the force of the covenant may be even greater because of the questions that the Holocaust raises about God? That the impetus for Jews to pursue justice in its internal life is even stronger precisely because of Jewish suffering, the memory of God's justice, and God's absence in the Holocaust?

The 614th commandment of Holocaust theology is a covenantal act of defiance and affirmation. It is defiance of the Nazis and their kin, defiance of the God who was not there. The affirmation is the carrying forth of the Jewish drama despite the odds, human and divine. The 615th commandment of Jews of Conscience is also a covenantal act of defiance and affirmation: defiance of the Nazis and the absent God, but also a refusal to allow the world of violence and atrocity to skew the fundamentals of the Jewish ethical tradition. The affirmation is a redoubling of the Jewish witness in the world as a prophetic vocation despite and because of Jewish suffering in the Holocaust. To cause suffering to others is to join the nations; it is to assimilate to the Constantinian formulations of the world, the cause of suffering to so many in history, including Jews.

THE NEW DIASPORA

In some ways Jews of Conscience have come to the end of Jewish history as we have known and inherited it. *After* the Holocaust and *after* Israel—and what Israel with the backing of the Jewish establishment has done and is doing to the Palestinians—the Jewish ethical tradition has been tried and has failed. Its failure is no more and no less than the failures of other traditions. Thus it is clear to Christian liberation theologians that the ethical center of Christianity was gutted as it assumed its Constantinian character. This is true for Islam in its various Constantinian incarnations as well. Constantinianism is a part of any and every religion; the joining of religion and state challenges the ethics of any and all traditions. After the Constantinian phase, there is little if anything left. Renewal is a possibility but it is then in the shadow of the previous Constantinianism, renewal thus forever defined by an initial failure. What is more, the elements of Constantinianism continue far into the future. Once embarked upon, Constantinianism defines the norms of religiosity; what it means to be Jewish, Christian, or Muslim is always contested and dissenters are defined as on the margins.

Perhaps we have reached a point where the designations of Jew, Christian, and Muslim need further identifiers—Constantinian Jew; Christian, Muslim, or Jew; Christian or Muslim of Conscience. Is there also something beyond this descriptor? Perhaps these descriptors hide the fact that those Jews who practice Constantinian Judaism and those who embrace being a Jew of Conscience, for example, are actually practicing different religions. Analyzed from another perspective, Constantinian Jews, Christians, and Muslims are practicing the same religion, albeit with different symbol structures. Might this be true for

Jews, Christians, and Muslims of Conscience, as they, too, practice the same religion with a different symbol structure?

Another layer of religiosity and practice needs to be explored here as well. Constantinian religiosity always sees its symbol structure and truth claims as intact, firm, and beyond dispute. Religious people of conscience know that their symbols and truth claims are in fragments, contested, compromised by power and chastened by suffering. The central question—perhaps the central religious question throughout history—is whether we as individuals and as communities move toward empire or toward community. Constantinianism moves toward empire and carries the certainty of empire; conscience moves toward community with the vulnerability and the constant search for a broader inclusion this entails. Thus the relationship between and among the various Constantinian establishments of our day is defined by various orthodoxies; the relationship between various communities of conscience is defined by action and compassion with those marginalized and the violated.

The very movement of conscience itself breaks down barriers, including the barriers of symbols and truth claims. It could be that new diaspora has been forming—perhaps is already formed but existing without articulation—that contains within it people of conscience from different religions and cultures. Jews of Conscience are there but they are not alone. Together with others of conscience, Jews carry their fragmented tradition into a new community. Since in this community no one overarching symbol structure or truth claim is recognized, Jews will be, along with others, carrying their own fragmented traditions with them.

Of course, Jews of Conscience, as Christians and Muslims of Conscience, are in exile from their own communities. They are also together in a new community that is not entirely their own. In exile, then, they are entering a new diaspora, a diaspora that is their new home. It is where the expression of their deepest longings will be realized and tested. It is where their quest for liberation, so frustrated in their own original community, will again be expressed and tested.

Chapter Review

1. How has history shaped Judaism, i.e., the Holocaust, the 1967 war?
2. Could the Holocaust have occurred if the state of Israel had existed?
3. How would a Christian deal with the belief that Jews were punished for their disbelief via the Holocaust?
4. Describe Jewish liberation theology.
5. Describe the new diaspora.

The Uniqueness of Christianity

By Eugene F. Gorski

Christianity and the non-Christian world religions are similar in that they are all "true" religions. But among them, there are, of course, significant differences from the point of view of the experience and interpretation of the Sacred, creeds and dogmas, liturgical practices, theology and spirituality, and so on. Since God makes himself available to all human persons, why are there many religions rather than just one? Richard McBrien explains these differences:

> Just as God is in principle available to every person (Rahner's "supernatural existential") and to every people (since we are essentially social), so also religion, as the structured response to the experience of God, is available to every person and people. But since "no one has ever seen God" (John 1:18), we can never be absolutely certain that we have had an actual experience of God or that we have correctly perceived, interpreted, and expressed that experience. Furthermore, God can become available to us only on terms consistent with our bodily existence, i.e., sacramentally.

Eugene F. Gorski, "The Uniqueness of Christianity," *Theology of Religions: A Sourcebook for Interreligious Study*, pp. 281–301. Copyright © 2008 by Paulist Press. Reprinted with permission.

> Every experience of God or, from the other side, every self-disclosure of God, is inevitably conditioned by the situation of the person or community to which God has become available in a special way. Those communities are differentiated by time, place, culture, language, temperament, social and economic conditions, etc. Revelation, therefore, is always received according to the mode of the receiver, to cite a central Thomistic principle ("Duodenum recipitur in aliquo recipitur in eo secundum modum recipientis," *Summa Theologica*, 1. q. 79, a. 6). Since religion is our structured response to the reception of God's revelation, our response will be shaped by that mode of reception. Indeed, the Son of God became incarnate in a particular time and place, in a particular culture and religious situation, in a particular man and a particular family, nation and ethnic community."[1]

While many differences exist among the religions, it is important for us in this study to focus on the basic difference between Christianity and the other religions. In what fundamental way is Christianity *unique*?

Central to the understanding of its uniqueness is Christianity's conviction that it alone is founded on Jesus Christ, who is believed to be the only and unparalleled redemptive mediator between God and humankind, the universal savior intended for all persons, as well as the perfection and fullness of God's revelation of truth. These beliefs are well grounded in the testimony of the scriptures and in the teaching of the church.

Scriptures and Teaching of the Church

In regard to Jesus Christ as God's revelation of truth, scripture asserts that in the mystery of the incarnate Son of God, who is "the way, the truth, and the life" (John 14:6), the full revelation of the divine truth is given: "No one has ever seen God. It is God the only Son, who is close to the Father's heart, who has made him known" (John 1:18); "For in him the whole fullness of deity dwells bodily" (Col 2:9). The Second Vatican Council teaches, "By this revelation, then, the deepest truth about God and the salvation of man shines out for our sake in Christ, who is both the mediator and the fullness of all revelation" *(Dei Verbum* [DV] 2). Furthermore,

> Jesus Christ, therefore, the Word made flesh, was sent "as a man to men." He "speaks the words of God" (John 3:34), and completes the work of salvation which his Father gave him to do (see John 5:36; 17:4). To see Jesus is to see his Father (John 14:9). For this reason Jesus perfected revelation by fulfilling it through his whole work of making himself present and manifesting Himself: through His words and deeds, His signs and wonders, but especially through his death and glorious resurrection from the dead and final sending of the Spirit of truth.

> Moreover, He confirmed with divine testimony what revelation proclaimed, that God is with us to free us from the darkness of sin and death, and to raise us up to life eternal ... The Christian dispensation, therefore, as the new and definitive covenant, will never pass away, and we now await no further new public revelation before the glorious manifestation of our Lord Jesus Christ (see 1 Timothy 6:14 and Titus 2:13). *(DV 4)*

Pope John Paul II taught that Jesus contains the fullness of what God wants to make known to humanity.

> In Christ and through Christ God has revealed himself fully to mankind and has definitively drawn close to it; at the same time, in Christ and through Christ man has acquired full awareness of his dignity, of the heights to which he is raised, of the surpassing worth of his own humanity, and of the meaning of his existence." *(Redemptoris Hominis* [RH] 11) ... God's revelation becomes definitive and complete through his only-begotten Son ... In this definitive Word of his revelation, God has made himself known in the fullest possible way. He has revealed to mankind *who he is*" *(Redemptoris Missio* [RH] 5).

In regard to Jesus being the sole redemptive mediator of humankind, scripture asserts with clarity, "And we have seen and do testify that the Father has sent his Son as the Savior of the world" (1 John 4:14); "Here is the Lamb of God who takes away the sin of the world" (John 1:29b). In his speech before the Sanhedrin, Peter proclaims, "There is salvation in no one else, for there is no other name under heaven given among mortals by which we must be saved" (Acts 4:12). And Saint Peter claims that Jesus Christ "is Lord of all," "judge of the living and the dead," and therefore "whoever believes in him receives forgiveness of sins through his name" (Acts 10:36, 42, 43). In addressing himself to the community of Corinth, Paul writes, "Indeed, even though there may be so-called gods in heaven or on earth—as in fact there are many gods and many lords—yet for us there is one God, the Father, from whom are all things and for whom we exist, and one Lord, Jesus Christ, through whom are all things and through whom we exist" (1 Cor 8:5–6). Moreover, John states, "For God so loved the world that he gave his only Son, so that everyone who believes in him may not perish but may have eternal life. Indeed, God did not send his Son into the world to condemn the world, but in order that the world might be saved through him" (John 3:16–17). According to the New Testament, the universal salvific will of God is closely connected to the sole mediation of Christ: "[God] desires everyone to be saved and to come to the knowledge of the truth. For there is one God; there is also one mediator between God and humankind, Christ Jesus, himself human, who gave himself as a ransom for all" (1 Tim 2:4–6). And about Jesus as redemptive mediator the Second Vatican Council teaches:

> The Church believes that Christ, who died and was raised up for all, (2) can through His Spirit offer man the light and the strength to measure up to his supreme destiny, Nor has any other name under the heaven been given to man by which it is fitting for him to be saved (3). She likewise holds that in her benign Lord and Master can be found the key, the focal point and the goal of man, as well as of all human history. *(Gaudium et Spes* [GS] 10)

Pope John Paul taught that if God's saving love fills the universe, its pipeline is Jesus—only Jesus. "Christ is the one savior of all, the only one able to reveal God and lead to God … Salvation can come only from Jesus Christ" (RM 5). Consequently, Jesus is both "history's center and goal" *(RM 6; Dialogue and Proclamation* [DP] 22, 28) and he who "reconciles" or repairs the "rupture in the relationship between Creator and creation … after original sin."[2]

The scriptures and the teaching of the church, then, give testimony that Jesus is the summit and fullness of God's revelation and the universal savior intended for all humankind. This means that in principle a person's knowledge of God in Christ is completely adequate. Nothing is to be discovered about God (about God's mercy, love, fidelity, justice) that had not already been disclosed through Christ. The Christ-event is the definitive and normative self-communication of God by which all other communications are to be measured and tested. In the Christ-event is found the sole and unparalled redemptive mediation between humankind and God.

Only Jesus Christ is the absolute savior, the fullness of God's revelation and salvation. Only Jesus of Nazareth is the one mediator between God and humankind—the one ultimately sought by that "seeking Christology" written into every person's being and consciousness by the grace of God's Christocentric self-communication. Christianity, established on the reality of Jesus Christ, is therefore unique among the religions of the world. The preeminence of Christianity resides not in Christians themselves but in Jesus' person, his message, and his saving life, death, and resurrection. An authentic pluralism is compelled to acknowledge the uniqueness of God's revealing and saving activity in Jesus Christ.

DOMINUS IESUS

These traditional truths, so important to the recognition of the unique character of Christianity, have been challenged by some theologians in the contemporary debate about religious pluralism. *Dominus Iesus* took a critical stance to their claim that these truths have been superseded.

It appears that the declaration had in mind the "pluralistic" theology of religions, often associated with John Hick's philosophy of religion.[3] Hick's type of theological thinking is based on the hypothesis that "the great world traditions constitute different conceptions and perceptions of, and responses to, the Real from within the different cultural ways of being human."[4] Religious terms for ultimate reality, like

Brahman, Sunyata and the *Dao, Yahweh, Allah, Shiva,* and *Kali* are different ways human beings have of naming and connecting with what Hick calls the "Real." As a consequence, *all* religions must be seen as partial and incomplete interpretations of a transcendent Reality that fully surpasses humankind's ability to name. No religion may legitimately claim to have the definite and entire revelation of God and therefore affirm superiority to any other religion as a path to salvation. Regarding this relativistic thinking about religious diversity and its implication for Christianity's evangelizing efforts, *Dominus Iesus* states that "the Church's constant missionary proclamation is endangered today by relativistic theories which seek to justify religious pluralism, not only de facto but also de jure (or 'in principle')" (4).

The pluralistic theology of religions has implications also for traditional Christology. These have been articulated, for example, in the recent work of Roger Haight.[5] To the question, "Is Christianity really a religion destined for all people?" Haight's response tends toward the side of pluralism. He proposes that

> Christians must believe that Jesus is a normative revelation from God, but they may also hold that God is normatively disclosed in other religious traditions as well. Jesus may mediate salvation for Christians, but he is not salvific for people who follow other religious paths. Consequently, Jesus of Nazareth is not a universal savior, the unique and unparalleled redemptive event intended for all. Other mediations of salvation proper to the other religious traditions exist and are not to be subsumed within the mediation Christians affirm. Many distinct and independent paths lead to a sole common salvation in God. Jesus, therefore, is not necessarily the only mediation of the divine empowered by the Spirit.[6]

Dominus Iesus takes a critical stance against contemporary theological thinking that claims Jesus of Nazareth "reveals the divine not in an exclusive way, but in a way complementary with other revelatory and salvific figures" (9). This position is rejected for being in profound conflict with the Christian faith: "There are also those who propose the hypothesis of an economy of the Holy Spirit with a more universal breadth than that of the Incarnate Word, crucified and risen. This position also is contrary to the Catholic faith, which, on the contrary, considers the salvific incarnation of the word as a trinitarian event" (12). In support of this view the declaration cites *Gaudium et Spes* 22: "The Holy Spirit offers to all the possibility of being made partners, in a way known to God, in the paschal mystery." *Dominus Iesus* also cites *Redemptoris Missio* where the pope notes that the Spirit, who is at work universally for the salvation of all human beings, "is the same Spirit who was at work in the incarnation and in the life, death, and resurrection of Jesus and who is at work in the church. He is therefore not an alternative to Christ nor does he fill a sort of void which is sometimes suggested as existing between Christ and the Logos" (29). It is necessary above all, the declaration states, to insist on the definitive and complete character of the revelation of Jesus Christ.

> In fact it must be *firmly believed* that, in the mystery of Jesus Christ, the incarnate Son of God, who is "the way, the truth and the life" (John 14:6), the full revelation of the divine truth is given: "No one knows the Son except the Father, and no one knows the Father except the Son and anyone to whom the Son wishes to reveal him" (Matthew 11:27); "No one has ever seen God; the only Son, who is in the bosom of the Father has revealed him" (John 1:18); "For in Christ the whole fullness of divinity dwells in bodily form" (Colossians 2:9–10). *(DI5)*

Conclusion: Christianity as Normative

Since Christianity, and only Christianity, is the response to faith in Jesus—who is the only mediator of salvation between God and humankind as well as the summit and fullness of God's revealed truth[7]—it is the normatively true religion.[8] The non-Christian religions, then, are relatively true and lesser and extraordinary means of salvation. While the other religions do not have the fullness of truth—ambiguities and errors are found within them—they nevertheless are true and valid insofar as they implicitly share and practice the truth and values of Christianity.

It should be noted here that in *Dominus Iesus* 22 the following qualification is included: "If it is true that the followers of other religions can receive divine grace, it is also certain that *objectively speaking* they are in a gravely deficient situation in comparison with those who, in the Church, have the fullness of the means of salvation." However, citing *Lumen Gentium* 14, the declaration goes on to caution that "'all the children of the Church should nevertheless remember that their exalted condition results, not from their own merits, but from the grace of Christ. If they fail to respond in thought, word and deed to that grace, not only shall they not be saved, but they shall be more severely judged.'" Convinced of the unique and normative status of Christianity, the declaration speaks in number 22 of the church's duty to bring the Christian gospel to the world. She is "duty bound to proclaim without fail Christ, who is the way, the truth and the life (John 14:6). In him, in whom God reconciled things to himself (2 Corinthians 5:18–19), men find the fullness of their religious life" *(Nostrae Aetate* 2). And in number 5 the declaration states that

> the encyclical *Redemptoris Missio* calls the Church once again to the task of announcing the Gospel as the fullness of truth: "In this definitive Word of his revelation, God has made himself known in the fullest possible way. He has revealed to mankind who he is. This definitive self-revelation of God is the fundamental reason why the church is missionary by her very nature. She cannot do other than proclaim the Gospel, that is, the fullness of the truth which God has enabled us to know about himself." *(RM 5)*.

THE TEACHING OF POPE BENEDICT XVI ON THEOLOGY OF RELIGIONS

Benedict XVI's career began in 1959 with his position as professor of systematic theology.[9] His life as teacher and scholar was strongly influenced by his experiences as consultant in Vatican II (1960–64); there he witnessed many developments inside the council, enabling him to help formulate certain texts and, later on, to comment on them with authority. Regarding his teaching on the non-Christian religions, we call attention, first, as an introduction, to a sermon Professor Ratzinger preached in 1964. It was entitled," Are Non-Christians Saved?" In light of the controversy that arose as a consequence of his later teaching on the subject as pope, it seems appropriate to make reference to this sermon.

"Are Non-Christians Saved?"

> Everything we believe about God, and everything we know about man, prevents us from accepting that beyond the limits of the Church there is no more salvation, that up to the time of Christ all men were subject to the fate of eternal damnation. We are no longer ready and able to think that our neighbor, who is a decent and respectable man and in many ways better than we are, should be eternally damned simply because he is not a Catholic. We are no longer ready, no longer willing, to think that eternal corruption should be inflicted on people in Asia, in Africa, or wherever it may be, merely on account of their not having "Catholic" marked in their passport.
>
> Actually, a great deal of thought had been devoted in theology, both before and after Ignatius, to the question of how people, without even knowing it, in some way belonged to the Church and to Christ and could thus be saved nevertheless. And still today, a great deal of perspicacity is used in such reflection.
>
> Yet if we are honest, we will have to admit that this is not our problem at all. The question we have to face is not that of whether other people can be saved and how. We are convinced that God is able to do this with or without our theories, with or without our perspicacity, and that we do not need to help him do it with our cogitations. The question that really troubles us is not in the least concerned with whether and how God manages to save *others*.
>
> The question that torments us is, rather, why it is still actually necessary for us to carry out the whole ministry of the Christian faith—why, if there are so many other ways to heaven and to salvation, should it still be demanded of us that we bear, day by day, the whole burden of ecclestical dogma and ecclesiastical ethics?.[10]

This sermon given during the time of Vatican II is a foreshadowing of Professor Ratzinger's later teaching on the theology of religions.

Cardinal Ratzinger and *Dominus Iesus*

Ratzinger's tenure as professor of theology ended in 1977 with his appointment as archbishop of Munich and Freising. In 1981, Pope John Paul II called him to Rome to assume the post of cardinal prefect of the Congregation of the Doctrine of the Faith. He occupied this post until he was elected pope in 2005.

The decade from 1992 to 2002 was one in which the Congregation for the Doctrine of the Faith, and therefore also its cardinal prefect, gave much attention to the theology of religions. There were several theologians who set forth unorthodox answers to the questions of religious diversity, and correcting them played the same role in the efforts of the congregation in these years as correcting the publications of some liberation theologians had during the preceding two decades.

And then, on August 6, 2000, the declaration *Dominus Iesus*, elaborated under the supervision of Joseph Cardinal Ratzinger, was published with the ratification of Pope John Paul II. There is hardly any doubt that Ratzinger had more a part in its composition than anyone else, and that its integral content represents his own theological thought. As we have seen, the document's main concern was precisely to combat inappropriately pluralistic theologies with a strong statement of the following basic claims of christological and ecclesiological orthodoxy: the unique and total salvific significance of the life, passion, death, and resurrection of Jesus; the close unity of the redeeming work of the incarnate Logos with that of the Holy Spirit; the profound intimacy between the church of Christ and the visible and hierarchically structured Catholic Church in full communion with the bishop of Rome; and the necessity of preserving the church's evangelical mission to bring the gospel to all and its imperative to engage in serious dialogue with other religions.

Cardinal Ratzinger's firm and explicit personal affirmation of *Dominus Iesus* should be noted. On September 14, 2000, he sent a letter, signed by himself, to the presidents of Bishops' Conferences explaining the purpose and authority of the declaration. He states that the declaration

> presents the principle truths of the Catholic faith in these areas; such truths require, therefore, irrevocable assent by the Catholic faithful; the text also … points out important questions that remain open to theological investigation and debate. Since it is a document of the Congregation for the Doctrine of Faith, the declaration has a universal theological nature.

Ratzinger goes on to indicate that he

> is confident that the conference itself, as well as individual bishops, will do everything possible to insure its distribution and favorable reception … Particularly in the areas of ecumenical and interreligious dialogue and in Catholic universities and faculties of theology, it is essential that the doctrinal contents of this declaration become a point of reference as well as a solid and

indispensable foundation for pastoral and missionary work which is convincing, effective and consistent with Catholic teaching.[11]

The thinking of Joseph Ratzinger on theology of religious pluralism is surely found expressed in *Dominus Iesus*. Further insights into his views on this subject can be found in one of his books, *Truth and Tolerance*, which was published in 2003.

Cardinal Ratzinger's Writings as a Theologian

During his career as prefect of the Congregation of the Doctrine of the Faith, Cardinal Ratzinger continued his theological writing. And when he reached the age of seventy-five, he evidently was ready to sum up his life's scholarly work. As he began to edit his writings, he made no major changes in his original texts. A text he edited and published shortly before his elevation to the papacy is of particular significance for us: *Truth and Tolerance: Christian Belief and World Religions*.[12]

This text is a collection of thirteen of his previously published essays on the various questions concerning the theology of religions. Some of these questions are, May a non-Christian religion be a real means of salvation for its adherents? May eternal salvation be separated from the life, death, and resurrection of Jesus? What may be said in regard to a devout non-Christian's relation to God? How can the Catholic Church's demand for the evangelization of non-Christians be reconciled with its requirement for serious dialogue with those who practice the other religions? What is the meaning of interreligious prayer? The essays of *Truth and Tolerance*, mostly from the 1990s, with his more recent comments and elaborations added, are learned restatements of basic Catholic orthodoxy on these questions raised by religious diversity.

As Cardinal Ratzinger himself indicates in *Truth and Tolerance*, when *Dominus Iesus* was published in 2000, there came "a cry of outrage from modern society, but also from great non-Christian cultures such as that of India; this was said to be a document of intolerance and of a religious arrogance that should have no more place in the world of today."[13] There was also (and this is not spoken of in the book) criticism of *Dominus Iesus* from prominent members from within the hierarchy. At least two cardinals, Edward Cassidy, then president of the Pontifical Council for Promoting Christian Unity, and Walter Kasper, the current president, publicly distanced themselves from the declaration.

In light of this context of tense conflict, the collection of Ratzinger's essays, which was published in German and Italian in 2003 and in English in 2004, is important. It holds firmly to the line of the fundamental claims of christological and ecclesiological orthodoxy expressed in *Dominus Iesus*. Consequently, it is a precise indication of what the former theologian and Vatican administrator who is now the pope thinks about the theology of religions, and it makes clear what is at issue between the pope and the critics of *Dominus Iesus*. *Truth and Tolerance* also expresses elements of Ratzinger's thought not directly related to the purpose of *Dominus Iesus*. Some of these elements we consider next.

Ratzinger and Rahner

For the lead essay of the collection, Ratzinger placed a piece he had written nearly forty years previously for the *Festschrift* dedicated to Karl Rahner on the occasion of his sixtieth birthday: "The Unity and Diversity of Religions: The Place of Christianity in the History of Religions." This time Ratzinger added some "preliminary remarks" that set forth his criticisms of Rahner, which he had intentionally omitted in the Festschrift as a mark of respect for his countryman. These criticisms refer to Rahner's famous lecture of 1961 on "Christianity and the Non-Christian Religions." Ratzinger speaks of two points in Rahner's approach with which he did not agree: first, Rahner's restricting his interest in the non-Christian religions to the salvation of the individual person, without much concern for the significance that other religions have in themselves; second, all religions, consequently, were equally summed up by Rahner in the single abstract concept of "religion." In fact, for the solution offered by Karl Rahner, the history of religions, as well as any concrete religion, becomes irrelevant. Ratzinger acknowledges that in light of the enormous amount of research being done in the field of the history of religions, a single theologian is unable to master all religions in detail. In his book, however, Ratzinger does reflect on the significance the other religions have in themselves. His reflection includes efforts to discover "whether there was any kind of continuous historical development here and whether any basic types of religion could (be) recognized, which we could then more easily evaluate" (18). He also reflects on the unique character of Christianity, "to show more clearly the place of Christianity in the history of religions" (16).

Two Types of Religions

One of the basic points argued by Ratzinger in his book, *Truth and Tolerance,* is that an impartial exploration of the world's religions discloses a fundamental difference between two types of religions: those that offer a "mysticism of identity" (33–34) and those that advocate a "personal understanding of God." In his review of the cardinal's book, Paul Griffiths, Schmitt Professor of Catholic Studies at the University of Illinois at Chicago, proposes that "Ratzinger tends too easily to identify religions of the former type [those that offer a 'mysticism of identity'] with those of Asia, especially Hinduism. This is dubious, descriptively and historically: Many Hindus have had what Ratzinger means by a personal understanding of God, and at least some Christians, Jews, and Muslims have lacked it." But Griffiths adds that the distinction is, nevertheless, "a powerful one and serves well Ratzinger's purpose of emphasizing difference and underscoring distinction: All religions do not commend the same goal or offer the same understanding of God and the human; and it is among the tendencies of those who advocate religious pluralism to obscure this."[14]

Uniqueness of Christianity

Ratzinger explains the uniqueness of Christianity in a precise and traditional way. Christianity's distinctiveness does not enter history like a bolt from the heavens. Nor does it simply abolish or lay waste the world's religions and cultures. Rather, as the principle and fullest presence in the world of the institutional form of the Christ's body, the church provides those who do not yet know her with the enticement of a fuller and richer understanding of what they already know, both religiously and culturally. The possibility of conversion offered by Christianity is, consequently, an offer that carries with it a culturally and religiously unique fulfillment of cultures as they existed before conversion. The church is called, therefore, to address Buddhists, Marxists, secular hedonists, and neo-Stoics in the same voice and with the same two attitudes: as a humble yet confident presenter of an outstanding gift, and at the same time, as an eager and sincere listener. These attitudes are those of proclamation and dialogue; they are inextricably linked in Ratzinger's thought, as they are also in the documents of Vatican II. Ratzinger notes that the only two partial exceptions are conversations with those to whom the church is already closely related—that is to say, the Jewish people and the Muslims. But he says little about the Jews or the Muslims in these essays.

Religious Truth

In the second half of *Truth and Tolerance*, Ratzinger turns to the question of religious truth. If God is triune, if Jesus of Nazareth was the second person of the Holy Trinity, and if the Catholic Church is the institution in which Christ's church subsists—if all these traditional beliefs are true, then the positions rejected in *Dominus Iesus* must be false. But he also concerns himself with the larger philosophical difficulties in regard to skepticism and relativism. At some length he speaks of the connections of relativism with the rejection of the very idea of truth as correspondence of the knowing intellect to its known objects, and he explores the connection of skepticism with the idea that it is impossible to know which religion is true even if one were true. One way he does this is by reflecting on Christianity's rivals in the Roman world of late antiquity. But Ratzinger does not think that people today can simply adopt, for example, Saint Augustine's response to the neo-Platonists. He recognizes that for modern persons, as for their fourth- and fifth-century forbearers, arguments to support the Christian affirmation of the basic comprehensibility and rationality of the world will no longer be convincing to the cultured despisers of Christianity. While this position is correct, it is to be held together, Paul Griffiths suggests, with Ratzinger's equally strong affirmation of Christianity's truth. The world is comprehensible by human rationality because of the nature of its creator and redeemer. "Faced with the Christian claim—with good arguments in support of it, for that matter—many will deny it. This interesting fact holds the key to at least some elements of the complex of questions raised by religious diversity."[15]

Buddhism and Hinduism

In the view of Paul Griffiths, many of Ratzinger's statements about Buddhism and Hinduism in *Truth and Tolerance* are characterized by a superficiality and generality he would himself criticize in comparable remarks about Christianity. But he adds, "These are matters that do not affect the merits of the work as a whole, which are great. *Truth and Tolerance* provides transparently lucid guidelines for the recognition of when orthodoxy has been abandoned. It rightly identifies the main intellectual and social pressures issuing in such abandonment."[16]

SUMMARY

In his writings as theologian and his work as prefect of the Congregation of the Doctrine of the Faith, Joseph Ratzinger held to traditional christological and ecclesiological truths in his reflection on the theology of religions.

PAPAL TEACHING OF BENEDICT XVI

There have been many occasions that seem to prove that, as the Supreme Pontiff, Benedict XVI is highly motivated to foster and develop what was initiated by his predecessors, especially John Paul II. In John Paul's time, there were many symbolic acts of respect: visits of synagogues and mosques, the prayer in Assisi, the Wailing Wall in Jerusalem, and in Yad Vashem. What John Paul II began, Benedict continued: he visited the synagogue in Cologne; he visited Auschwitz, where suddenly a rainbow appeared; he prayed in the Blue Masque in Istanbul facing Mecca. At the same time, however, we witness disturbing consequences of his lecture at Regensburg.

On September 12, 2006, Benedict XVI delivered an academic lecture in Regensburg, Germany, that argued for both the reasonableness of faith and that faith separated from reason can result in behaviors contrary to God's will. In this context, the pope quoted the opinion of a fourteenth-century Byzantine emperor, Manuel II Paleologus, that "not acting reasonably is contrary to God's nature." The emperor had illustrated his assertion about unreasonable religious behavior by discussing the use of violence to coerce conversion, attributing such practices in polemical terms to Islam, and this language was quoted by the pope: "Show me just what Mohammed brought that was new, and there you will find things only evil and inhuman, such as his command to spread by the sword the faith he preached."[17]

The lecture sparked protests in many Islamic countries. Apparently the protestors had concluded or were advised that Benedict himself believed Islam to be, in the quoted words from the fourteenth century, "only evil and inhuman." Because the lecture did not include any examples of unreasonable Christian practices or repeat formal Catholic teaching from the Second Vatican Council that the church regards Muslims with esteem, the probability of unintended negative interpretations of the lecture was increased.

On September 16, 2006, the Vatican secretary of state, Cardinal Tarcisio Bertone, issued a statement about criticism in the Muslim world over Pope Benedict XVI's remarks about Islam and violence.

> As for the opinion of the Byzantine emperor Manuel II Paleologus ... the Holy Father did not mean, nor does he mean, to make that opinion his own in any way. He simply used it as a means to undertake—in an academic context, and as is evident from a complete and attentive reading of the text—certain reflection on the theme of the relationship between religion and violence in general, and to conclude with clear and radical rejection of the religious motivation for violence, from whatever side it may come.[18]

Bertone stated that the position of the pope concerning Islam is unequivocally that expressed by the councilor document *Nostra Aetate*:

> The Church regards with esteem also the Muslims. They adore the one God, living and subsisting in Himself; merciful and all-powerful, the Creator of heaven and earth, who has spoken to men; they take pains to submit wholeheartedly to even His inscrutable decrees, just as Abraham, with whom the faith of Islam takes pleasure in linking itself, submitted to God. Though they do not acknowledge Jesus as God, they revere Him as a prophet. They also honor Mary, His virgin Mother; at times they even call on her with devotion. In addition, they await the Day of Judgment with God will render their deserts to all those who have been raised up from the dead. Finally, they value the moral life and worship god especially through prayer, almsgiving and fasting. (3)

The Holy Father sincerely regrets, Bertone insisted, that certain parts of his lecture could have sounded offensive to the sensitivities of the Muslim faithful and were interpreted in a way that does not at all correspond to his intentions. On September 17, 2006, the pope stated, "At this time, I wish also to add that I am deeply sorry for the reactions in some countries to a few passages of my address at the University of Regensburg, which were considered offensive to the sensibilities of Muslims. These in fact were a quotation from a medieval text, which do not in any way express my own person thought." In a general audience on September 20, 2006, the pope stated:

> In no way did I wish to make my own the words of the medieval emperor. I wished to explain that not religion and violence, but religion and reason, go together. I hope that my profound

respect for world religions and for Muslims, who "worship the one God" and with whom we "promote peace, liberty, social justice and moral values for the benefit of all humanity" (*Nostra Aetate*, no. 23) is clear. Let us continue the dialogue both between religions and between modern reason and the Christian faith![19]

Notes

1. Richard McBrien, *Catholicism: Completely Revised and Updated* (San Francisco: HarperCollins, 1994), 380.
2. From the pope's November 1999 apostolic exhortation *Ecclesia in Asia* 11.
3. A comprehensive statement of Hick's pluralist approach is his book, *An Interpretation of Religion: The Challenge of Other Religions* (Oxford: Blackwell, 1989).
4. Ibid., 376.
5. Roger Haight, *Jesus: Symbol of God* (Maryknoll, NY: Orbis, 1999).
6. Philip Kennedy has also articulated implications of pluralistic theology for Christology. He holds that religious pluralism is an unavoidable fact of reality. Since God is illimitable, no historical reality can manifest the full richness of God. "Jesus Christ is not the complete revelation of God in history, but a partial manifestation of what God may be like. Since Jesus is not the unveiling of the fullness of God in the world, other religions may have their way about God's salvific nature. Even according to classical dogmatic theology, Jesus Christ is the enfleshment in history of the Second Person of the Trinity. The fullness of the Trinity is not incarnate in Jesus. Consequently, there is more to God, so to speak, than has been shown in Jesus Christ. God remains a *Deus absconditus*, a God who always escapes human attempts to picture God." Philip Kennedy, cited in Martin E. Marty, "Rome and Relativism," *Commonweal* 125:18 (2000). Gerald O'Collins has made a similar point about Christology. In one sense, surely, Jesus Christ embodies and communicates the fullness of revelation, but in another sense he does not. "The final vision of God is still to come. As St. John puts it, 'it does not yet appear what we shall be ... when he appears, we shall be like him, for we shall see him as he is' (1 John 3:2). As we wait in hope for the complete and final revelation, we see and know 'dimly' and not yet fully. Looking forward to the fullness of God's saving self- manifestation. St. Paul writes: 'Now we see in a mirror dimly, but then face to face. Now I know in part: then I shall understand fully, even as I have been fully understood' (1 Corinthians.13:12)." Gerald O'Collins, "Watch Your Language" [review *The Meeting of Religions and the Trinity* by Gavin D'Costa], *Tablet* (November 4, 2000), 1490.
7. Jacques Dupuis has reflected with great insight and originality on Jesus Christ as the unique and only savior of humankind as well as the fullness of God's revelation. Since Dupuis's contributions will surely play an important role in the ongoing development of a theology of religions compatible with

scripture, tradition, and Magisterium, as well as effective in promoting inter- religious dialogue, it is included here.

Because Jesus' "personal identity" is that of the Word of God, Son of God, the second person of the Trinity, Dupuis states that "the Christian cannot stand without claiming for Jesus Christ a constitutive uniqueness." *Toward a Christian Theology of Religious Pluralism* (Maryknoll, NY: Orbis, 1997), 304. (Because the quotations in the next three paragraphs are taken mostly from this text, page numbers only are given in parentheses.)

This uniqueness of Jesus means that only he "opens access to God for all human beings" (387). It means, too, that in Jesus God has delivered the fullness of revelation: "It is the very person of Jesus Christ, his deeds and his words, his life, his death, and his resurrection—in a word, the total Jesus Christ-event itself—that constitutes the fullness of revelation. In him God has uttered to the world his decisive word" (248–49).

This fullness is not to be understood qualitatively, as though after Christ everything related to the divine mystery were already known and there was nothing further to learn. It is, rather, to be understood qualitatively, in the sense of being unsurpassed and unsurpassable in strength, concentration, and focus: "This plenitude … is not … one of extension and all-comprehension, but of intensity … It does not—cannot—exhaust the mystery of the Divine" (382). Our knowledge of God as revealed in Jesus is, then, not absolute: "It remains limited. On the one hand, Jesus' human consciousness, while it is that of the Son, is still a human consciousness and therefore a limited one. It could not have been otherwise. No human consciousness, even the human consciousness of the Son of God, can exhaust the Divine Mystery. On the other hand, it is precisely this human experience that Jesus had of being the Son, in relation to the Father, that enabled him to translate into human words the mystery of God that he revealed to us" (249). Consequently, the qualitative and limited fullness of God's revelation in Jesus "is no obstacle, even after the historical event, to a continuing divine self-revelation through the prophets and sages of other religious traditions, as for example, through the prophet Muhammad. That self-revelation has occurred, and continues to occur, in history. No revelation, however, either before or after Christ can either surpass or equal the one vouchsafed in Jesus Christ, the divine Son incarnate" (249–50). The revelation in Christ is central and normative for Christians.

While God's self-disclosure in Jesus has normative authority, it is nevertheless relational, in the sense that "the 'transhistorical' character of the risen humanity of Jesus Christ notwithstanding, the event [of God's becoming flesh] is limited by its insertion in history, without which its singular significance and density would vanish. It is, then, at once particular in time and universal in meaning and, as such, 'singularly universal,' yet related to all other divine manifestations to humankind in one history of salvation—that is, relational" (388). Therefore, while the fullness of what God wants to make known to humankind is focused in Jesus, to increase the depth of understanding, Christians have to relate what they have in Jesus to what the Spirit is disclosing in the other religions. The universal enlightenment of the Word of God and the disclosing of his Spirit "make it possible to discover, in other saving figures and traditions, truth and grace not brought out with the same vigor and clarity in God's revelation and manifestations in Jesus Christ. Truth and grace found elsewhere must not be reduced to 'seeds' or 'stepping stones' simply to be nurtured or used and then suppressed in Christian revelation. They represent additional and autonomous benefits" (388).

Dupuis clarifies the relationship between what God has to say through other religions and what God speaks in the Spirit. Since Christ, not the Spirit, is at the center of the way to God, whatever God discloses through other religions in the Spirit must be understood "in view of, and in relation to" what God has disclosed in Jesus Christ. It does not take the place of Christ (197).

"Complementarity" exists between the other religions and Christianity. Dupuis uses the term *complementarity* to indicate how some elements of the one Divine Mystery can be vividly expressed by the practices and sacred writings found beyond Christianity. Nonbiblical scriptures "may contain aspects of the Divine Mystery which the Bible, the New Testament included, do not highlight equally. To give some examples: in the Qur'an the sense of the divine majesty and transcendence, of adoration and of the human being's submission to the holiness of God's eternal decrees, and in the sacred books of Hinduism the sense of God's immanent presence in the world and in the recesses of the human heart." Jacques Dupuis, *Christianity and the Religions: From Confrontation to Dialogue* (Maryknoll, NY: Orbis, 2002), 135. While this complementarity may be considered reciprocal, it is not understood to mean "that anything is lacking with Christianity that it would have to receive from other religions, without which it would not enjoy the fullness of divine revelation, rather in the sense that God has provided gifts to human beings in the other religious traditions as well, which even though they find their fulfillment in the revelation of God in Jesus Christ, nonetheless represent authentic words of God, and additional autonomous gifts from God. Such divine gifts to human beings do not in any way impede the transcendence and unsurpassability of God's gift to humankind in Jesus Christ. The complementarity between the seeds of 'truth and grace' in the other religious traditions and the 'fullness' of the divine manifestation in Jesus Christ, attested by the Christian sacred scriptures, is thus to be understood as mutual 'asymmetrical' complementarity" Dupuis, *Christianity and the Religions*, 136.

8. Francis X. Clooney puts into context the traditional teaching that asserts Christianity as normatively true. "It is not a peculiarly Roman Catholic insight to hold that the content of faith is true or that truth about reality can be normatively apprehended. I have known many Hindus over the years who are quite willing to assert the truth of what they believe. In my years of study of Indian Hindu theologies, too, I have encountered numerous claims by theologians as to the truth of a community's faith … When we claim that 'my faith is true, unique or even superior' we may be correct, but the claim itself is not unique or even particularly unusual. Catholics who make this claim are in important ways like Ramanuja and his community who make a comparable claim." "Implications for the Practice of

Inter-Religious Learning," in *Sic et Non: Encountering Dominus Iesus*, Stephen J. Pope and Charles Hefling, eds. (Maryknoll, NY: Orbis, 2002), 160.
9. The sources for this section are the following:
Mathew Bunson, "Pope Benedict Speaks to Muslims," *Catholic Culture*, available at: http://www.catholicculture.org/library/view.cfm?recum=7536
Paul J. Griffiths, "Rehabilitating Truth" [review of *Truth and Tolerance: Christian Belief and World Religions* by Joseph Cardinal Ratzinger], First Things (May 2005), 49-51.
Michael Ireland, "Pope Benedict XVI Apologizes for Speech Offending Muslims," *StreamingFaith*, September 19, 2006, available at: http://www.streamingfaith.com/community/news.aspx?NewsId=420&bhcp=I
"Pope Benedict and Islam," Boston College: Center for Christian-Jewish Relations, available at: http://www.bc.edu/research/cjl/eta-elements/texts/cjrelations/topics/Benedict_Islam.htm
Joseph Ratzinger, "Are Non-Christians Saved?" (1964), *Beliefnet*, available at: http://www.beliefnet.com/story/209/story_20936.html
Cardinal Joseph Ratzinger, "Letter of Cardinal Ratzinger regarding *Dominus Iesus*" Vatican, September 14, 2000, *Catholic Culture*, available at: http://www.catholicculture.org/library/view.cfm?recnum=31323
10. Ratzinger, "Are Non-Christians Saved?"
11. Ratzinger, "Letter of Cardinal Ratzinger regarding *Dominus Iesus*"
12. Joseph Cardinal Ratzinger, *Truth and Tolerance: Christian Belief and World Religions* (San Francisco: Ignatius Press, 2004).
13. Ibid., 9.
14. Griffiths, "Rehabilitating Truth," 51.
15. Ibid., 51.
16. Ibid.
17. Excerpts from the papal lecture, "Faith, Reason and the University: Memories and Reflections," September 12, 2006, Boston College: Center for Christian-Jewish Relations, available at: http://www.bc.edu/research/cjl/meta-elements/texts/cjrelations/topics/Benedict_Islam.htm
18. Ibid.
19. Ibid.

CHAPTER REVIEW

1. Differentiate between the types of Christian groups.
2. What is canonicity?

3. Explain the different ways Christians look at heaven, hell, purgatory and salvation.
4. In what ways does religion divide us? In what ways does it join us together, with regard to Christianity?
5. Explain Predestination.

Islam

By Irfan A. Omar

In the twentieth century, Western technology and scientific advancement were promoted to an unprecedented degree for the purpose of bringing about an equal distribution of its fruits. But in actuality, it was only an extension of the previous Western modes of hegemony and domination of the Third World (the "two-thirds world"). Scientific achievements of the West were being utilized, according to Herbert Marcuse, "to serve the interests of continued domination." Thus only "the modes of domination have changed: they have become increasingly technological, productive, and even beneficial" (1955:vii). When Marcuse wrote these words the economic globalization had not yet fully revealed its face, resulting in an unprecedented concentration of wealth and power in the hands of the few. In the twenty-first century this objective of "continued domination" by some Western entities has become manifest at all levels of human existence: environmental, economic, sociopolitical, and increasingly cultural.

At the same time, in the twenty-first century, it is futile to speak of the "West" (primarily understood in cultural terms) or even the "North" (understood in economic terms) as well as their opposites because

Irfan A. Omar, "Islam," *The Hope of Liberation in World Religions*, ed. Miguel A. De La Torre, pp. 91–112. Copyright © 2008 by Baylor University Press. Reprinted with permission.

these terms have lost a good deal of meaning. Today the West and North are found everywhere; they exist not only within their own historically claimed domains but also within the heart of their polar opposites, the "East" and the "South." The rapid dissemination of Western culture through the mass media and the concentration of economic power through the globalized reach of the corporations have penetrated many other cultures, societies, and markets. These two have established themselves as a set of normative global cultural and economic patterns, demanding that all other systems must give way. Globalization has taken over.

It is pertinent to speak of liberation theology as a phenomenon that has manifested and reappropriated itself in many parts of the "two-thirds world" as a response to these systemic and structural processes. It is of particular importance to understand the different ideologies and movements that have provided a medium for such manifestations and reappropriations. Religion has played a key role in many such movements. While Latin American struggles were first framed in the context of Marxism and Christianity, the struggles in the Middle East and North Africa began in experimentation with westernization, secularism, socialism, and Arab nationalism, culminating in various forms of religious resurgence. Islam became the channel through which resistance and resurgence, revivalism and discontent were expressed. Islam undoubtedly remains one such powerful medium in the contemporary world. Today such struggles and challenges have lost all sense of geography and ethnic alliances. Today's liberation struggles cut across national boundaries, as well as political and sectarian divides, and are marked by conflicts which are both internal—among Muslim groups, as well as external—between Muslim and non-Muslim groups.

In the period after the cold war until the events of September 11, 2001, the Western political talking heads and some policy makers in both the legislative as well as the executive branches of government regarded Islam as the next "enemy" of the United States and the Western world. The earlier threat posed by the Soviet Union, which no longer existed, had been replaced by Islam. It was argued that Islam was a challenge not only to Western economic interests but also to its cultural interests, which are in the end one and the same. The alleged manifestations of these so-called challenges have been reported in many Western countries, such as France, the Netherlands, Germany, and the United Kingdom, for in these countries, due to incidents involving Muslims, the issue of cultural differences has been raised in racial and ethnic terms. The story of Islam in the West continues to be written with earnest speed, and more so now than ever before. With Western/American involvement in Afghanistan and Iraq and the impending designs for Iran, the geopolitical focus on both Islam as a religious tradition and the Muslim societies continues to be a source of anxiety and unease for many Muslims, especially those Muslims who are part of the West (even though they may not necessarily be located *in* the "West").

In a post-September 11 world, the situation has worsened for many Muslims as they increasingly come under suspicion for being who they are. The countless attacks on Islam and Muslims have put many on the defensive. But as modes of oppression change as well as increase, so do the forms of resistance. In recent years, Muslims in the United States in particular have become proactive in seeking to engage in dialogue across all levels of the social, religious, and political landscape. Interreligious and intercultural dialogue has caught on in many communities and better awareness of their political rights is being disseminated through civil rights and community organizations across North America. Indeed, one of the greatest challenges facing Muslims worldwide is to continue to engage in liberationist forms of struggle against bigotry both from within and without.

The Universality of the Theme of Liberation: A Broader View

The term *liberation theology* arose within the context of a Christian struggle that sought to revive the human-centered values within a highly ritualized and particular world of Christianity. Thus applying the term to discuss the same phenomenon in other religions is problematic at best. However, the crux of what liberation theology stands for—the search for and revival of the liberative principles that place human beings at the center of religious discourse, and the struggle associated with these—is part and parcel of all religious movements. Even as the Latin American liberation theology was taking root, African and Asian countries witnessed their own forms of resistance movements—i.e., the struggles against the colonial domination of the nineteenth and early twentieth centuries. Thus the phenomenon that liberation theology refers to has always been present in many societies and has often been expressed through religious symbols and activism. Even in their origins, the world's major religious traditions themselves arose out of a fundamental need for human liberation from whatever it was that displaced the people involved; be it spiritual decadence, economic greed, racial prejudice, cultural and political imperialism, lust for power, or simply the forces of the ego marshaled against the very core of human morality.

Historically, Islam also began as a liberationist movement in seventh-century Arabia where tribal customs had created a hierarchical social structure which systematically discriminated against people of other races and classes and even against those from other tribes. Slavery and patriarchy were the defining characteristics of that society in which Muhammad, the founder of Islam lived, and although a few women of power were able to assert their rights, a vast majority of women did not have any recourse to justice in a male-dominated power structure, living in a gendered hierarchy with fewer possibilities for exercising their individual freedoms. Similarly, as prophet Muhammad's movement, based on the revelatory event, grew, its monotheistic message was determined by the ruling establishment of the city of Makkah to be a threat to their economic and social interests. The freedom to believe in and live according to an alternative worldview, other than the unjust system perpetrated by the hierarchy at the time, was not granted. Instead, Muhammad and his followers had to endure persecution and hardships on account of their peaceful movement which sought to establish a just and equitable society, and which ultimately stressed the notion of "struggle" (*jihad*) for freedom to practice one's faith. This struggle was carried out through nonviolent resistance to persecution: with patience, fortitude, and steadfastness, as the Qur'an demanded its followers to do.

In the first phase of Prophet Muhammad's ministry (610–622 C.E.), the struggle on behalf of Islam did not involve any violent response to persecution; once the level of persecution reached unbearable levels, however, and when the Prophet and many of his followers were forced to migrate out of their native city of Makkah and moved to Madinah, divine sanction was given to take up arms, and even then, only to defend their lives and their freedom to practice their religion. The paradigm of struggle and resistance to injustice established by prophet Muhammad and his early followers was clearly a movement of liberation. Many other Islamic movements developed in later centuries have attempted to follow that prophetic paradigm, and together these have become important sources of inspiration for many contemporary Muslim liberation struggles.

Many twentieth-century Islamic movements had their roots in their experience of being the target of Western hegemonic adventures in the Muslim world in general, and the Middle East in particular. These experiences of course are built upon and sometimes draw succor from the memories of the previous three centuries of colonial and postcolonial enterprise. Increasingly though there have emerged a number of liberation movements, even "theologies" in a sense because they do acknowledge the divine dispensation in how and what they set out to achieve. Thus one can speak of a Palestinian theology of liberation which began as a "nonviolent" intifada in the 1980s but has taken on various manifestations since then. One could also consider the liberation struggles of many communities living in African and Asian countries to cope with the realities of economic and cultural globalization. In more ways than one, globalization has uprooted traditional forms of social and economic structures and has quite successfully shaken indigenous moral and religious systems, often replacing them with the Hollywood version of the "good," the "bad," and the "ugly."

In addition, myriad smaller movements within Islam seek to liberate from within. These are the Muslim reformist movements working to alleviate the age-old tensions between the polarized views on a host of issues, from women's rightful place in Muslim societies and in the religious hierarchy, to theorizations of an appropriate political and economic configuration of a Muslim state. Many such movements and struggles are being carried out in all parts of the world from Afghanistan to the United States, from Denmark to South Africa. At the same time, there is an attempt to construct an overarching unified struggle that all Muslims are beginning to feel part of due to an incredible amount of Islamophobic activities which have emerged since the horrifying terrorist attacks of September 11, 2001. The level of prejudice and biased attacks against Islam and Muslims are now quite well known in public and are often tolerated at the highest levels of civil society in some Western countries. All Muslims face this common struggle regardless of their particularized situations. In fact, this struggle goes beyond any specific religious, cultural, and ethnic divide; it poses a challenge to all concerned with basic human rights and freedoms.

It is beyond the scope of this essay to discuss these and other various forms of Islamic/Muslim liberation theologies. Here I will limit myself to the discussion of the Islamic scriptural imperatives that speak to themes of liberation. I will focus on two contemporary attempts/theologies that sought to revive and reframe Islamic liberation themes from the perspective of religion. These themes are reflected in the work of Asghar Ali Engineer (India) and Ali Shari'ati (Iran). Showcasing these major initiatives will help to draw parallels between the Islamic and Christian liberation theologies and to highlight the parity that exists between their respective objectives and methods, their reliance on scriptural authority, and their focus on the concern for the masses.

A Theology of Praxis

Theology is always about God and about us at the same time. But it is not solely metaphysical; in theology, human beings are talking about the divine. It is the human seeing oneself in relation to God, or the divine reality. God is at the center but this center is perceived from the perspective of a believer. This perspective, however, may have originated from and on the basis of revelation. Thus theology is a reflection upon pastoral work. It is a practice, a doing, so to speak.

Understanding of religion may go beyond and indeed goes beyond any mainstream theology. There are always marginal theologies, including what has sometimes been referred to as "a people's version of theology," that flourish parallel to mainstream theology (Ferm, 1992:5). The latter theology almost always remains abstract and metaphysical, whereas the alternate or people's theologies often relate to the historical situation of the people and arise as a response to fundamental social and human needs. For any theology to be completely useful and satisfying it has to fulfill both these functions: the metaphysical as well as the existential. As is evident from historical examples found in many religions, however, mainstream theologies have often neglected the prophetic and pastoral aspects of their challenge and thus have given rise to people's theologies. If theology remains metaphysical in all circumstances, then it simply becomes a tool in the hands of the privileged, implicitly supporting the status quo. On the other hand, people's theologies are not always liberative in the immediate sense, but they bring awareness of the needs of the masses who are often dispossessed to the point of having little or no voice in determining their destiny.

According to Asghar Ali Engineer (b. 1939), one of the pioneer theorists to address the notion of an Islamic liberation theology, Islam also has had its own marginal theologies that have taken a radical stance at many a point in the history of Islam. He identifies Sufi theology as one that tends to be closer to the heart of the people, although in certain modes it is even more metaphysical than the mainstream theology. Not all manifestations of Sufism provide simple and straightforward answers to the problems and questions confronted by an average believer, especially with respect to the daily struggle for survival. In its devotional aspects, however, Sufism is closer to the heart of the people where there is less of a concern with "understanding" and a greater emphasis on praxis of spirituality.

Since mainstream (orthodox) theologies are almost always rigid and legalistic, or to be more precise, rigidly "otherworldly," these marginal theologies help to complement the mainstream theologies. But often they are also in conflict regarding the emphasis; the former usually focuses upon the metaphysical and the latter on the present social and economic conditions. These two theologies can and must work closely in cases where these marginal theologies directly relate to or emerge from the original sources of the orthodox theology, that is, the scriptures. A truly liberative theology must evolve out of or at least be connected to what Cornel West calls "the core message" of the tradition. Thus a genuine Islamic theology of liberation must be grounded within the historical examples of the tradition. It must derive from the primary sources of the Islamic faith—the Qur'an and the Sunnah (traditions and the example) of Prophet Muhammad—and yet remain in conversation with the historical understandings of the core message and, more importantly, how this core message manifests itself in the daily lives of the people needing this theology.

Islamic Appropriation of Liberation Theology

Liberation theology is intended to historicize the struggles and meanings that are already present in the lives of the people. For many Latin American theologians, it was a kind of Marxism that did not undermine the authority of the metaphysical principles upheld by the Christian religious tradition. In other words, it is an attempt to strike a balance between the two opposing poles: "metaphysical destiny beyond historical process" and the "human freedom to shape temporal destiny." It is a praxis borne out of such an interaction (Engineer, 1990:1). The Boff brothers defined liberation theology as "an organization for the whole of society ... no longer from a point of departure of the capital held in the hands of the few, but an organization of society based on everyone's labor, with everyone sharing, in the means and goods of production as well as in the means of power" (1984:8). Gustavo Gutiérrez's seminal work *A Theology of Liberation*, which appeared in 1973, was the first systematic presentation of the idea of liberation on the basis of religion. Before Gutiérrez, Paulo Freire, the author of the *Pedagogy of the Oppressed*, introduced the idea of a liberationist theology through his interest in the social transformation of his people. Freire was primarily interested in promoting literacy among his people.

For Freire, promoting literacy meant equipping people with tools for liberating themselves from their immediate miseries (both economic and social) so that they could withstand the systems of oppression. He wanted to acknowledge that basic understanding and intelligence are already present in all human beings. What is left for them to attain are the "tools" of literacy in order to give an expression to their already existent intelligence. The fundamental understanding of the idea of resistance to oppression—which is perpetuated by power—is a necessary tool since resistance can dislocate power. Based on the belief that every individual is born with intelligence, liberation theologians began a process of empowerment by way of this struggle, whereby eventually people would become agents of their own liberation (Boff and Boff, 1984:28). To this end, liberationist theologians argued, any theory that would provide a remedy to the eradication of poverty should be applied, be it Marxist or socialist. For them this would not change their basic understanding of God, or the purpose of religion. Instead it could only strengthen them by enabling them to express their will. Moreover, any language that would help express these concerns and help develop a pedagogy/theology may also be used. Thus the language that was used to express these forms of liberationist theology was Marxist and socialist, since these ideologies provided the liberation theorists with the social-scientific method as well as the terminology for an appropriate representation of the poor as the oppressed vis-à-vis the oppressor.

One way to construct a theology of liberation within the Christian context was by way of reflecting upon the time when Jesus lived and his social circumstances, highlighting his own poverty, and his association with and ministry among the poor. In that context one is also reminded of the three stages one goes through in order to effect a change: seeing the reality, taking sides, and acting upon it. Liberation theologians not only take sides with the poor, they also promote activism in order to realize the fruits of this ideological stance. In their view this is the only way to understand Jesus' mission since Jesus always took the side of the poor and the oppressed. Jesus also fought for the poor against the oppressors; he fought against hierarchy (Gutiérrez, 1984:19ff, 122–23). Thus for Gutiérrez, as a Christian one cannot afford to stay passive to injustice. Similarly, Enrique Dussel asks, in his classic work *Ethics and the Theology of Liberation*, "what does it mean to be Christian?" and answers in the following way: "Indeed, in reality, one does not be a Christian but is always in the process of *becoming* a Christian." And this *becoming* is synonymous with the movement of liberation (1978:90; italics in original). Thus one might say our being religious is not a static thing; rather it is acting out in ways that liberate. In its classic mode, liberation theology seeks to focus on becoming economically independent and liberating oneself from poverty, because it identifies as its chief goal the "preferential option for the poor."

Similarly a Muslim too must understand one's religiosity as a process of becoming; it is a movement toward God in spiritual terms, but it is never dissociated from one's responsibility toward people. Who among those in need would require more attention than the poor and the destitute? The Qur'an asks this question; in fact the Qur'an instructs that a Muslim must always take the side of those who are weak and oppressed regardless of their religion and race. One of the five obligatory acts of worship is *zakat*, commonly translated as almsgiving. It symbolizes an act of purifying oneself (spiritually) by giving a specified portion of one's wealth to those in need. The Qur'an 9:60 (*Surat al-Tawbah* [Repentance]) states: "Alms are meant only for the poor, the needy ... to free slaves and help those in debt, for God's cause, and for travellers in need. This ordained by God; God is all knowing and wise."

For Boff, Gutiérrez, and many other liberation theologians, Marxist philosophy through its social analysis provided a desirable lens for seeing the Christian religious teachings as a remedy for the treatment of social inequality. Many Islamic theologians too sought inspiration from what some have called the "socialistic" tendencies of the original sources of the Islamic tradition which contain liberative elements within themselves. Ali Shari'ati (1933–1977), the Iranian intellectual and activist, was one such influential thinker in the twentieth century who spoke extensively *against* the Marxist vision and yet *in favor* of the socialistic impulses within the Islamic message. In fact, Shari'ati argued that throughout Islamic history from the time when Islam was still in its infancy, the ideals of the revelation of God and injunctions of prophet Muhammad were still seen to have been focused upon the task of restoring justice, equality, and peace. Numerous Islamic revivalist movements of the last hundred years have attempted in one way or another to revert to this early idealistic outlook of the Islamic message.

As with Latin American liberation theology, Islamic theology of liberation sees the historical, religious, and cultural contexts as seminal in providing the ground on which the liberative elements will develop. Thus there is a strong regional/local flavor to these elements. This local grounding is possible because of an important characteristic of liberation movements: they must be rooted in the people and their experiences and struggles, and their tenets are not handed on from the top down. Thus, as Thomas Schubeck, S.J. in his seminal work *Liberation Ethics* aptly notes, liberation theology reverses the order in which traditional theologies are framed. In liberation theology, dogma comes last and is in fact judged on the basis of the suffering of the oppressed, which is at the center. Dogma is viewed from the vantage point of the suffering rather than the other way around (1993:59). In fact classical dogmatic theologies have often served as an impediment to liberation rather than facilitating it. According to Engineer, "dogmas are the product of human urge for security rather than that of spiritual quest for inner certitude." For religion to be an instrument of change, it must be framed within the discourse of liberation theology. Once a religion is defined through the principles of liberation, it can become a powerful medium of resistance to oppression of all kinds. Since liberation theology particularly concerns itself with the practical conditions experienced by the masses, it inevitably looks critically at the mere metaphysical theorization of ethical behavior and the abstraction and ambiguity of the notions of justice. Instead it advances itself from the bottom up, by looking at the reality on the ground and constructing a theoretical framework from there. In other words, it consists of a dialectical interaction between what is and what ought to be (Engineer, 1990:6).

Muslim liberation ethics demands that Islamic normative tradition be interpreted in light of its application to the sociopolitical and historical dimensions of life. In other words, if the charity prescribed in the Qur'an is not visible in the lives of Muslims in how they interact with others, it is of no use to be talking about that ideal; the more pressing issue is to see how that ideal manifests itself in one's daily life. The discussion of religious values and theological concepts must take into account the social context as well. Early Islamic theology was preoccupied with metaphysical aspects of human religious endeavor. Although the concepts of social justice and human freedom were part and parcel of the teachings of the

Qur'an and the prophetic tradition, when it came to the sophisticated discussions of law and theology, the jurists, the grammarians, and the philosophers became primarily concerned with ideological and abstract ideas. The social spirit of the Qur'an and Prophet Muhammad's teachings became the subject of speculative analysis. The simple concerns for the human condition—spiritual and socioeconomic—gave way to complex discussions focusing on grand theories of law and philosophy. Take, for example, the notion of justice, which is central in the Qur'an but has often been reduced to a neat metaphysical discussion of the qualities of God. Classical theologians have often remained aloof from the sociopolitical and economic realities. Muhammad Husayn Fadlallah, the Shi'a cleric and leader of the sociopolitical party, Hizbullah of Lebanon, is one of the many contemporary critics of metaphysical discussions of justice. He and other justice-oriented Islamic revivalists have argued that any conversation about justice must take into account the ground realities faced by the masses. From the belief that God is just, it does not necessarily follow that the rulers and the elites in a given society will be just. Unless some sense of self-determination is experienced by the masses, the struggle to achieve justice must remain a proactive one (Abu Rabi, 1996:232).

Early Islam as a Movement for Liberation

As one considers the primary sources of Islam, one is unmistakably drawn to the concern displayed for social justice which was the basis for the normative tradition in the beginning. Later the same concerns and values were manifested in a variety of movements in Islamic history that resemble the nature of liberation principles promoted today. Muslim theologians, even those not directly addressing the concerns of liberation, have argued that the beginning of Muhammad's career as a prophet was essentially a revolutionary attempt to transform the social conditions of his time. The Prophet came from among a poor, though noble, family. He challenged the rich and those who legitimized the status quo in that society. Therefore his struggle attained wide support from among the poor and the oppressed, including many slaves (Engineer, 1990:2ff.).

Engineer and others argue that the foundation upon which Islamic tradition rests contains liberative elements. The ideals which Islam puts forward as its primary objective are in their essence egalitarian. The earliest Islamic society was established on the basis of divine authority; all other worldly authorities were seen as subservient to that divine authority. This divine authority, however, was represented, in the time of Muhammad, by the revelation given to Muhammad, which later formed the scripture, the Qur'an. In a sociological sense, since Muhammad was the recipient of the revelation, he, as a prophet and a messenger, was the authority. In theory, all human beings are equal and they were considered superior or inferior only in terms of their proximity to the divine. Here piety becomes a way to achieve full humanity, a means of attaining perfection. But piety is not a tangible or measurable entity, therefore no one person may claim to judge the other. Only God knows who is righteous and who is not; God is the final judge of all beings.

Hence there is no justification for one human being's exploitation, subjugation, or oppression of another human being on the basis of claims of superiority in any respect.

Further at the ontological level, Islam liberated human beings from the worship of manifest objects and nature spirits. It turned the focus of attention from the material to the immaterial/metaphysical. In doing so, Islam caused human beings to think freely and more creatively. Islam also discarded the many rituals that had been part of various traditional religious systems at the time of its inception. Rituals that sacralized existence before were deemed unnecessary since existence itself is sacred. In this way, too, it forced the destruction of the status quo in the existing religious hierarchy.

Scriptural Basis for a Theology of Liberation: Justice in the Qur'an and the Normative Tradition

> [God] sent Our messengers with clear signs, the Scripture and the Balance, so that people could uphold justice. ...
>
> (*The Qur'an 57:25, Surat al-Hadid [Iron]*)

One of the main concerns of liberation theology is justice as it applies to both the society and the individual. In the Islamic view, justice is a key factor in constructing a society that comes close to the ideal. In the Qur'an, 7:29 (*Surat al-A'raf* [The Heights]), "Say, 'My Lord commands righteousness ... Just as He first created you, so you will come back [to life] again.'" The command to be just comes along with the reminder of a time of accountability at the moment of resurrection on the Day of Judgment (*yawm al-akhir*). Similarly, the Qur'an 49:9 (*Surat al-Hujurat* [The Private Quarters]) reminds the believers, "God loves those who are even-handed [just]." Again, in Qur'an 5:8 (*Surat al-Ma'idah* [The Feast]), justice is upheld as equal to being pious. "You who believe, be steadfast in your devotion to God and bear witness impartially: do not let hatred of others lead you away from justice, but adhere to justice, for that is closer awareness of God." Thus piety without consideration for others' rights is not real piety.

The concepts of *'adl* (justice) and *ihsan* (righteousness) are two very important concepts in the Qur'an. Being just implies in the Qur'anic sense being so in all spheres of life, especially in social dealings. Hoarding of wealth is considered a serious act of injustice toward the underprivileged and the disadvantaged. In this regard the Qur'an says: "...tell those who hoard gold and silver instead of giving in God's cause that they will have a grievous punishment" (The Qur'an 9:34, *Surat al-Tawbah* [Repentance]). Justice is primarily understood as economic justice since one's economic circumstances affect most other aspects of this worldly life. Justice also implies honesty in social dealings. With respect to the ethics of trade and business transactions, the Qur'an says, "...you may not exceed in the balance—weigh with justice—and do not fall short in the balance [or measure]" (55:8–10, *Surat al-Rahman* [The Lord of Mercy]). Justice here is understood comprehensively; it implicates one's affairs in all aspects of life—social, economic, and religious.

In the Islamic normative tradition, practical concern for the poor and the dispossessed is just as important as religious piety. Prophet Muhammad's message, when he began his ministry, was for everyone, but it appealed particularly to the poor and the oppressed. He spoke on behalf of those who were without power. He spoke against the establishment for the sake of justice. It was a revolutionary message sparked by the metaphysical force that called people to be just. After all, the core of each heavenly message had always been the establishment of an ethical society that implies justice as its very basis and operates on the principle of accountability.

Some Christian thinkers seem to propose that Christianity and Marxism share the same ideals while they differ on ideology and strategy as understood through the lens of liberation theology, especially in the 1970s and 1980s when Marxism was unduly valorized among some Latin American Christians. Islam does not share much with Marxism, however, it contains some vital concerns for social justice—ideas that at least theoretically speaking are shared between the two. For example, in Ali Shari'ati's understanding of the Islamic message, the Qur'an often addresses its message to the masses (*al-nas*) which indicates a concern for the welfare of the universal human community and not just for any select group. Thus the Qur'anic sociology, in his view, reflects a socialistic message (1979:64).

The Qur'an also speaks of the notion of *jihad* (spiritual and social struggle) in many different contexts. In one instance the Qur'an says that "those who commit themselves and their possessions to striving in God's way" are noble (4:95, *Surat al-Nisa'* [Women]). *Jihad* is not a struggle to promote one's own interest or for political gain; rather it must be taken up for promoting the cause of the oppressed and the weak. Again, the Qur'an commands: "Why should you not fight in God's cause and for those oppressed men, women, and children who cry out [for help]" (4:75, *Surat al-Nisa'* [Women]). Therefore, *jihad* is primarily to be "waged" to protect, safeguard, and secure the interests of the oppressed and the weak or to defend against aggression. Thus, the cause of justice is highlighted within the normative tradition.[15]

At the very beginning of Islamic history the first leader of the Muslim community after Prophet Muhammad was Abu Bakr. His words, as he addressed his people collectively, resonate the scriptural injunction mentioned in the Qur'an 4:75 cited above: "No doubt I have been made your ruler (wali) and though I am not better [than] you. If I render good (to you) help me, if I indulge in (something) bad, correct me ... those of you who are weak are powerful unto me until I restore their right unto them with ease and those of you who are powerful are weak unto me until I snatch from them what (they unjustly claim) to be their right."[16] This is a good example of a leader who, inspired by the normative ideas of the tradition, leaves himself open to criticism, and who clearly sides with the poor in order to bring about an economic (and thus sociopolitical) equilibrium in society. Therefore, the theory or the normative principles introduced in the Qur'an met with the practice of those early Muslims who claimed to adopt them. The Islamic tradition emerged from those modest beginnings and these examples remain the foundation upon which Islam as a faith rests. The history of the early Islamic ethical principles and their social manifestations, although imperfect, point toward a strong basis for conceiving an Islamic paradigm for a theology of liberation. Any contextual analysis of Islamic history would reveal that normative Islam has been the source of inspiration for many theologies of liberation in the past and it continues to be so in the present.

Islam and the Challenge of Poverty

It may be said that liberation theology is a product of piety, the experience of poverty and political awareness. It is a product of piety because it authenticates the struggle of individuals who are either themselves victims of poverty or who empathize with such victims. Piety allows one to channel the hope for the betterment of humankind, and the practice of one's faith tradition to bring this about, to meaningfully engage with the problems faced by oneself and others.

The experience of political and social oppression, and in particular that of poverty, which is one of the worst forms of violence, is what first brought the voices of liberation to the forefront of a religious struggle for justice. The process of viewing the struggle for justice through the lens of religious teachings represented an awareness of greater possibilities for reenergizing and redefining such struggle in concrete and meaningful terms. The Islamic tradition places a strong emphasis on the marriage of piety and action (or political awareness). Piety is considered hollow without some level of involvement in the struggle for justice. The Islamic imperative for social justice is as important for faith as the one found in the Christian message: "It shall be those who feed the hungry, clothe the naked, care for the sick, and defend those who are wronged who will inherit the Kingdom of God" (Matt 25:34ff.).

Poverty is a condition in which people live in undersupplied resources. It is characterized by poor housing, premature aging, hunger, insufficient means of survival, and so on. This describes sheer bodily poverty or material deprivation. But since this poverty has consequences that dominate other spheres of human existence, it is an important indicator for evaluating the overall human condition. The issue of the impoverishment of the human being became one of the main concerns in the Latin American context in the face of extreme poverty. An entire discourse has been generated related to impoverishment.

Liberation theology developed out of looking at the poor. It was to imply that poverty is bad; it must be eradicated and eliminated. In Islamic mystical understanding, poverty is not necessarily a sign of misfortune; it implies that one has fewer reasons to be tested by God. The mainstream Islamic social teachings, however, call for establishing equitable economic systems under which the gap between the poor and rich must always be in the process of shrinking and not expanding.

The Qur'an speaks of the prophets as coming from among their own people, the masses. "It is He who raised a messenger, among the people who had no Scripture. ..." (62:2 *Surat al-Jum'a* [Day of Congregation]). With the exception of David and Solomon, the prophets of the Qur'an are all said to be sent for the people, from among them, and they did not identify themselves with the rulers or the ruling classes. Thus Islam constantly assumes a struggle between the two main types of social groups: the rulers, who are called *mustakbirun,* or the arrogant, and the masses—the *mustad'afun,* that is the weakened and the oppressed. As Ferid Esack aptly notes, this "contrast" between the powerful and the oppressed masses appears in many parts of the Qur'an (7:136–37; 28:5). In fact, "the Qur'an makes a clear choice for the *mustad'afun* against the *mustakbirun* even though the former may not be Muslim" (1997:98). Thus according to the Qur'an, all prophets as liberators sided with the former. Islam, in standing up for the weak and the poor, restricts the accumulation of wealth by the few. Similarly a Muslim is enjoined by the Qur'an to reflect on the needs of the dispossessed in society. One of the obligatory five pillars in Islam is almsgiving (*zakat*). It is not voluntary but every Muslim of a certain economic status must give a portion of his/her wealth for the sake of the welfare of others. The Qur'an 51:19 (*Surat al-Dhariyat* [Scattering Winds]) speaks of "the rightful share of the beggar and the deprived" in the general wealth of the rich, implying that the right to wealth and property is not absolute, but rather subject to a reasonable distribution among all sections of society.

Echoing some of the early liberationist thinkers, left-leaning Muslim liberationists would argue that modern faces of poverty are the direct result of the imposition of the capitalist economic model, presented as the best mode for all. The capitalist system is considered unjust because exploitation, which is the essence of capitalism, is unjust. Marx and later Marxists have condemned and radically denounced capitalism, primarily in their critique of exploitation. Liberation theology also seeks to critique exploitation and, in doing so, it appropriates the language used by Marxists. Insofar as the issue of exploitation is concerned, the Islamic worldview agrees with the Marxist social analysis. Where the question of metaphysical materialism arises there is no agreement. Islam as an ideology of this world ultimately points to the reality beyond this world, and hence could not possibly be compatible with the Marxist worldview. Within a capitalist system, the laborer almost ceases to be human. A person exists as an "appendage of capital," as the ordinary instrument of labor, which has to be maintained and "begotten" (just like pigs in a piggery or dogs in a "puppy mill"); the laborer exists as a "beast of burden." Exploitation, in a capitalistic society, is thus a "process of divestiture," depriving workers of their potentialities as human beings and imposing upon them "degraded and almost servile conditions," converting them into "mercenaries and, of their means of labor, into capital" (Marx, 1973:322ff.). Insofar as the eradication of such exploitation is concerned, Islam may be said to inspire a similar passion for resistance against all forms of injustice. In an ideal Islamic society, it is arguably the most important task for those who seek to change or abolish the system that perpetuates the exploitation of the masses by the few. Needless to say that the lofty ideals proposed by Marxist social thought never really materialized, or ever benefited the masses in the way they were thought to have done. And while the theme of liberation forms the very foundation of the Islamic understanding of society in history, realities on the ground never seemed to have reflected the ideals adequately.

ISLAM AS A BASIS FOR MODERN LIBERATION MOVEMENTS

Despite the above, Islam has been the source of liberative struggles in the past and it continues to inspire movements and ideas in the present. One such movement was that of Ali Shari'ati.[17] In the twentieth century, postcolonial struggles for economic and political independence defined the challenges many Muslim societies faced. During the latter half of the twentieth century, Shari'ati and other Muslim theologians attempted to discover liberative elements within an Islamic historical framework. These elements could then be made to operate in fashioning a worldview which allows others to see the drive to liberation rooted within that framework. Ali Shari'ati reappropriates themes of liberation in Islamic terminology, just as Enrique Dussel and other Latin American theologians reappropriated them in Marxist terminology and the language of the Left. Incidentally, they both studied at the Sorbonne around the same time, and possibly studied under some common teachers including the Jewish philosopher Emmanuel Levinas.[18]

Shari'ati was a theologian, a reformer, and a *mujaddid* ("renewer" of faith) in his own right. Thus he was aptly suited to use the Qur'an and other Islamic sources to formulate his brand of liberation theology. Shari'ati regarded the language of the Qur'an to be symbolic. He believed that multiple layers of meanings must be deduced from the scriptures for the purpose of establishing equality and justice in society. Islam, says Ali Shari'ati, is a progressive ideology. Thus he posits his discourse within a foundational assertion that "Islam, very simply, is a philosophy of human liberation. Its first summons, 'Say, 'there is no god but God,' and prosper' propounds *tawhid* [oneness of God] as the necessary means to that end" (1980:73). And as a "philosophy of human liberation," it leads one to a state of self-awareness.

Among Islamic ideals, justice is one of the key principles. As discussed above, justice is central among all the themes arising out of the Qur'an. Thus in the modern period, Marxism did not reveal any profound truth by claiming the cause of justice, albeit economic justice. In Shari'ati's view, Marx's understanding of social analysis may be acceptable insofar as it does not stand upon his critique of religion or the divine.[19] Islamic progressivism is revealed in its fundamental notion of the unity of being (*tawhid*). This principle of unity reflects, more than it represents, the complete—that is, a meaningful and purposeful—harmony in which Islam situates God, humanity, and nature (1980:86). Shari'ati writes, "Marxism because it is founded on an absolutely materialistic worldview, is incapable of raising humanity in its essence, attributes or evolutionary state beyond the narrow confines of materiality; it ranks human being along with all other beings in the confines of an unconscious and purposeless nature" (87). Shari'ati's "dialectic of man," so to speak, attempts to view human existence in a balanced manner; the human being is both a material as well as a spiritual being.[20] Whereas the *ulama*—the religious leaders of Muslims—paid too much attention to the spiritual and the ritualistic side of the human effort, Marxist social analysis focused upon the economic realities and rejected the spiritual dimension of human beings altogether. Both have their reasons in history. *Ulama* perpetuate their stay in power by diverting the attention of the masses toward the reality beyond and enjoy in the here and now their empowering role in religious societies. The Marxist one-dimensional view, on the other hand, stems from its origins in an increasingly industrialized Europe, where modernity as its main propeller caused the separation between the domains of the scientific and the unscientific; in effect, between the mythical and the religious, between dogma and belief. Islam, through its basic worldview of *tawhid*, sees human beings as expressing this divine essence, with transcendental attributes and infinite potential of evolution, and hence situates humanity in a "living, meaningful, and infinite universe which extends far beyond the domain of the sciences" (Shari'ati, 1980:87).

The close affinity between Islam and the liberation elements are also seen in the fact that in the Islamic tradition, at least in the beginning, there was no distinction between the ideologue, the activist, and the worker. The class mentality developed later due to the influence of regional customs. The leader is at the same time also an activist and a worker. Early leaders of Muslim societies were humble in their lifestyle; in that they identified with the masses rather than the ruling elite. With the rise of hereditary rule in the Umayyad period this began to change (Shari'ati, 1980:105).

Islamic Revivalism: Toward a Praxis of Liberation

Arising within the last three decades, Islamic revivalism is seen as operating on the principles of liberation theology. One main reason given for such a view is that revivalist movements challenged and continue to challenge the prevailing political conditions and dominant worldview that sought to determine the destiny of the masses with regard to their economic, social, and cultural conditions. Revivalist ethics was built around the notion of self-determination, confronting and resisting Western political influence which has been present in the Muslim world throughout the postcolonial period. Their basic claim is to liberate people from the dependency upon the West.[21] In essence they are "ideological revolutions" in their own right and pose a diverse set of challenges in different contexts. As James Scott points out, "Wherever there is domination there is also resistance."[22] Just how this resistance has surfaced in various parts of the world and at various points in history is a matter of observation. The Islamic fundamentalism, or to be more appropriate, Islamic resurgence, has many faces of its own as well. As one party to the revolutionary spirit and postrevolutionary struggles, the student movement of Iran, "Mujahidin-i Khalq" had an extensive struggle against the status quo of the ruling upper classes in Iran. Their motto, according to their official publication *Mojahed*, is "onwards towards the annihilation of exploitation and oppression of every kind and the realisation of the classless society in *Towhid*" (Engineer, 1990:64). Another example of a resistance movement is the "Black Power" movement of the sixties which may also be compared to the "Muslim Brotherhood" of Egypt. Both spoke of the return to the texts (the Word/Jesus) and called for the reinterpretation of these texts in light of the contingencies of the modern world. Insofar as they also believed in the application of their revivalist theories in their own societies, they are also labeled as "fundamentalists" and/or "extremists" (Yadegari, 1986–1987:39).

Liberation theologians assert that Jesus came to liberate humanity not only from spiritual decadence but also from the bondage of material poverty and social injustice. Muslim revivalist movements also began as a struggle for social, political, and economic liberation. They sought liberation from oppression by the hands of the colonialists, as Muslim lands were colonized for most of the nineteenth and early twentieth centuries. Nonetheless, the dominant perception was that the Muslim reformers simply wanted to defend the Islamic faith against its erosion in the wake of imperialism and cultural annihilation. Jamal al-Din Afghani, the first active Muslim reformer and revivalist (d. 1897), divided the world into two categories: the oppressor and the oppressed. This dichotomy exists in the worldview of many other thinkers and activists, most of whom are mainstream liberation theologians—for example, Hugo Assmann of Brazil, Enrique Dussel of Argentina, Allan Boesak of South Africa, and James Cone of the United States. They all speak of the oppressors and the oppressed (Yadegari, 1986–1987:39).

For liberation theorists, especially in the early developmental days of liberation theology, the language most suitable for its expression is filled with directly appropriated Marxist terminology. For the Islamic liberationists the language most viable was that of the early Islamic experience of struggle against injustice and religious persecution. Where the former used the Bible, the latter used the Qur'an. This use of these texts to justify the notions of justice and equality and to critique the present unjust social structure, characterizes both the Latin American theologies of liberation and the Islamic revivalist movements. Another common denominator between the two is their understanding of modernity. The fundamentalist/revivalist group opposes those aspects of modernity which it deems as an infringement upon Islamic cultural space—for example, some Western values and social mores, they argue, undermine their view of Islamic social ethics. In some ways this thinking differentiates itself from the liberation theologians' main resistance to modernity. The liberation theologians are primarily opposed to the modern means of economic production and distribution that perpetuates class society. The basic operative element in both movements is power.

To a large extent Islamic revivalism has been the answer to many modern challenges that emerged across the Muslim third world. These challenges are generally constituted by three main factors. Firstly, it answers the challenge posed by nationalism; through the nation-state theory Muslim lands were carved up and divided into artificial nation-states by the colonial powers. Secondly, it responds to the challenge of liberalism, both political and economic; through modern means of production and distribution political control of these nation-states has been continuously perpetuated, hence economic globalization has arisen. Thirdly, and most importantly, it answers the challenge posed by a more recent process of cultural domination, that of cultural globalization—the Western cultural ethos now has a vast reach through the use of mass media and the Internet—which, in addition to, and with the help of the above two factors, also hastens the process of westernization. Therefore, some of the main premises of Islamic revivalism arose in response to the above challenges. Firstly, Islamic revivalism seeks to reactivate the Islamic reasoning for the social analysis of its own societies. Secondly, it proposes to reconstitute the political authority of

Islam which has been made to disappear in the wake of colonial and postcolonial hegemonic enterprises. Thirdly, it maintains the need to revive the Qur'an and the *hadith* as the primary sources for the development of the Islamic theory of knowledge. These and other aspects of revivalist movements in Islam are understood as attempts to liberate people from the hegemony and domination of the masses by the few who directly or indirectly benefit from such domination. The issues are framed in the context of the notion of justice. Revivalist movements seek to transform their own societies, on the basis of fundamental values to which their respective societies adhere. They seek to challenge Western influences which often come in the garb of economic incentives and plans for development and increasingly manifest themselves in the form of social and cultural practices. The comparison between Islamic revivalism and liberation theology continues to be made, and it may be granted that they share some similar traits. But they are not one and the same. In the twenty-first century, both have been transformed and are being reshaped continuously by the fast pace of technology. The fact remains, however, that liberation theology can easily be read into the Islamic revivalist movements despite the shifting nature of some of the claims made by these movements.

Conclusion

Many contemporary Muslim thinkers have already attempted to develop a theoretical framework for their own brands of theologies that strongly resonate with Christian liberation theologies. Those attempts are by no means exhaustive; in fact the struggle to define and understand various themes of liberation continues to be played out. In the post-September 11 era, Muslim liberation thinking has taken off into many different directions simultaneously. One of the major areas of struggle is intra-Muslim dialogue on the topic of what constitutes a "moderate" Islam. Western talking heads define it based on their understanding of secularized religion prevalent in many European countries; many Western Muslim thinkers argue for it in the form of a "civil Islam" that consciously seeks a change of posture in legal and social norms. Yet others, both in Western as well as in many Muslim countries, are trying to find a balance between the demands of an increasingly secularized and westernized world and the fundamentals of Islamic ethics. In the end, liberation from expressions of religious behavior that are intolerant and noninclusive is perhaps as necessary as liberation from the many kinds of fundamentalist secularism such as the one promoted in some French civil and political discourse.

Thus liberative principles can be based on both religious as well as extra-religious elements and can be expressed in religious as well as secular language. It is not imperative that all issues of contemporary reality be settled on the basis of religious principles. There is clearly a need to understand that not all values must be justified through religious texts and/or the prophetic tradition. It is essential that today we begin to acknowledge the "extra-religious values"—such as democratic model of polity—which do not go against the spirit of the overall teachings of Islam.[23]

These reformist trends, it is hoped, will continue to work through the Muslim intellectual and social landscape in the coming decade. As Muslim societies move ever closer to a greater understanding of the need to reinterpret their religious tradition in the light of our contemporary realities, there is yet hope that the liberative principles will become manifest in the real lives of people in many parts of the world, who continue to experience oppression at the hands of the few. Herein lies the challenge for all those who seek to uphold justice and freedom, peace and security, as basic human rights for all, to continue the struggle—the *jihad*, although nonviolently—yet with full determination and power, drawn from any creed, religious or secular, that gives them this power.

CHAPTER REVIEW

1. Explain *zakat*.
2. How does Muhammed's life mirror liberation theology?
3. What is the meaning of *jihad*?
4. How does Islam view poverty?
5. Differentiate between a moderate Muslim and an extremist Muslim.

CPSIA information can be obtained at www.ICGtesting.com
Printed in the USA
LVOW11s2001040114

368094LV00001B/43/P

9 781621 317531